Pursuing Digital Literacy in Compulsory Education

new literacies ¶
AND DIGITAL EPISTEMOLOGIES

Colin Lankshear and Michele Knobel
General Editors

Vol. 43

The New Literacies and Digital Epistemologies series
is part of the Peter Lang Education list.
Every volume is peer reviewed and meets
the highest quality standards for content and production.

PETER LANG
New York • Washington, D.C./Baltimore • Bern
Frankfurt • Berlin • Brussels • Vienna • Oxford

Pursuing Digital Literacy in Compulsory Education

EDITED BY Lampros Stergioulas
AND Helen Drenoyianni

PETER LANG
New York • Washington, D.C./Baltimore • Bern
Frankfurt • Berlin • Brussels • Vienna • Oxford

Library of Congress Cataloging-in-Publication Data

Pursuing digital literacy in compulsory education /
[edited by] Lampros K. Stergioulas, Helen Drenoyianni.
p. cm. — (New literacies and digital epistemologies; v. 43)
Includes bibliographical references and index.
1. Internet in education. 2. Internet literacy. 3. Computer literacy.
4. Education, Compulsory. I. Stergioulas, Lampros K. II. Drenoyianni, Helen.
LB1044.87.P87 372.3'4—dc22 2009025959
ISBN 978-1-4331-0619-4 (hardcover)
ISBN 978-1-4331-0618-7 (paperback)
ISSN 1523-9543

Bibliographic information published by **Die Deutsche Nationalbibliothek**.
Die Deutsche Nationalbibliothek lists this publication in the "Deutsche Nationalbibliografie"; detailed bibliographic data is available on the Internet at http://dnb.d-nb.de/.

The paper in this book meets the guidelines for permanence and durability of the Committee on Production Guidelines for Book Longevity of the Council of Library Resources.

29 Broadway, 18th floor, New York, NY 10006
www.peterlang.com

Printed in the United States of America

Contents

Prolegomenon

Pursuing Digital Literacy in the School: Reconstructing the School to Provide Digital Literacy for All

In the last two decades, advances in information and communication technologies have been continuously raising society's expectations from the so-perceived transformative wave of the emerging "Knowledge Society", an ideological construct that carries a promise for a better future, and places knowledge, and alongside it education, in the driver seat of humanity. Yet, by the end of 2008, the world was hit by the most severe economic, and by extension social and political, crisis in more than half a century, with rising unemployment and social welfare under threat. The view of an ever-prospering society riding the ICT/"Knowledge" wave has now to face a sudden reality check, forcing reconsideration of individualism and its consequences of cynicism and greed. Similarly to other crises in history, it is now likely that people will attempt to rediscover their values and visions and to reinstate "their hope for a better future". Just like other defining historical moments, these recession years might be marked by the unique opportunity it offers for ushering in a period of radical economical and societal transformations.

It is within this context of the universal desire to reinstate and reposition our hope for a better future and hence to promote a transformative vision of education, which was the motivation for this book and where aims and themes of its discourse lie. Digital technology and digital media are inevitably and inextricably part of our future, a future which is literally defined by the way we educate our children. As such, the aim to provide "digital literacy for all" underpins the need, and the challenge, of re-constructing the school.

What may be the characteristics of the school in the 21st century? What may be the role of digital media, tools, contents and equipment in that school? What will be the role of the teacher and what the role of the student? Responses to these exceedingly complicated and pedagogically stimulating questions usually range from the over-optimistic to the over-pessimistic. In any case, however, they always appear to induce thoughtful scepticism over issues that lie beneath debates and discussions about the modern school crisis, the need for educational reform and the innovative role and radical value of ICT use in education.

Starting from the acknowledgment that there are many different standpoints, this edited tome is an attempt to explore the challenging landscape of a newly established and highly promoted compound term, strongly related–if not identical–to ICT use in education, inextricably associated with the media and information literacies, which is often described as the solution to the socio-economical, political and cultural problems involved in the phenomenon of "digital divide", namely the term "digital literacy".

Drawing upon this problematisation, the book aims to inform on current views and developments, disseminate recent research and practice in the area of digital literacy in compulsory education, and give a voice to a distinguished, as well as diverse, body of educators working in this intricate and important subject. We hope that the book will appeal to a wide spectrum of readers from many walks of education, including teachers, academics, local education authorities, education students, ICT coordinators and advisors, researchers, academics, practitioners, educationalists, consultants, policy makers, and others with an interest in school education.

Helen Drenoyianni and Lampros K. Stergioulas

Acknowledgments

The editors are indebted to Carole Bromley and Georgios Xydopoulos of Brunel University for their many hours of editing work, for their support, and for making sure that the manuscript was completed. Many thanks, Carole and Georgios.

We would also like to thank our series editors Colin Lankshear and Michel Knobel, Chris Myers, Managing Director of Peter Lang Publishing, and Sophie Appel of Peter Lang Publishing for their kind and continuous support, their patience, and for making the production of this book possible.

Synopsis

PURSUING DIGITAL LITERACY IN COMPULSORY EDUCATION

Positioned within the generic subject of digital literacy or "literacies", this edited collection has a distinct focus on compulsory education, which is an important and wide area of interest in its own right, and can be a useful resource to a broad audience, including university education departments and their students (both undergraduate and postgraduate), as well as in-service teachers and training bodies.

The book explores a wide spectrum of issues related to digital literacy: its conceptualization and its relation to other literacies, as well as to the broader area of ICT use in education, the pursuit of digital literacy in educational practice and the influence of the school environment, educational policy and practice for the purposeful development digital literacy towards increased equality and democracy in the school, how digital literacy can be a part of a modern curriculum, and what forms digital literacy will take in the future.

The challenges and the unanswered questions in pursuing digital literacy in the 21st century are many. What capacities should individual learners develop in order to collaborate as equals and (co-)create, publish or share content with their peers and their social networks? What are the characteristics of the relationship between digital literacy and e-exclusion in compulsory education? In particular, what should the pursuit of digital literacy in a democratic school be like, and how could it counteract the multi-dimensional digital divide in the school? Most educationalists recognize the close relationship between digital literacies and the rich concept of media literacy, and advocate the digital reconfiguration of the school environment, while many now recognize that this needs to come about with new paradigms of bottom-up change and not via the traditional top-down routes.

We are currently witnessing major digital shifts in all aspects of life and education, including in our primary and secondary schools. We are also facing many present and future challenges in teacher education, as well as in redefining the roles of teacher and student. The role of the teacher is shifting away from the traditional, mainly transmissive, role to that of learning facilitator or learning companion. The student-teacher relationship is also changing as a result, assuming a more equitable nature, as students become more independent (even self-organized, or self-directed in their learning) and empowered by the new tools to participate and interact/collaborate as equals, as well as to create, (co-)produce, publish, create or share content. The potential of this trend of open pedagogy looks rather promising for the development of new democratic, inclusive, participatory and more effective forms of school education.

To address the above challenges, more research is needed on:

- How pedagogical practices in the school can change due to the emergence of digital media in social life and what mechanisms are the most appropriate to effect such changes.
- What aspects of knowledge, skills and competencies should be included in the curricula of compulsory school education for being a fully participating citizen in the digitally immersed society of the 21st century.
- The changing role and function of the school as a place of knowledge assimilation and construction in a digitally enriched world, and the needed changes in the organizational structure of the school to support this.
- How to link most effectively theory with practice, and research with policy.

The book offers a rich mosaic of ideas on digital literacy and can be used in flexible ways as a main or complementary text for teaching relevant subjects. It has four main parts, covering different aspects of digital literacy in compulsory education:

I. Digital literacy, its relationship to other literacies, and the pedagogical use of ICT

Melpomeni Tsitouridou and Konstantinos Vryzas provide us with a good primer on the conceptualization of digital literacy, and its challenges in relation to educational practice and countering the digital divide. They trace the origins and emergence of digital literacy from earlier conceptualisations of literacy and present us with a powerful depiction of digital literacy as a concept in continuous flux. Their approach is to consider the generic concept of literacy and examine its transitions towards the current notions of modern literacies. Digital literacies are regarded as socio-cultural practices and conceived from an educational point of view. The chapter studies the educational dimensions of these new literacies, and their dependence on a whole range of factors—social, political and economic. It concludes that terminology does not matter so much, and agrees with other commentators that what is important is that understanding, meaning and context should all be fundamental to the concept of literacy (David Bawden).

From this perspective, literacy is inseparably connected with social and cultural practice, as well as the power structures of society, and thus the development of digital technology requires a more complex conceptualization of digital literacy, which will take into account the richness and diversity of the many different factors.

In their refreshing and insightful take on the challenge of digital literacy, David Bawden and Lyn Robinson begin their examination of digital literacy from the viewpoint of fighting off the "dark side of information", which they eloquently decompose into a plethora of modern-day information "paradoxes and problems", and end up with a comprehensive set of core elements—a description of digital literacy that is practical/functional as well as profound, and that will appeal to many readers. They too seem to subscribe to the necessity of the development of digital literacy in school-age children and the importance of the moral and social elements, particularly attitudes, values and perspectives, in providing the personal empowerment and independence that are much needed in order to deal effectively with the digital world and its challenges.

Alivisos Sofos approaches digital literacy through analysing the concepts of "Competence" and "Literacy". Digital literacy is viewed as a focus category of media literacy, where the term "media" refers to a holistic approach of media. First, the chapter reviews the various uses of the term "literacy" in the pedagogy literature, revealing numerous related derivative approaches to this term, such as "reading literacy", "mathematics literacy", "scientific literacy", "ICT literacy", "photography literacy", etc. Each of these approaches specifies actions, abilities and aptitudes that students and citizens must acquire in the modern information age with regard to media categories and services. The chapter then goes on to examine different approaches of the concept "media literacy" taken by theoretical research and educational organizations, and provide different classifications of digital literacy as a separate/specific category of media literacy and media competence, systematized under five different perspectives. The main focus here is on the conceptual framework on which all these approaches are based and on the identification of the partial aims of digital literacy. Finally, the chapter analyses the prerequisites for digital literacy, in the form of conditions, at three levels: (a) macro-social, (b) micro-social and (c) inter-personal.

II. Digital literacy practice: The pursuit of digital literacy in the school and the roles of the learners, teachers, and the school environment

Ela Orstad puts digital literacy in the context of transitive social and knowledge practices and looks at the implications to schooling and how literacy and knowledge practices change due to technological developments. He highlights the close relation between current digital literacy discourses and media literacy traditions, and how the development of digital literacy in the school draws upon local literacies and former social understandings, mediated through the emergence of new technological but also cultural tools. His examples from a number of projects studying ICT and digital competence development in Norwegian schools illuminate the complexities of the pursuit of digital literacy in the school, the importance of media education and the creative and critical aspects of digital literacy, and the need to address the emergent digital rift between teachers and students, through building a culture of equality and independence of learning in the school.

Joe Cullen examines the potential of social networking, and in particular Web2.0 technologies, in supporting digital literacy—particularly in the context of digital exclusion. He reviews the emerging "Web2.0 for learning" landscape, which includes the so-called Learning 2.0 technologies, examines the new literacies supported by such technologies, and assesses the general contribution of Web2.0 to the e-inclusion agenda. He discusses a number of recent Web2.0 developments and their impact on learning, and observes that there are indications that Web2.0 technology changes the nature of digital literacy, and, in some cases at least, can reduce the problem of digital divide for excluded groups, although in some other cases it seems to have an adverse impact and reinforce social problems. The study examines use and objective (purpose of use) of Web2.0 for learning, and makes an insightful attempt to analyse the different types of Web2.0 learners and develop a typology of Learning 2.0 applications. The review's findings are encouraging, in that a wide range of Web2.0 tools are shown to have been used to support digital literacy and in particular digital inclusion—supporting new forms of learning and social relations—with demonstrable positive effects in some cases at least. Cullen concludes that there is some evidence that Web2.0 is beginning to make an impact on developing of new educational structures and environments and to change how the educational enterprises operate, raising important issues for digital literacy. It certainly looks like an emerging trend that will make an impact on the digital literacy field.

Problematised by a related phenomenon, that is, digital literacy engagement being more advanced in outside-the-school settings rather than inside the schools, Don Passey's chapter starts by posing the question of motivation: "why would learners want to be digitally literate?" and discusses ways that ensure successful pursuit of digital literacy within the school environment. He revisits recent results on the shifting nature of digital literacy and its impact factors, reviews available data from previous studies on access and use of digital technology, and finally focuses on two recent studies, which he uses as exemplars, to show that specially designed projects within the school can offer meaningful and realistic opportunities to develop digital literacy within the school, particularly when there is an element of realness or authenticity, in the sense of relevance to real life: "real purpose, real audience and real value". These empirical studies show that such an approach can provide the desired high level of engagement, and help the learners make the transition from "digital natives" to "learning natives". It is shown that a wide range of (sometimes unexpected) educational outcomes can arise from such possibilities, and an important challenge ahead will be to identify and evaluate effectively the nature and extent of such outcomes in relation to digital literacy development. The need to research this problem further looks indeed pressing.

III. Digital literacy policy, e-inclusion and curriculum development

Ellen J Helsper deftly questions the need and indeed the appropriateness of attempting to construct an exact conceptual definition of digital literacy. She has used the data from the Oxford Internet Survey (OxIS) to show that different cultures can influence digital engagement in different ways. Her insightful findings raise important issues for the successful pursuit of digital literacy in modern society. She concludes that definitions of digital literacy that ignore the differences in digital engagement cultures are missing an important factor and will lead to less effective practices and policies.

Focused on the European landscape, Laura Cervi and José Manuel Pérez Tornero provide us with a comprehensive historical and geographical tour of the media and digital literacies across time and across Europe. They take us briskly through the journey of the evolution of the various literacy concepts and their connections between them, offering a wealth of well-documented and detailed information documents, references, and sources, along the way, and taking up the challenge of conceptualization, to arrive convincingly at the emerging paradigm of an all-encompassing media literacy. This expanded concept of media literacy embraces the emergent digital literacies, as well the classic literacy (reading and writing) and the conventional media literacy. Examining both the barriers and the promising enablers, the authors make a formidable case for the pursuit of digital literacy in European schools, and their recommendations call for the attention of both policy makers and practitioners.

Drawing from a review of the evolution of curriculum development in the US, Georgios Grollios argues for an alternative perspective on curriculum planning which is viewed to give rise to a new kind of digital literacy development that could effectively address social problems related to social inequalities, power relations, and dominant ideology. The chapter embarks on a critical—historical as well as pedagogical—analysis of the main perspectives on curriculum planning, as experienced in the US along the course of the formation of the field of curriculum studies in that country. Based on this insightful analysis, the chapter goes on to expose positions of an alternative perspective on curriculum planning, which differs significantly from the dominant perspectives in the field. The proposed approach to curriculum planning aims to provide a curriculum connected to the social reality that the students experience in their local/everyday context, and lead to a more open, democratic school. Such a perspective may be crucial for the development of an alternative approach towards the pursuit of digital literacy, one which could tackle effectively the current problems of social inequalities.

Anastassios Liambas and Ioannis Kaskaris argue for a vision of "digital literacy for critical consciousness" and consider the nexus between pedagogy and ICTs, which evokes a complex theoretical framework, thus building a rich problematisation oriented towards realizing emancipation and utopian discourse for both the school and society. It is argued that the public dialogue on digital literacy could be enhanced within range of the compelling perspective that engages technology, historically, into the realms of the social forces of production (i.e., correlating the forms of culture and knowledge with the relationships of production), the means to contour pedagogic methods, students' meaningful praxis, and broad class and gender themes. The chapter further argues that a critical discourse on digital literacy could be annihilated to the extent that the discourse on digital literacy: (a) becomes the ideological vehicle to accommodate the needs of the market and economic antagonism; or, (b) becomes the platform to neutralize the possibilities in empowering social forces, and therefore be inclined to regulate consensus and uniformity. Finally, the chapter concludes that the only way to integrate digital literacy into the school setting is via an emancipatory democratic route where the process towards critical consciousness, creative capacity and epistemological curiosity of the learner would be considered as a basic commitment of the school—represented within the historical and the socio-political that addresses education.

Tapio Varis takes on the issues of the development and evaluation of digital literacy in the school environment. He adopts a similar approach to Laura Cervi and José Manuel Pérez Tornero, taking the view that digital literacy is complementary to media literacy, can be considered as (part of) media literacy, and therefore focuses on critical and creative abilities. Taking Finland as an exemplary case in terms of successful literacy and inclusion outcomes, Varis makes a case for the adoption of this expanded media literacy as the main type of literacy for the school, which will include all aspects of digital literacy, and for the need of new policies to promote, but also perhaps even more importantly, to evaluate/measure digital literacy using social indicators. In his conclusion, he stresses Pérez Tornero's point: that our society is going through a literacy transition, which involves the most profound "tekne" transformation humanity has ever faced.

IV. Visions of the future: Digital literacy and the school in the 21st century

The advent of precipitous changes in the way we perceive and practice digital literacy is also the theme of Keri Facer's chapter. Employing future studies and critical discourse analysis, Keri Facer vividly explores the possible alternative futures of digital literacy in the 21st century and arrives at some compelling narratives, which she then examines with the lenses of operational, cultural and critical literacies. It is difficult to disagree with her argument that the current converging discourse on the "21st century literacies" is not as helpful as many people might think, as it seems to represent an overgeneralizing, Western/hegemonic and ultimately narrow and limited view of what's to come, which ignores the many different social contexts emerging around the world. The narratives of the three scenarios—"global knowledge economy", "rise of localism", "rise of superhumans"—are thoroughly challenging and engaging, and probably indicative of the hard and sometimes unexpected choices that today's society has to make. Facer then poses some difficult questions about the purpose of the school in these alternative futures and offers a stark depiction of the digital literacy challenges that compulsory education faces in these contexts. She observes that the development of critical capacities is consistently important and relevant, regardless of what the future may hold, and urges us to rethink our approach to digital literacy. Elaborating on this position, she concludes that, although outside-the-school digital literacy education is beginning to matter more than what actually happens in the school environment, the future of digital literacy at school lies more within a critical literacy context and on exploring diverse cultural practices.

Neil Selwyn examines the same, "school as digital disappointment", problem—i.e., the school losing out to outside-the-school environments when it comes to digital literacy—from the perspective of what changes schooling needs to go through to rise to the digital challenge, and re-imagines the school as a "loose space" for digital literacy. He reviews the recent trends in the educational community towards the radical re-construction of the school settings aimed to meet today's digital literacy challenges (known as "re-schooling" or even "de-schooling"), and after outlining the weaknesses of such arguments, he proposes a "subtler readjustment" to digital literacy practice towards a less formalised, "loose space" operative environment, that does not destroy the existing institutional structures of the school. The chapter explores ways in which the pursuit of digital literacy may become as a focus for democratic dialogue, cooperation and trust between learners and teachers. Selwyn's arguments make a convincing and realistic case that such loosening up of the schools' digital literacy activities, in a gradual and thoughtful manner, will reconcile more successfully the formalities of the existing industrial-era school structure with the digital literacy challenges.

It is our aim and hope that the contributions in this collection will be helpful companions to our readers to assist them to find some of the answers, but also rather more importantly, to identify, understand and formulate the important issues and questions, and to gain some valuable knowledge, clarity and insight on the highly complex challenge of pursuing digital literacy in the school.

Lampros K. Stergioulas

PART I

Digital Literacy, Its Relationship to Other Literacies, and the Pedagogical Use of ICT

• CHAPTER ONE •

Digital Literacies: Definitions, Concepts and Educational Implications

Melpomeni Tsitouridou and Konstantinos Vryzas

Introduction

In contemporary society the traditional concept of literacy has expanded to acquire new meanings, as the world enters a new age—variously known as the information age (Kubey 1997), the electronic era (Snyder 1998a), the digital world (Tyner 1998), the cyberliteracy (Gurak 2001) or the digital era (Warnick 2002).

Formerly a person was described as literate if he was able to read and write, but with the rapid advance of technology in recent years and the changes this has brought to society, the concept of literacy has now become broader. In today's world the literate person must possess digital skills in order to navigate successfully the multi-dimensional digital environment. In contrast to their children—the so-called digital generation—today's adults, who grew up in the world of the printed book, are often bewildered by cyberspace, which fills them with the same feelings of anxiety that they experience when confronted by a foreign language. The modern world, with its bewildering array of means of communication and automation, requires a new concept of literacy, one that goes beyond the ability to read and write. A digital world is emerging that requires digital skills. These involve not only the ability to use the new technologies, but also new skills in the field of education. The world of high technology calls for individuals equipped with the highest caliber of digital skills, regardless of race or culture (Prensky 2001).

Digital literacy is a concept that is still evolving. Originally it was understood as technological literacy, the need for individuals to master the technological tools enabling them to make use of the changes technology was bringing to society. However, digital literacy is not merely a superficial cognitive skill possessed by the individual; it is a whole set of social practices. Its objectives are not confined to the individual, but extend to the building of skills and the development of critical thought within the framework of the emerging knowledge society. Its significance is interrelated to that of a whole range of factors – social, political and economic. From this perspective, literacy practices are inseparably connected with social and cultural practices, as well as the power structures of each society. The impact of the new literacy cannot be divorced from the social and cultural context in which it is introduced. We cannot, therefore, think solely of the technical aspects, in isolation from the cultural and social framework (Rosado & Bélisle 2006).

The objective of this study is to approach digital literacies starting with an understanding of the concept of literacy itself. Digital literacies are regarded as socio-cultural practices and conceived from an educational point of view. This study is made up of three sections: the first describes the evolution of the concept of literacy, the second covers the transition from the traditional forms of literacy to the new digital literacies, and the third studies the educational dimensions of these new literacies.

Literacy: An Evolving Concept

Literacy is a concept that is still evolving, its meaning determined, on each occasion, by the social requirements of a specific community. Given that the term can only be understood within its social, economic, political and cultural context, its definitions must take into account the changing and increasingly demanding needs of society (Behrens 1994).

Defining Literacy

The term 'literacy' is not easy to define. Use of the term is confused, and moreover, many authors fail to define clearly the concept to which they are referring (Virkus 2003). It is essential that an attempt be made to define the concepts we use if we are to avoid confusion. The way in which a term is defined will have consequences on many levels. Thus the way in which we choose to define the concept of literacy will impact on issues of theory and practice, as well as issues of educational research and policy.

Literacy is generally understood as the ability to read and write to a competent level, or competence with written language in both reading and writing. It is defined as 'the ability to read and write' as well as 'competence or knowledge in a specific area' (Oxford Dictionary of English 2005), or as 'the ability to read and write, or the knowledge of a particular subject, or a particular type of knowledge' (Cambridge Advanced Learner's Dictionary 2009).

Definitions of literacy should not be confined to the individual skill of being able to read and write, but should take into account also the social contexts of the term. Literacy does not have a universal, a-historical or a-social character. On the contrary, it forms part of a specific culture, is continually evolving and represents a life-long cumulative process. It extends its reach across media, modalities and other language and sign systems (Luke 2003a).

Literacy is not an innate human skill, but an ability that is learned, most often through formal education. It is not a neutral, abstract skill, but is related to the value which the society itself, over the passage of time, has attributed to the processes of reading and writing. In its turn, this value effects both the dissemination and limitation of literacy. It is impossible to establish what proportion of the population was able to read and write in the ancient world. We are dependent for our knowledge on random scraps of information, for example, the system of voting for ostracism in ancient Athens, which provides evidence that most Athenian citizens were expected to be able to write a man's name. In the Athenian democracy the existence of a relatively high level of reading matter is likely to have been paralleled by a high rate of basic literacy among adult citizens. The literacy level might to some extent have been linked to social functions where writing was required. In this sense the Spartans would have been considered relatively illiterate, given that they kept very few written records, at least up until the Roman period. The contexts in which writing was used are of importance in evaluating the role of literacy in the ancient world. In itself, literacy was not evidence of high social status. Thus in the time of the Roman Empire much of the work involving reading and writing was performed by slaves. (Thomas 1992, 1998, 2009; Woolf 2009).

In the mediaeval period literacy was understood as the ability to read and write, with the concept of the learned person participating in the activities of the community of the literate. The definition of literacy has undergone substantial change since then. Mass literacy was first achieved in the modern industrial era. With the coming of the industrial revolution, the literacy of the middle class was directly linked to the management of roles within the context of the industrial society. The second half of the 20th century saw increased efforts to tackle problems of illiteracy among, mainly, less-privileged social groups and individuals. Literacy was now seen as a tool for economic, social and cultural advancement (Martin & Madigan 2006).

Through most of history, literacy has meant the ability to read and/or write to a specific level of competence. Conceptions of literacy and uses of the term have been closely linked to the historical context at any time. In the Europe of the Middle Ages and Renaissance the term *literatus*, or *lettered*, would have referred to competence in Latin and been used mainly of the clergy or aristocracy. Later, as local languages developed and the use of Latin was sidelined, the monopoly on literacy of the clergy and aristocracy was gradually eroded (Graff 1979, 2001).

Before Gutenberg, writing activities consisted mainly in recording and transcribing oral speech or copying classical manuscripts (McLuhan 1962). Reading was often done publicly, slowly and out loud (Olson 1994). The notions of reading and writing began to change from the 12th century, with development accelerating dramatically in the wake of the invention of the printing press in the mid-15th century—an invention which changed the whole concept of reading, writing and scholarship. The transition had begun from oral performance to silent comprehension, from copying manuscripts to original creation, and from the mastery of certain religious texts to the examination of a wide field of knowledge (Eisenstein 1979).

Notions of literacy have continued to change following the era of mass industrialization. A progress paradigm of literacy emerged and literacy was viewed as a form of self-expression (deCastell & Luke 1986). This paradigm was in constant conflict with a more technocratic paradigm, which eventually prevailed, and in which literacy is viewed as one of the 'survival skills' necessary if an individual is to function in society (Cuban 1993).

Literacy is said to separate prehistory from history (Goody 1987, Goody & Watt 1968), primitive societies from civilized societies (Levi-Strauss 1983), and modern societies from traditional societies (Lerner 1958). It allows people to master the logical functions of language and to think abstractly (Goody 1986; 1968).

Literacy might be defined simply as the ability to use the written language. It is the capacity to use a set of techniques for decoding and reproducing printed material. This is print or alphabetic literacy. The concept of literacy, originally self-evident in meaning, acquires a much broader range of significance with the passing of time. We can distinguish three concepts of literacy: the capacity to read and write, a skill or competence, and an element in learning. A literate person is someone who is capable of reading, writing and understanding his mother tongue. But the concept of literacy is always relative; it will not mean the same thing in different countries. This is because it is closely related to the culture of each country. Cultural literacy is a term used to describe knowledge of the rules and values of a culture. Moreover, the mutually exclusive polarity of literate-illiterate has been abandoned in favour of a conception of literacy as a continuum. At one end of this continuum lies some ability to reproduce letter combinations, and at the other end lie language skills such as logical thinking, higher-order cognitive skills and reasoning (Clifford 1984, Hillerich 1976). The term literacy is dual in nature: firstly it indicates the ability to read and write, secondly it means the capacity to read with meaning and to understand. For many centuries the word 'literate' was used to refer to persons who were well-read in literature. Today it has acquired the sense of being able to acquire and use effectively information, in order to play an active role in the life of society.

According to the UNESCO definition (1986; 1965), a person is functionally literate when he is able to use reading, writing and calculation in order to function effectively within his group or society and thereby contribute to his own development and that of the community. A functionally literate person is one with the reading and writing skills necessary to act effectively with the context of his culture and group (Gray 1956).The OECD (2000) sets out five levels of literacy. The first covers persons with elementary skills, the second persons with simple skills able to carry out not very complicated tasks. At the third level are persons who respond satisfactorily to the requirements of daily life and work in a complex, advanced society. Levels four and five are occupied by persons who show a command of higher-order information processing skills. According to an OECD (2000) study at least one in four adults fails to reach the lowest literacy level. Of course, the definitions and measurements of literacy, especially for comparative purposes, are difficult. Despite the tests used in recent years, measurements often remain problematic and contradictory (Graff 1987, 1995).

The question of literacy involves the manner and purposes of public participation in society. The concept of literacy is related to three processes, shaped in both historical and cultural terms: the symbolic and material representation of knowledge, culture and values, the dissemination of interpretative skills and abilities within a population, and the state management of power (Livingstone 2004).

The notion of literacy is relative and varies across historical and socio-cultural contexts. Definitions of literacy change in an increasingly technological world. In the contemporary era the concept of literacy is expanding and acquiring different meanings for different people, depending on economic and historical conditions. The concept varies from society to society and group to group, mutating in line with the historical evolution of society itself. Hence it is suggested that what alphabetic literacy was to preindustrial society and print literacy to industrial society, digital literacy is to post-industrial society (Gee 1996).

Those who attempt to define literacy find it is an elusive concept. It means lots of things to lots of people. Moreover, there are many literacies which are associated with tools used for writing and reading. Literacy depends on the availability of a writing technology. It has an economic basis. It requires a cultural context within which it can be defined and measured. Responding to the needs of society, literacy enriches and strengthens the ability of people to think critically and seek meaning for their lives (Hillerich 1976, McGarry 1994).

There are five distinct stages in the process of storing and transmitting information in society: the oral stage, alphabet stage, manuscript stage, print stage and electronic stage. These stages co-exist in a non-linear harmony. At each stage the concept of literacy changes, as people are obliged to acquire particular skills and knowledge in order to make use of information (McGarry 1993).

Traditionally, literacy has been closely associated with written communication and contrasted with oral communication. However, reference is frequently made today to different forms of literacy such as media, computer, internet or cyber literacy. Many people have claimed that we need to combine more than one literacy in order to meet the demands of contemporary life. Literacy is often seen as a sign of modernity; it acquires a symbolic, ideological and even mythical value. Interpretations of its meaning are sometimes contradictory. Thus despite the fact that literacy has been associated with the idea of progress, it has also been used as an instrument of authority, preserving inequalities of class, ethnicity and gender (Thomas 1998).

While there is no disputing that literacy has contributed to human progress, it has also frequently been used by powerful social groups as an instrument of authority to reinforce their own social and economic interests (Livingstone 2004, Vryzas 2006). It has served both as a means of liberation and a means of subjection and social control, to defend the social hierarchy. It is a concept that carries its own ideological and political charge. It is not and never has been a purely personal characteristic or ideologically neutral 'skill' acquired by an individual; instead, it is a social practice (Gee 1991; 1988, Hartley 2002, Street 1995; 1993; 1984).

Skills or Social Practices

The term 'literacy' is sometimes used as if it were synonymous with the concept of 'competence', or even 'skill' (Buckingham 2003). A narrow approach would confine the meaning of literacy to the acquisition of skills.

Thus in the case of information literacy, some authors accept that the terms 'information literacy' and 'information skills' are synonyms and are used, in essence, to describe the same concept (Stubbings & Brine 2003). The definition and understanding of the concept of information literacy would appear to be linked to the way in which the concepts of competence and skills are defined and perceived. The concept of competence also has a variety of meanings and it is not always clear whether it refers to identifiable skills or is linked with patterns of behaviour (Virkus 2003).

The New Oxford Dictionary of English (2001) defines competence (or competency) as the ability to do something successfully or efficiently; the scope of a person's or group's knowledge or ability; a skill or ability. The term 'skill' is defined as a person's ability to do something well, and also as an expertise. It would appear that there is no significant difference between competence and skill, and that the terms can be described as synonyms (Virkus 2003). Concepts closely related to competence and skill are those of ability, capacity, expertise and know-how. It is difficult to establish whether these concepts form an ideological hierarchy or are all on the same level of generality (Savolainen 2002). Some authors have claimed that skills include the ability to apply our knowledge in practical settings. In such settings, skills can be perceived as the technical aspects of competence. Other researchers approach competence as a complex phenomenon and introduce a distinction between competence and competency (Cheetham & Chivers 1998, 2000; Koper 2000).

A competency is the ability, within a certain domain, to make use of both already-learned and new knowledge and skills. Many terms are also used interchangeably, and it is not always clear what the various authors mean by the terms competence and skill (Felstead, Gallie, Green & Zhou 2007). Nevertheless, it is asserted that the term information literacy is not confined to a single skill or competence but refers to a broader and more complex set of attitudes, approaches and skills (Virkus 2003). However this may be, the fact is that alternative terms such as competence, human capital, cognitive skill, etc. are not fully satisfactory, since the concept of literacy involves mainly the textuality and technology that mediate communication (Livingstone 2004).

The skills-based definition of literacy is focused on the abilities of the individual (whether as reader, listener, spectator or computer user) rather than on society's management of knowledge through structures and institutions (media, state, education, work) (Livingstone 2003). The perception of literacy as a set of skills developed by the individual and detached from the social context was challenged by a critical approach to literacy which takes into account its social parameters and sees the individual as part of a social and cultural framework from which literacy practices take their meaning (Heath 1983, Luke & Freebody 1997, Street 1993; 1984).

For many years now the concept of what it means to be literate has been undergoing a process of redefinition in parallel to changes in society and culture. Literacy does not consist merely in the acquisition of a set of functional and cognitive skills, but rather a set of social and cultural practices by which information is encoded and communicated (Gallego & Hollingsworth 2000). Formerly, to be literate meant to possess the skills of encoding and decoding written texts. From this perspective, once a person had become literate he was ready to embark on the process of learning. Literacy was seen as neutral, to be used for any purpose, whether good or ill, personal or collective. It was, in other words, an autonomous model of literacy (Street 1984).

However, literacy is not a context-free, value-neutral skill, but is linked with mastery of the processes by means of which culturally significant information is coded. Literacy is not confined to a set of detached skills; on the contrary it can be seen as a framework of socially organized practices in which individuals are involved. The notion of literacy as social practice spread among social psychologists and educationalists in the early 1980s, resting on the evolving theories and methodologies of socio-linguistics and the ethnography of communication (Scribner & Cole 1981). Since the 1970s and 1980s, a socio-cultural approach to literacy has been emerging in which the concept of literacy is related to social practices and conceptions of reading and writing (Street 2000; 1995, Vincent 2003; 2000).

We need, then, to understand literacy as something much broader than an enhanced form of skill. It should be seen rather as a set of social practices, not a narrow cognitive skill (Barton & Hamilton 2000, McLaren & Lankshear 1993). All literacy practices are incorporated within a social context. The objectives of literacy are holistic and not confined to individual outcomes (Markauskaite 2006). Everyday, intimate experiences of literacy influence and are influenced by the broader socio-cultural framework in which they occur (Reder & Davila 2005). Literacy is regarded as a socio-cultural practice. Theorists of literacy often prefer to use the term literary practices, instead of literacy skills, since the former lays emphasis on the importance of the actual application of literacy in a social context (Warschauer in press). Literacy as a social practice comprehends a whole range of skills, knowledge and resources, and literacy learning has a social basis. Access to literacy is closely tied to social, political and economic conditions (Freire 1970; Myers, Hammett & McKillop 1998).

Literacy as multiple socially constructed practices embraces three interrelated dimensions: the operational, the cultural and the critical. The operational dimension pertains to competency with language, the cultural dimension competency with regard to the meaning system, and the critical dimension the socially constructed nature of all human practices and meaning systems (Green 1988; Lankshear & Knobel 1997). It is worth pointing out that although the critical dimension of literacy is basic to the generation and transformation of meaning, schools pay it scant attention. Yet since the main purpose of education is the shaping of future citizens who can play an active part in and contribute to democratic processes and practices, the critical dimension of literacy must acquire a central place in education (Snyder 1998a). Literacy is a set of intellectual social practices; it is not confined to the skill of functional information acquisition. What interests us, therefore, is the transition from information retrieval to critical analysis, evaluation, and knowledge creation.

Literacy or Literacies

Literacy is a discourse—one of the most complicated discourses within a multicultural and multilingual society. In the past the term literacy was used to refer mainly to alphabetic literacy, and this was because the main technologies of literacy, such as the printing press, conceded a primary role to the written language in relation to other forms of semiosis, distinguishing verbal from iconographic information and representation. In recent years there has been a tendency to expand the notion of literacy beyond its initial application to the medium of writing. Literacy concerns the interpretation of all mediated symbolic texts (Livingstone 2004, 2003).

Since the 1980s the term emergent literacies (Spencer 1986) has come into use and many authors refer to new or multiple literacies (Buckingham 1993a; Tyner 1998). We thus hear mention of visual literacy (Moore & Dwyer 1994), television literacy (Buckingham 1993b, 1993c), cineliteracy (British Film Institute 2000) and information literacy (Behrens 1994, Bruce 1997). Finally, the emergence of the concept of multiliteracies (Cope & Kalantzis 2000) is related both to the social differentiation of the contemporary forms of literacy, and to the fact that the new media require new forms of cultural and communicational competence (Lotherington 2007).

The traditional definition of literacy appears to have met the requirements of a world dominated by the written word. But with the emergence of a whole host of new media, the traditional concept of literacy has been challenged and confusion has arisen, with new versions of literary appearing—such as computer literacy, cyber-literacy, internet literacy, network literacy, digital literacy and information literacy—as difficult to relate to each other as to the previous concepts of print literacy, audiovisual literacy, critical literacy, visual literacy, oral literacy, cultural literacy or social literacy (Livingstone 2003; 2002).

If we wish to understand oral, print and digital literacies in the context of our own times, it is useful to see literacy as a set of social events, with varied and sometimes opposing uses, in different contexts. There are different types of literacy, not only over the course of time but also within the same society. This is why theorists more frequently use the word in the plural 'literacies'. Furthermore, some authors have, metaphorically, expanded the concept of literacy to include the culture of reading (Hirsch 1987) or even more the 'reading of the world' (Freire & Macedo 1987).

Literacy is in fact a set of 'literacies', since print-based activities take many different forms. Literacies do not function outside of social and cultural contexts, nor are they neutral, since as practices they are interwoven with values, objectives and expectations (Martin-Jones & Jones 2000). We neither learn, nor teach nor use literacy skills in context-free ways (Snyder 1998b). Finally, it is worth mentioning that the concept of literacy is related to the concept of authority. Even the most commonplace significance of the term literacy, i.e., 'to be able to read and write', cannot conceal the fact that in historical terms literacy was related to authority in terms of possibility of access to, interpretation of and production of printed material (Luke 1989).

The concept of literacy evolves in line with historical and social change. What is regarded as literacy at one time will change at another, in accordance with the prevailing attitudes. We are currently experiencing the transition from exclusive print literacy to multimodal literacy (Kress 2003; 2000). Multiliteracies address literacy needs in the emerging digital era (Cope & Kalantzis 2000). However, it is argued that such proposed literacies as computer, media, visual and digital literacy are often provisional, speculative and distinguished by the subtle ideological and professional differences of their various constituents (Tyner 2003).

Those who claim that there is only one form of literacy, i.e., print literacy, believe that the term literacies causes confusion (Paul 2006). The metaphorical use of the term in such phrases as economic literacy, emotional or spiritual literacy, may have a certain charm, but it raises important questions, since all resemblance to the original meaning of the term is lost. The expressions may make sense in the English language, but in other languages the term literacy is much more closely related to the concept of writing, as, for example, in the French word alphabetization (Buckingham 2003). And thus some authors have insisted that the concept of literacy should continue to be confined to writing (Barton 1994; Kress 1998), while others claim that the visual media require a process of cultural learning which does not differ significantly from the learning of the written language (Messaris 1994).

Historically, the definition of literacy has been based on print and been monocultural. In general, definitions of literacy are associated with the symbolic system of a culture. However, competence in the symbolic system of just one culture is no longer enough in today's globalized world. In contrast to the position taken by Kress (2003), in which the concept of literacy should be based exclusively on writing, since this is the main practice of meaningmaking, others assert that literacy today is more than writing and reading competence in the script of a national culture (Luke 2000a). We now live in a transnational culture, where global networks of symbols, information and knowledge transcend traditional national frontiers (Cameron 2002; Castells 2000; Clyne 1994; Luke & Luke 2000). The traditional concept of literacy, then, involved just one literacy, in one medium, and in a monocultural national context, whereas the contemporary concept of literacy involves multiliteracies in multiple media and in a multicultural (transnational) context.

A classification of the different forms of literacy will distinguish between tool literacies and literacies of representation. The former relate to the general spread of new technological tools in society, including computer, network and technology literacy. Literacies of representation involve the need to analyze information and understand how meaning is created; they involve such areas as information, visual and media literacy (Tyner 1998).

Some authors have pointed to the multiplicity and complexity of literacies and propose a taxonomy of three components: broad or generic forms of literate practice (word, sound and image processing; e-mailing, netting and gaming); particular aspects of these practices and more specific activities falling within them; are procedures or techniques involved in these practices (Lankshear & Knobel 1997). This is a taxonomy which attempts to identify a number of new literacy skills necessary for proficient and critical participation in the emerging knowledge society. The spectrum of literacy includes: alphabetic literacy (writing of one's name), functional literacy (reading and writing), social literacy (communication in a cultural context), information literacy (critical location, evaluation and use of information) and digital information literacy (application of information literacy in the digital environment) (Bruce 1997).

The complexity of the current information environment, as we move into the digital age, requires a broad and complex form of literacy, one which does not only involve skill-based literacies and is not confined to any individual technology or set of technologies. In the complex and interrelated world of today the notion of literacy has been considered a monolith, while diverse alternative constructions of multiple literacies have been proposed (Hawisher & Selfe 2000). The new and traditional literacies combined will form a necessary condition of social participation. Thus the teaching of these literacies will need to be the objective of the education system (Kellner 2002). Moreover, long before the appearance of computers, the internet or debates on multiliteracy, children learned from mass media texts such as TV, movies, cartoons and comic books (Drotner & Livingstone 2008; Greenfield 1984; Livingstone 2002; Subrahmanyam & Greenfield 2008; Ware & Warschauer 2005).

Towards Digital Literacies

The last twenty years have been a period of unprecedented technological change. The process of digitalization has led to a convergence of the various media and brought significant changes to almost all areas of society, the economy and culture. The internet is becoming a cultural crossroads for work, play and social interaction (Livingstone 2009). Mobile phones are bringing new services, increasing mobility and transforming consumer habits. Digital technology transcends the boundaries of time and space in a manner never seen before, while also reshaping patterns of social life and cultural identity. As new communication behaviours evolve and access to information grows ever easier, new prospects for the dissemination of information and knowledge overturn the traditional structures. Thus a multidimensional information environment is taking shape, to deal with what requires a complex and broad form of literacy (Rosado & Belisle 2006).

Literacies and Technology

The ties between technology and literacy are close; some form of technology is involved in every form of literacy. From alphabetic to digital literacy, technologies are involved. The instruments used in encoding, decoding and making meaning, such as pens and printing presses, are forms of technology. Digital literacy mainly involves practices in which digital technologies are integral. Formerly, the technological means involved were regarded as ancillary to literacy, but we now realize the intimate inter-relationship between the two (Green & Bigum 1996). In the contemporary world literacy depends on understanding the multiple media and developing the skills to use them creatively. Each medium represents a unique environment, presenting the world from its own distinctive perspective. The medium we shape shapes us in turn. Press, television and new technologies all influence our perceptions, attitudes and behaviour.

The new media have not replaced their forerunners. Internet does not replace book (Grafton 2009) just as computer has not superseded television, and television has never replaced print. On the contrary, contemporary man lives in a media environment within which print, audiovisual and computer media are all incorporated. With the increasing convergence of the media, owing to digitalization, the boundaries between the media that were until recently quite discrete are now hard to trace. The increasing convergence of the media makes necessary the acquisition of skills and competencies corresponding to the multiple literacies required by the varied forms of contemporary communication. Media literacy offers a conceptual framework linking the various media and interpreting complex, mediated symbolic texts. By media literacy we mean the ability to access, analyze, evaluate and create messages (texts, images, sounds) through which we come face to face with everyday life. It covers the whole spectrum of media, including print, radio, television, cinema, music, the internet and other digital communication technologies (Aufderheide & Firestone 1993, Frechette 2002, Kubey 1997, Livingstone 2004).

It is argued that literacy changes in line with changes in the media. Thus the changing technologies entail changing literacies. From this perspective, literacy is not simply a characteristic of the individual user, but is medium-dependent. This is a view characterized by some degree of technological determinism. In reality there is a reciprocal process of influence between medium and user, between technology and society. Both technology and literacy are shaped by a complex process of transposition from modernity to post-modernity (Gee 2000, Poster 2001, Turkle 1995).

The new technologies are the symbol of progress into the information age. In technocratic discourses, technology is frequently presented as a universal remedy for social and educational problems, through a perspective of technological messianism. In reality, however, technology and literacy cannot be separated, and the reciprocal influence between them is unceasing. Moreover, in one sense reading and writing are also technology, since they convert thought and speech into records. Thus literacy is a technology of which records are the end products (Clanchy 1993). Almost all human activities are mediated by tools. What is important is not the properties of the tools in themselves but rather the way in which they are incorporated in and transform human activity.

Literacy retains close and reciprocal links with technology. An examination of these relations identifies three approaches: transformative, transactional and deictic. In the first approach, technology leads to a reshaping of literacy; in the second, technology and literacy reciprocally shape one another. The third approach, finally, assimilates both the previous approaches and proceeds even farther, asserting that literacy is continuously changing as the technology of literacy rapidly evolves, offering new opportunities but creating new challenges (Leu 2000).

As new technologies have developed and, in recent years, become increasingly complex, new literacies have appeared. New forms of literate practices are not simply a matter of technology. Technologies do not determine culture. On the contrary, they are products of specific cultural practices and literate traditions (Luke 2003b, 2000a). Many terms have been used in the literature to describe the new literacies. These terms are all related and some of them are used with synonyms, such as: information literacy, computer literacy (synonyms: information technology/electronic/electronic information literacy), library literacy, media literacy, network literacy (synonyms: internet literacy, hyper-literacy), digital literacy (synonym: digital information literacy) (Bawden 2001).

The development of computer literacy has followed the development of computer technology. Four stages can be discerned in the development of computer technology: the introduction of minicomputers, personal computers, the Web, and portable and wireless computing. In the 1970's most people did not have access to computers and computer literacy courses were confined to the need to know about computer technology. In the following decade the introduction of PCs allowed broader access to computers. Computer literacy courses included such topics as computer applications (word processing, spreadsheet etc.), history, basic computer operation, computer confidence, and the role of computer technology in the business world. The web made its appearance in the early 1990s but did not start to influence computer literacy courses until the end of that decade. The main topics included the use of applications to solve problems in specific knowledge domains and the social and ethical aspects of computers and computing. The availability of information technology led computer literacy to the idea of information literacy. In the last few years, portability and mobility have improved access to information and strengthened the ability to communicate. Computer literacy courses now include use of the web among their main topics (Hoffman & Blake 2003).

Use of the term computer literacy is limiting in that it focuses on technology while overlooking information content (Carbo 1997). The term first appeared with the spread of the PC, but was later questioned in the educational sector since it was identified with the most basic forms of computer operation. Computer literacy was described as a skill-based literacy, and unfortunately a narrow approach to the subject can still be found today. Technology continues to shape the definition of computer literacy. The development of technology changes not only the nature of computing but also how the technology itself is perceived by society (Bawden 2001).

With the development of information technologies in the early 1970s, the term information literacy also began to be used (Virkus 2003). While computer literacy was confined to the use of specific hardware and software applications, the term information literacy focused on the search for, analysis and evaluation of information. There is no commonly accepted definition of information literacy. The term is used in the literature widely and confusingly. This confusion is due to the fact that the words information and literacy are both vague and ambiguous. The term information literacy is often used without specific content, is the object of controversy and is continually being challenged (Snavely & Cooper 1997; Virkus 2003).

The concept of information literacy is not static but dynamic. It is continually being adapted to the requirements of different historical, social, cultural and technological contexts. It is regarded as part of a wider literacy continuum which has presented different degrees of development over the course of time (Behrens 1994). First appearing in the literature in 1974, information literacy incorporates abilities, knowledge and values related to the search for, access to, evaluation, organization and diffusion of information and knowledge. The contemporary meaning of the term is difficult to define, but among the many definitions perhaps the one encountered most frequently is that of the American Library Association:

> To be information literate, a person must be able to recognize when information is needed and have the ability to locate, evaluate, and use effectively the needed information. (ALA 1989:1)

In this definition, information literacy is regarded as a survival skill for the information age. Those who are information literate know how to choose the right information from the deluge of facts which inundate contemporary life and how to use to it solve problems or take decisions, regardless of whether the information in question is taken from a PC, a book, a film or any other source.

Information literacy is a natural extension of the concept of literacy to the information society (Bruce 2002). It is conceived as a behaviour which permeates all phases of human life. The essential characteristics of information literacy involve attitude, knowledge and skills (Boekhorst 2003). The term often focuses on strategies for searching for information. However, it mainly involves cognitive skills which users must possess if they are to evaluate information effectively. In a way, information literacy functions as a filter which can identify false, irrelevant or biased information. Information-literate individuals think critically and can question even information that is presented as valid and reliable. Information literacy is more of a knowledge than a skill and has more to do with education than training (Hornby & Clarke 2003).

In her exploring of the character of information literacy, Bruce (1997) distinguished seven different ways of experiencing information literacy. The features of each conception below describe both the meanings attributed to experience and the way people's awareness is structured:

i. The information technology conception. Information literacy is seen as using information technology for information retrieval and communication
ii. The information sources conception. Information literacy is seen as finding information located in information sources.
iii. The information process conception. Information literacy is seen as executing a process.
iv. The information control conception. Information literacy is seen as controlling information.
v. The knowledge construction conception. Information literacy is seen as building up a personal knowledge base in a new area of interest.
vi. The knowledge extension conception. Information literacy is seen as working with knowledge and personal perspectives adopted in such a way that novel insights are gained.
vii. The wisdom conception. Information literacy is seen as using information wisely for the benefit of others.

In addition to the term information literacy, many other related terms have been used by various authors: 'infoliteracy', 'informacy', 'information empowerment' 'information competence', 'information competency', 'information competencies', 'information literacy skills', 'information literacy and skills', 'skills of information literacy', 'information literacy competence', 'information literacy competencies', 'information competence skills', 'information handling skills', 'information problem solving', 'information problem solving skills', 'information fluency', 'information mediacy' and even 'information mastery' (Virkus 2003). The term information literacy is the most widely used (Bawden 2001). However, some authors have already abandoned the term in favour of alternatives such as information competency or mediacy.

These terms appear to be proposed either in order to avoid the constraints entailed by use of the word literacy, or to express a broader concept which embraces the whole spectrum of media (Webber & Johnston 2000).

Information literacy today is inseparably associated with information practices and critical thought in the ICT environment, and is regarded as the essential literacy for life in the 21st century (Bruce 2002). Information literacy supports and enriches lifelong learning through skills related to the use of technologies without this use, however, constituting a necessary condition. The descriptions of information literacy which have appeared since the early 1970s may be summarized in the form of three concepts: the ICT concept, the information (re)sources concept and the information process concept. In the first concept information literacy involves the competence to use ICT to retrieve and disseminate information, while in the second concept it involves the competence to find and use information independently or with the aid of intermediaries. The third concept, finally, involves both the previous concepts and is the most useful one. In this third concept information literacy involves the process of recognizing information need, retrieving, evaluating, using and disseminating of information in order to acquire knowledge (Boekhorst 2003).

Information literacy consists in the ability of individuals to recognize their information needs, locate and evaluate the quality of information; store and retrieve information, make effective and ethical use of information, and apply information to create and communicate knowledge. Information literacy involves broader issues and is not confined to ICT skills. These involve receiving and transmitting information using ICT, whereas information literacy involves the process of transforming information to create new knowledge before transmitting the new information. People may be information literate without possessing ICT skills, but the increasing role of digital information in the emerging knowledge societies makes it necessary that everyone should acquire information literacy skills. Thus the function of information literacy in knowledge society presupposes both access to information and the ability to use ICTs. (Catts & Lau 2008). ICTs have developed as a hybrid of printed text, sound and graphic imagery, just as print technology in the fifteenth century emerged in hybrid form as part script and part print (Luke 2003b, 2000a) .

ICTs have changed literacy practices as well as the concept of being literate in contemporary, technological society (Snyder 2000). Literacy practices based on computers and the internet are referred to as electronic literacies (Warschauer 1999). These are not isolated from print literacies, but serve as an umbrella term for many other generic literacies of the information era (Warschauer 2004). Electronic skills can be divided into three main categories:

ICT practitioner skills, ICT user skills and e-business skills (Hoffman & Blake 2003).

We can identify similarities between literacy and ICT access. Both are linked to advances in communication and the generation of knowledge. Just as literacy was a condition of participation in industrial capitalism, so ICT access is a condition of participation in information capitalism. Both suppose a connection to a physical artifact, to sources of information and to a skill level in order to utilize information. Both are to do not only with receiving information but also producing it. And both are associated with concepts of societal divides (the great literacy divide and the digital divide) (Warschauer in press). With the rapid evolution of the ICTs, a new form of literacy is emerging, which has been given a variety of names: computer literacy, internet literacy, cyber-literacy or digital literacy. This new form of literacy—if indeed it is new and if it is appropriately described as a literacy—is the subject of keen discussion both in the academic community and in the political and public space (Livingstone 2003, 2004).

Digital Literacies

There is no commonly accepted definition of the term digital literacy. It is a polysemic concept, used differently by different authors (Aviram & Eshet-Alkalai 2006). Moreover, terms such as IT literacy, computer literacy, digital skills, e-Skills or digital competence often describe similar phenomena. The term digital literacies concerns new forms of 'writing,' 'reading,' and 'research' which are based on digital media and are emerging alongside oral and print literacies. The digital literacies are to the digital media what literacy was to the printed media. They are associated with broader cultural, institutional and ideological changes characteristic of the transition from a culture of print literacy to a culture permeated by digital technology. Moreover, literacy is not only a technology but also a social institution. In the modern world people need a greater range of technical, cognitive and social skills if they are to carry out their duties and solve problems in digital environments. These skills are described in the literature as digital literacy (Gilster 1997; Inoue, Naito & Koshizuka, 1997; Pool 1997; Tapscott 1998).

Like any form of literacy, digital literacy refers to a person's ability to use and communicate information effectively and creatively. The term has a broad range of uses in the literature (Bawden 2008). Some of these are confined to purely technical aspects of the term, while others refer to its cognitive, psychological and social facets (Gilster 1997, Tapscott, 1998). Often the definitions of digital literacy are understood in a purely functional sense and only involve a set of skills relating to effective operation of hardware or software (Buckingham 2006). Thus digital literacy is seen as the person's ability to perform tasks effectively in a digital environment, or as the ability to find information efficiently on the web. Other definitions focus not so much on the technical skills required as on the broader cognitive skills and critical evaluation of digital information (Junge & Hadjivassiliou 2007).

Digital literacy is not confined to a simple ability to use software or machinery, but embraces a whole range of cognitive, social and emotional skills necessary if users are to perform effectively in digital environments. The term digital literacy is somewhat vague and changes with advances in technology. Often unclear use of the term causes confusion and thereby makes it harder to design and develop digital learning environments. Deviations in the terminology and the appearance of pleonasms are due mainly to the fact that digital technology is a relatively new phenomenon and there is a lack of extensive and in-depth research into digital literacies (Eshet-Alkalai 2004).

According to Gilster (1997:1) digital literacy is:

> ...the ability to understand and use information in multiple formats from a wide range of sources when it is presented via computers.

Digital literacy is

> ...the ability to access networked computer resources and use them. (Gilster 1997, xii)

Digital literacy does not consist merely in the skills involved in searching for information, but also involves the ability to use that information in daily life. Digital literacy

> ...refers to a way of reading and understanding information that differs from what we do when we sit down to read a book or a newspaper. The differences are inherent in the medium itself, and digital literacy involves mastering them. (Gilster 1997:28–29)

Digital literacy, like any other form of literacy, is not confined to a simple reading skill, but always involves the ability

> to read with meaning, and to understand. It is the fundamental act of cognition(Gilster 1997:1).

> Just as the hypertext is an extension of the traditional reading experience, so digital literacy is the logical extension of literacy itself (Gilster 1997).

Digital literacy involves the ability to use digital technology, communication tools or networks to identify, evaluate, use and create information. It represents the ability of a person to use digital information in the performance of tasks within digital environments, and to evaluate and apply the new knowledge he has acquired in those environments. In a digital era, literacy per se involves the ability to understand information in any form in which it may be presented. Digital literacy is not skill-based literacy, like computer literacy, but a literacy requiring a broad range of capabilities (Bawden & Robinson 2002). Often the term digital literacy is used to refer to competencies which ensure effective use of tools, practices and symbol systems of digital technologies. The features which characterize digital technologies are: the potential for nonlinear browsing, the random juxtaposition of content, interactivity, and the manipulation of text, sound, image, and the moving image. The digital media differ from print media in both the volume of source materials and the speed of information retrieval. Digital technology favours the interactivity, the immediacy, and the integration of multiple media. The term digital literacy refers to an ability to read and understand hypertextual and multimedia texts (Bawden 2001).

The invention of printing allowed the duplication, reproduction and distribution of information on a wide scale. Until then the bulk of information and knowledge had not been in written form, it had been handed down orally from generation to generation. Digital reproduction and distribution of information opened up new opportunities and new horizons. Hypermedia offered the ability to access information in a non-linear way. Of course, the roots of hypermedia lie in the era of the bound book, long before the invention of printing. While papyri were read in linear fashion, line by line, the bound volume allowed readers to leaf through a book and thus favoured a non-linear way of seeing the text that was easy and accurate (Eshet-Alkalai 2004, Eshet-Alkalai & Geri 2007).

Digital technologies favour the creation of new forms of social practices and immediacy. They abolish the constraints of time and space and reorganize spatial and temporal relations on a macro-transnational level and on a micro-level for inter-subjectivity (Luke 2003a). Digital literacy differs from print literacy since the same digital source may generate sounds, images and words in a way impossible with print. Digital media represent the world and offer particular interpretations of reality which contain particular values and ideologies. Digital media, like all media in fact, are related to broader social, political and economic forces.

The concept of digital literacy is expressed in terms of sets of particular skills to be learnt, and competences to be demonstrated. However, this approach is particularly limiting, since literacy transcends the bounds of mere skill acquisition (Bawden 2001). Attaining the objective of digital literacy does not involve obtaining more tools or skills or competencies. Digital literacies are socially and culturally constructed practices (Lankshear & Knobel 2006). Digital literacies are regarded as social practices in which texts are constructed, transmitted, received, modified, shared, within processes employing codes which are digitised.

The phrase 'digitally literate' can be misunderstood as an equivalence to traditional forms of print-based literacy—'digital reading and writing'. The digitally literate person is not someone who simply has the skill to practice digital reading and writing by analogy with the traditional form of print-based literacy. Digital literacy involves an interest, an attitude and an ability on the part of individuals to use appropriately the new digital technology for seeking and using information, constructing new knowledge and communicating with others—so that they can play an active role in society (Junge & Hadjivassiliou 2007).

Discussions about digital literacy focus more on information than on the cultural uses of the digital technology. From this perspective, a digitally literate individual is one who can search efficiently and manage and use information. However, this view appears to overlook the symbolic and emotional dimensions of digital media uses. Digital literacy is not confined to purely functional skills but means, above all, the ability to understand and evaluate critically the digital world (Livingstone, Bober, & Helsper 2005).

Information literacy and digital literacy are both related to information overload, the management of information, the creation of new knowledge and lifelong learning, within the context of the emerging knowledge society (Bawden 2009, Bawden & Robinson 2001). Information literacy is a long-standing concept, whereas digital literacy is more recent. Although both digital literacy and information literacy remain distinct, they are also converging. Information literacy and digital literacy, although linked to simpler skills-based literacies, are based on knowledge, perceptions and attitudes (Bawden 2001).

The vagueness of the concept of digital literacy is due to two factors. The first is the absence of a comprehensive conceptual framework and theoretical foundation. The second is the rapidly changing, continually evolving nature of the digital media, with the devices becoming ever more complex and containing ever more extensive and varied content (Martin & Grudziecki 2006). Until now discussion of the question of digital literacy has focused mainly on practical issues; there has not been a comprehensive conceptual framework, a theoretical foundation. In the literature we can discern two main strategies: the conservative and the sceptical The first rests on the assumption that digital literacy represents a set of skills, while the second assumes that there is something much more profound underlying those digital skills (Aviram & Eshet-Alkalai 2006, Eshet-Alkalai 2005 2004).

The first strategy is based on a belief that effective ICT-based learning presupposes specific skills, whereas the sceptical strategy poses more critical questions, challenging the very concept of digital literacy. The second strategy involves two different sceptical assumptions. According to the first of these, so-called digital literacy is no more than a signpost concealing personality characteristics such as learning styles, intelligence, capacities or personality types. According to the second, the term digital literacy conceals deeper cultural trends and conflicts, such as that between industrial culture, based on the book, and contemporary post-industrial digital culture. More systematically conceived digital literacy includes five types of literacy: photo-visual literacy, digital reproduction literacy, information literacy, branching literacy, socio-emotional literacy (Eshet-Alkalai 2004, Eshet-Alkalai & Amichai-Hamburger 2004). This conceptualization indicates that digital literacy is not confined merely to PC use or the searching for information on the internet, but mainly involves cognitive, critical and social skills.

Digital literacy is no longer an end-point to be achieved, but should be seen rather as part of a broader literacy continuum. It is a new form of literacy necessary in a world where digital technology plays an ever more significant role. We need to develop a multidimensional vision of the new technology-mediated literacy, a vision that includes its operational, cultural and critical aspects. Discussions of literacy involve, in reality, the manner and objectives of participation in society. A democratic and critical approach to literacy might lead to the framing of a strategy for transforming the user from passive to active, from receiver to participant, and from consumer to citizen (Livingstone, Bober & Helsper 2005).

Digital Literacies and Education

Formerly, literacy was defined as reading and writing, and was mainly the privilege of an elite. With the onset of the industrial revolution, mass education became necessary in order to train learners for the workforce (Agnello 2001, Vincent 2000). As we now pass from the industrial era of modernism towards post-modernism, society, under the impact of the ICTs, is becoming ever more complex (Gee 2001). Within this social context the question of literacy is being posed in new terms: what does it mean to be literate in our contemporary, multicultural, multilingual, digitally infused society?

Information, Knowledge & Learning in a Digital World

The ICTs have changed the nature and role of information and knowledge in society. The main changes involve accessing information, processing information and developing information and knowledge. In the new society that is emerging, knowledge is created, reproduced and transmitted at high speed. The development of ICTs has impacts on culture, economy and employment. Every so often new media make their way into our daily lives, blending with the old media in a complicated way and affecting the formation of young people's cultural identities.

The knowledge-based economy requires competencies related to the management and processing of information. As access to information is becoming more and more easy, and less and less expensive, the skills and abilities required for the choice, interpretation, critical evaluation and effective use of information acquire a vital importance. More and more, access to the world of work requires the possession of suitable technological skills. People without these skills find it difficult to participate in economic and social life, and are at risk of marginalization (European Commission 2000, OECD 2000, 1996).

In the contemporary world, a literate individual is one who can critically assess information in whatever form it is presented. Technology is the vehicle for information, and the evaluation of information assumes a special importance. Information literacy involves the adoption of that pattern of behaviour which will allow acquisition of the appropriate information through a medium, together with critical knowledge and ethical use of the information in society (Webber & Johnston 2003).

Information literacy is not a set of skills, competencies and characteristics. It is a complex of different ways of interacting with information which might also include knowledge about the world of information, a set of competencies or skills, a way of learning, contextual and situated social practices, power relationships in society and social responsibility (Warschauer &Ware 2008). A person who is information literate recognizes the need for information, recognizes that full and accurate information is the basis for intelligent decision-making, recognizes the potential sources of information. He develops successful research strategies, has access to information sources, including computer-based and other technologies, evaluates information and organizes it for practical application. Finally, he incorporates the new information in an existing system of knowledge, using it for critical thought and the resolution of problems. The information-literate person is one who possesses analytic and critical skills to frame research questions and evaluate the results, as well as skills enabling him to seek and access various types of information in order to meet his needs. The stages involved are those of need recognition, search formulation, source selection and interrogation, information evaluation and information synthesis and use (Webber & Johnston 2003).

An information-literate person is engaged in independent, self-directed learning and uses a variety of technologies and information systems. He has internalized values which promote the use of information; he has a robust knowledge of the information world, approaches information in a critical spirit, has a personal information style which makes it easy for him to interact with the world of information. He is characterized by the ability to acquire and use the appropriate information for any situation, on both local and global levels, and is able to survive and respond successfully to each information technology environment, to find the right information to solve problems on the personal and professional levels, to deal effectively with rapidly changing environments (DeBlock & Buckingham 2007).

The need to find, evaluate and make effective use of information has always existed, but in the contemporary ICT environment the fulfilment of this need requires more—as well as more complex and more important—abilities. The skills involved in the location, evaluation and use of information employing ICTs consist in the ability to develop research questions, determine the most likely places to seek information, select the correct search tool, formulate appropriate search queries, rapidly evaluate the result of a search query, including the reliability, authorship, and currency of a source, save and archive located information, and cite or refer to located information (Virkus 2003, Warschauer in press).

What characterizes digital technology is that it allows information to be generated faster and in greater quantity than ever before, but at the same time it causes the problem of information overload (Martin & Madigan 2006). The information overload which is particularly related to the development of digital information has created a new problem—information fatigue syndrome (Wilson 2001).

With the enormous increase in access to information, the ability to evaluate that information has now become a critical issue. Of course, the need for correct evaluation was always important, but in the information explosion of today it has assumed a critical role. The ability to assess and evaluate information correctly has become a necessary skill for participation in the information society. The huge volumes of information being moved across digital networks at dizzying speeds often make it difficult to evaluate the reliability and authenticity of the data. We are passing through a transitional period between the late age of print and the post-typographic society. It is a time at which the phenomenon of learning will be complex, as we move to post-industrial forms of knowledge acquisition and generation, without having left behind the educational contradictions of the industrial age (Warschauer 2007a).

Digital literacies influence the sciences, education at all levels and learning environments; they also facilitate lifelong learning. The rapid dissemination of new technologies transforms the nature of learning and literacy. However, technology does not transform learning and literacy by itself, but only in conjunction with other social, economic, political and cultural factors. Digital literacies involve ICT-specific knowledge but also broader critical literacy skills, some of which obviously preexisted the digital age but now acquire particular significance. Digital literacies are not confined to mastery of ICT tools but also involve competences and understanding to cope with the significant changes brought about by the knowledge society. In this society, the generation and reception of knowledge is more and more assisted by digital technology. The interactive use of ICTs offers the potential for the elaboration and construction of knowledge. ICTs create new opportunities for learning and can be used to represent knowledge in different contexts. In the contemporary world learning skills are focused on working with information to produce knowledge. The concept of information was always related to learning, but with the development of digital technology it has acquired a special role (Eshet-Alkalai, 2004, Rosado & Belisle 2006, Warschauer 2006).

The development of digital communication has created new opportunities for cooperative learning. The internet and digital communication offer many learning opportunities, but also create new problems (anonymity, use of false names, crackers or hackers). Socially literate users of the ICTs are able to benefit from the strengths of digital technology while avoiding the pitfalls.

In the contemporary living environment, children mix and match knowledge drawn from different media. Multimodal experiences originating in the use of these media constitute the social practices of everyday life. However, these practices often clash with the functions of formal education. Children do not learn to use computers only through formal education, but also alone, without a specific institutional context (Livingstone 2000). Informal learning is at least as important as formal learning, especially when procedural knowledge, such as computer use, is involved. What is important, then, is the development of more effective connections between children's experiences of technology in their leisure and in the classroom (Buckingham 2005a; 2005b, Facer, Furlong, Furlong & Sutherland 2003).

Digital technologies are not just a matter of 'information' or of 'technology'. Their consequences depend to a great extent on the manner and purpose for which we use them. Technological change mainly impacts on children, but affects adults too. However, the term 'digital generation' applied to younger people is in many respects one-dimensional, since it recognizes a decisive role for technology. But technology is a result, or rather a function, of other social processes and cannot be separated from economic, political and cultural conditions. There thus seems to be no basis for the rhetoric which claims that technology has a decisive and irrevocable impact on children (Buckingham 2008, Buckingham & Willett 2006). The transformation of society into a knowledge society is effected through complex interactions between technological, social, economic and human factors and does not blindly follow deterministic patterns. Society seems in fact to be moving towards the possible and the promising, without simple linear causality (Vryzas 2006).

Digital Literacies: A Challenge for Education

Education and literacy are very closely related. Literacy involves the acquisition of skills and knowledge and the acquiring of mental tools and capacities for effective learning and use of socially constructed forms of communication and representation. Literacies are socially constructed educational and cultural practices, which evolve in line with social and cultural change. In the constructivist approach to knowledge and learning, learning takes place in socio-cultural contexts and knowledge is constructed in and through social interaction, dialogue, negotiation, and contestation. This approach locates knowledge and learning, rather than technology, at the centre of pedagogy (Luke & Freebody 1997).

The term literacy is not confined to mechanical skills or functional competencies but is linked with a broader humanistic view. Literacy is not the teaching of a set of skills but rather a process which might transform for the better both learning and culture. The analysis of the role of literacy in contemporary education is a complex issue. The complexity is due to the confluence of literacy and technology issues and, moreover, to the intertwining of literacy issues with those of education. When more importance is attached to the performance of technique than to the relevant purpose, the gap between technology and literacy grows wider (Warschauer 2006).

In educational institutions, from ancient times to the present day, the curriculum and teaching methods have tended to be defined in terms of mastery and engagement with dominant modes of information. The domination of pedagogy by mode of information (spoken language and gesture, inscription and print, or visual image) will need to be reversed, i.e., it is pedagogy which will need to acquire the upper hand. Different conceptions of literacy lead to different pedagogical approaches. The modern world is marked by the gradual shift from printed culture to the culture of digital media. This change influences the framework of educational research. Today's children live in a mixed-media environment, watching television, videos and DVDs and playing electronic games. In other words they grow up in a multimedia, multimodal literacy. Literacy is activated in many ways and manages a combination of different symbolic systems (Luke 2001, Webber & Johnston 2000).

ICT has changed literacy practices as well as the very idea of being literate (Lankshear, Snyder & Green 2000). The younger generation have literacy experiences different from those of their teachers and parents. Digital technologies tend to appeal most to children and young people, while causing confusion among older adults. Thus it may well happen that in the classroom digitally literate children are being taught by technologically retarded adults. The fact that digital technology is so much more appealing to the young may lead to a digital gap between students and their teachers. The culture of the book and the printed word in which teachers were formed may prompt resistance or hostility to the new forms of literacy (Luke 2001; 2000b). We should not underestimate the importance of informal educational experiences, since they help to familiarize children with digital literacy practices (Knobel & Lankshear 2003). Moreover, before literacy became part of formal education, reading and writing were taught in the church, in trade and in other informal networks.

The media cannot be properly understood if we see them merely as hardware and software. Digital technologies offer new ways of mediating and representing the world. Children engage with the digital media in their everyday lives not as technologies but as cultural forms. The use of digital media at school cannot ignore these experiences. Digital literacy does not merely involve access to digital technologies or their use as learning tools, but is related to a broader critical understanding of the inherent characteristics of the digital media and with their social, economic and cultural impact. Within this perspective what is important is not the development of technical skills but the in-depth understanding of how the media work and the promotion of more reflective ways of using them (Buckingham 2007a).

Using media and engaging in literate practices is a way of engaging with the world. The digital media provide new ways of constructing and communicating meaning through multiple forms. Multiliteracy or the multimodal teaching approach do not mean simply that more than one mode of representation is used. On the contrary, they involve multiple ways of signing, such as image, voice, motion and print, to animate social life and social action (Kajder 2007).

Traditionally, literacy was understood as reading and writing. Today the scope of the term has expanded and we now speak of multi-literacies, a development which may cause confusion in terms of the meaning of the concept in the educational context. In the past, the school culture was centered on the book; literacy was print-based and the learning of literacy involved the understanding and generation of written texts. In our day, literacy practices extend beyond the tradition of print- and book-based knowledge. Literacy now extends beyond learning to read a printed text and involves multiple literacies in multiple modes. These multimodal practices involve a broad range of skills, knowledge and understanding (Luke 2007).

Learning and innovation are the key factors of the emerging knowledge society (Kalantzis & Cope 2008). Digital literacy is now a necessary condition of participation in the local and global economies and cultures. Our relations with the media are not autonomous but depend on the social contexts in which we live. The media are not neutral tools for delivering information and should not be used in a functional or instrumental way. The use of digital technologies in teaching presupposes an education in media so that students can understand and criticize them (Buckingham 2007b).

Since, thanks to digital technology, the traditional and new media are converging, new fields of educational research are opening up. The increasing convergence of the media and the range of contemporary forms of communication require skills and competencies which are linked with multiple literacies. New forms of literacies are not a pre-requisite to learning, but are linked to modifying, changing or constructing new learning experiences. They concern not only learning to use technology, but rather learning to use technology to support learning (Bruce 2002).

With the rapid advances in ICTs, the information environment is becoming more and more complex. Yet the availability of information and information technologies is still not sufficient. With the increasing access to digital technologies, the discussion now needs to turn from the quantity of available data to the quality of the contemporary experiences of literacy. The response to the sheer quantity of digital information by the educational establishment is definitely not a question of complete adaptation or outright rejection. Between these two extremes there lies a broad range of options. Schools do not appear to be taking fully into account the increasing availability of digital information in daily life; they are confining themselves to training in the use of digital tools. However, they need to promote the in-depth understanding of digital literacy necessary in the knowledge society (Rosado & Belisle 2006, Tyner 2003).

Schools usually encourage the reproduction of normative knowledge. A critical multiliteracy pedagogy, however, will not confine itself to 'deconstruction', but will also proceed to reconstruction. It is not only about decoding message systems into micro-components, but about encoding as well (Luke 2007). The school must favour the creation of a learning environment in which the students creatively and critically browse, research, organize, select, and produce various forms of expression using all the available literacy tools. Incorporating digital tools in the school culture will mean tackling the problem of 'commodification'. Educational technology has been criticized in the past for being used to replace or weaken the role of teachers, to disseminate and establish the values and interests of the dominant social forces, and to promote the idea of education as a commercial product rather than a process of lifelong learning (Apple 1995, Cuban 1986).

Educational approaches to the understanding and treatment of digital information are still evolving. There is no agreement on the inherent characteristics of the digital technologies, on the best ways of incorporating them into the educational environment, or even on what to call this new literacy. Debate on digital technologies and their educational uses is becoming ever more complex, since it involves symbolic systems of representation and pedagogical approaches (Tyner 2003).

Incorporation of ICTs in education has failed to attain its objectives owing to logistical, administrative, and pedagogical obstacles. Many studies have shown high levels of access and positive attitudes to the role of digital technologies in learning. However, the availability of the hardware does not alone guarantee creative use by students (Cuban 2003). There is little consensus on how ICTs should be incorporated in the learning environment. The use of digital technology in education is not simply a matter of skills, equipment, training and resources; it is linked with fundamental visions and perspectives, necessary for any real change in the educational system (Lankshear & Knobel 2006).

Because they are unfettered by constraints of space and time, the digital technologies allow access to education for learners who are isolated by distance, poverty, or disability. They offer a range of methods of expression and allow access to a wide spectrum of views beyond those of the teacher and the book. They offer new resources and experiences, and put forward alternative perspectives. As digital technology changes the way information is stored and processed, teaching and learning cannot remain the same. The new media influence the way we think. The role of digital technology in school depends, essentially, on the way in which it is used. The question, then, is not one of including digital technologies in the context of the traditional teaching approaches, but of incorporating them into suitable frameworks of creative learning and teaching, frameworks which favour critical, independent and creative use of information (Tsitouridou & Vryzas 2004; 2003).

Digital literacy involves much more than how people learn to use digital technologies. It is not so much a matter of acquiring more tools, skills or competencies, as a problem of approach to knowledge. As the context of information and knowledge changes, and access to information is made easier, students need to reflect on how they come to know things, what type of knowledge they have constructed, how knowledge changes them and what type of knowledge they will need in the new society that is emerging. However, the educational environment today does not seem to be creating the right conditions for such maturing and awareness (Rosado & Belisle 2006).

Digital literacy is seen as a critical factor in the promotion of the knowledge society. Although the school is no longer a key means in digital learning processes, it remains a primary institution for the generation and dissemination of knowledge. The term digital literacy is used in the planning of curricula and teaching approaches in a rather vague way. Yet the term ought to be founded on robust, well-founded research and on rational scientific discourse. It is not a matter of adding digital literacy to the curriculum or teaching ICTs as a separate subject; what we need is a broader re-conceptualization of the concept of literacy in a world inundated with digital devices. It is therefore necessary to re-conceptualize relations between means of learning (technologies), literacy objectives and contexts of learning (formal, informal, semi-formal). When the objectives of literacy are clarified, the choice of tools to promote critical literacy can follow (Buckingham 2006).

There is no single model of education for digital literacy that could be applied in all circumstances. A critical pedagogical approach requires that both students and teachers should be active generators of information, not passive consumers (Whitworth 2006). Literacy instruction is most effective when its content responds to the needs and social conditions of the learners (Freire 1970). We might say that the same is true in the case of digital literacy. Digital literacy curriculum is presented in terms of skills, competences, understandings, higher-order thinking skills, or meta-cognitive processes. Digital literacies are at the same time a set of semiotic practices, a set of socio-cultural practices and a set of meaning-making practices (Rosado & Belisle 2006).

In a digital world it is not enough that learners have access to different forms of information; they need to be able to use that information efficiently and critically, to be able to interpret and construct meaning. Studies of the integration of digital literacy tools in education have indicated that the rate of transition from alphabetic to digital literacy practices is very slow. While students acquire substantial expertise in digital technologies through informal use, in the school environment such expertise is confined to basic information retrieval strategies derived mainly from print literacy. The gap between textbooks and digital media can be overcome through the structuring of adequate learning environments that match learning goals, pedagogical approaches, and communication technologies. Digital literacy possesses the almost magical aura of technology. Yet it must incorporate elements of critical thinking (analysis, synthesis and evaluation). The educational challenge is not only one of technical know-how but also, and mainly, the acquisition of critical skills to assist users in becoming discriminating (Snyder 1998b).

In each case of literacy, technology and pedagogy must be harmonized in pursuit of a common goal: a democratic education, based on critical literacy, education through experience and critical pedagogy, improving the life opportunities of each and every child. Critical literacy practices are the basis for a democratic society, since the exchange of information requires individuals who are not interested only in efficiency and productivity, but in social justice (Freire 1970).

Critical media literacy does not only involve learning via media but also their appropriate use in constructive ways and the acquisition of an ability to resist possible media manipulation. In this way it contributes to the forming of citizens who are motivated and competent, able to create their own meanings, shape their own identities and influence the social conditions in which they live. Thus the media can be used to promote education, democratic involvement and social progress (Kellner & Share 2007; 2005, Poter 2005).

The requirements of literacy have changed and will continue to change, as the ICTs penetrate further into and transform our daily lives. And if education does not develop suitable pedagogical frameworks to include the digital media and new forms of communication, there is a risk that it will be the corporate experts and not the educators who determine how people learn, what they learn and what ICTs consist in (Luke 2007, Luke, Luke & Mayer 2000).

Literacy is not viewed only as social practice but also as social action. Literacy is not only about 'reading the word', but also about 'reading the world'—and not only about reading the world but also writing it and rewriting it (Freire & Macedo 1987). In Freire's perspective, technology-based literacy is not only surfing the net, but also about making waves (Shneiderman 1997).

Bridging the Digital Divide

Digital technologies are really nothing other than a different way of seeing the world, of interaction with and access to new ways of learning. ICTs not only offer new opportunities but also bring with them new forms of social exclusion. They are regarded as a multiplier of economic and social factors and processes, with the potential to help individuals, groups and even nations to develop. At the same time, however, dissemination of technology can also multiply existing inequalities, since the effective use of ICTs requires human and social resources which may magnify the differences in their distribution (Warschauer 2008).

The issue of the development of ICTs is related to the question of the digital divide. This is found not only in access to technology, but also in the ability to use it effectively. There are many perceptions of digital divide (Warschauer 2007b). Among the factors which contribute to the digital divide are access to equipment, skills, confidence and ability to use ICTs, attitudes towards ICTs and use of technologies (Selwyn 2004). The digital divide is regarded first of all as a divide between those who have access to new technologies, and those who do not. However, we must go beyond this dichotomy, taking into account not just access but also use, and types of use of technology (Muir & Oppenheim 2002). We must appreciate the different gradations of access to and use of technology, and how it relates to other forms of social exclusion (Selwyn & Facer 2009; 2007). However, digital technologies might facilitate access to information and communication for people who traditionally did not have such opportunities.

The digital divide has been featured in discussions on the topics of social exclusion, economic growth and the role of technology in the solving of social problems. It lies at the intersection between technology and inequality. It is a complex phenomenon which is related to processes of social reform, equity and inclusion (Warschauer, Knobel & Stone 2004). It has deep social roots which relate to relations of inequality and power; it is not susceptible to an exclusively technological approach.

Digital literacy is, first and foremost, social in character. It is seen as a social stratification due to unequal ability to access, adapt, and create knowledge via use of information and communication technologies (ICT) (Warschauer in press). This is a particularly interesting definition, since it recognizes the digital divide as a social problem linked to technology, not a technological problem with social consequences. The digital divide has an obviously economic dimension, since big business and capital dictate who has access to the new technologies and who does not. Thus the digital divide is not exclusively a matter of digital technology, but a far more complex problem

(Selwyn, Gorard & Furlong 2005), a problem that cannot be tackled in isolation, since account must be taken of the social, cultural and economic factors. Millions of people do not participate in digital culture, nor do they benefit from it. However, gaps in information access cannot be eliminated through the mere provision of more digital tools to more people. What is necessary is that we frame policies to support research into the relations between literacy and the digital media (Warschauer 2006). The optimal uses of digital media in society are not attainable except on the basis of a combination of digital capital and access to tools.

In their attempts to bridge the digital divide governments have managed to incorporate ICTs in education. However, the tackling of the digital divide must not focus solely on the provision of hardware, but must also take into account economic and social needs. The emphasis should not be on hardware and the purchase of equipment, but on teacher training and the curricular frameworks that determine what is needed and how it is to be used (Rosado & Belisle 2006).

Tackling the digital divide is not just a matter of acquiring a PC. It involves more than provision of a computer or the possibility of internet access. It is linked, rather, with the development of new forms of critical digital literacies, acquired through active involvement in practices which involve social interests. It is vital to develop suitable literacies, because otherwise social inequalities will not be overcome and social groups will remain excluded from the emerging networked society and culture. The response to the digital divide must take into account a whole range of factors, such as technological cost and affordability, public access, content, social networks and communities, mediating institutions and literacy (Warschauer 2008, 2004).

Education is called on to play a crucial role in bridging the digital divide. This will involve not only preparing the younger generation for employment, equipping them with the technical skills needed, but also, and even more important, developing reflective awareness of values and ethical choices in the digital world. However, social inequalities of access to ICTs tend to be reproduced in school, since teachers use ICTs on a limited basis, thereby benefiting only the most able or privileged students. Access to useful information is more than a question of infrastructure. What matters is the learner's relation to knowledge and literacy and the role of the learner in constructing his or her knowledge (Cope & Kalantzis 1993).

Digital literacy is a priority for the European Union. Since 2000 a series of initiatives has been undertaken to promote the digital literacy of the population in preparation for the emerging knowledge society. However, digital literacy remains a problem for the EU. Despite significant initiatives to improve access to ICTs and the way they are used, there is still a by no means negligible percentage of the European population who lack basic ICT skills. Levels of digital literacy are low among women, in particular, among the elderly and among those with little formal education. Moreover, a significant proportion of the unemployed of the EU lack basic ICT skills (European Commission's Digital Literacy Review 2008, Junge & Hadjivassiliou 2007).

Digital technologies are seen as a warning as well as a promise. Digital literacy may be liberating—or confining. The results will depend on whether it is used as a tool of creativity or of conformity (Kaestle 1991).

Conclusions

In brief, we might say that the concept of literacy, as defined by Warschauer (in press), has five main features:

i. There is not just one, but many types of literacy
ii. The meaning and value of literacy varies in particular social contexts
iii. Literacy exists in gradations, rather than in a bipolar opposition
iv. Literacy alone brings no automatic benefit outside of its particular functions
v. Acquisition of literacy is a matter not only of education and culture, but also of power.

With the development of technology, new media are continually appearing, which do not supersede the old media but interact with them. The new digital media which are associated with the new forms of literacy in fact make the traditional literacies more valuable than ever before. Furthermore, competence in traditional literacies is often a gateway to successful entry into the world of new literacies (Warschauer 2007a). Technology of itself is not, of course, a solution to the problem of education; but it does provide opportunities which might be exploited in the context of a critical pedagogic approach.

Until the mid-1980s the approach to the use of information technology was seen mainly in the guise of acquisition of specialized programming knowledge. Today, however, there is a need for more critical and reflective approaches to digital literacy. The development of digital technology requires more complex conceptualization of digital literacy, as well as a whole range of skills (Martin & Grudziecki 2006).

The definitions of digital literacy in the literature display a confusion caused by varied terminologies, meanings and mutually contradictory definitions. But what counts is not so much the denomination attached to concepts as the concept itself, and its significance for practice. Digital literacy is associated with such issues as information overload, lifelong learning, knowledge management and the growth of the information society. To meet the demands of a complex information environment, we need a broad and complex form of literacy; one that is not confined to skill-based literacies or to specific technologies. It does not matter whether we call it information literacy, digital literacy, or simply literacy for an information age. What is important is that understanding, meaning and context should all be fundamental to the concept of literacy (Bawden 2001).

Bibliography

Agnello, M. F. (2001). *A postmodern literacy policy analysis*. New York: Peter Lang.

American Library Association (ALA) (1989). Presidential Committee on Information Literacy. Final Report. Chicago: *American Library Association*.

Apple, M. (1995). *Education and Power*. London: Routledge.

Aufderheide, P. and Firestone, C. M. (1993). *Media literacy: A report of the National Leadership Conference on Media Literacy*. Washington, DC: The Aspen Institute.

Aviram, R., and Eshet-Alkalai, Y. (2006). Towards a theory of digital literacy: Three scenarios for thenextsteps. *European Journal of Open Distance E-Learning*, available at http://www.eurodl.org/materials/contrib/2006/Aharon_Aviram.htm.

Barton, D. (1994). Literacy: *An Introduction to the Ecology of Written Language*. Oxford: Blackwells.

Barton, D. and Hamilton, M. (2000). Literacy practices. In D. Barton, M. Hamilton & R. Ivanič (eds.), *Situated literacies: reading and writing in context*, pp.7–15. London: Routledge.

Bawden, D. (2009). The dark side of information: Overload, anxiety and other paradoxes and pathologies. *Journal of Information Science*, 35(2), 180–191.

—— (2008). Origins and concepts of digital literacy. In C. Lankshear & M. Knobel (eds.), Digital *Literacy: Concepts, policies and paradoxes*, pp.17–32. New York: Peter Lang.

—— (2001). Information and digital literacies: A review of concepts. *Journal of Documentation*, 57(2), 218-259.

Bawden, D., and Robinson, L. (2002). Promoting literacy in a digital age: Approaches to training for information literacy. *Learned Publishing* 15, 297–301.

Bawden, D., and Robinson, L. (2001). Training for information literacy: Diverse approaches Online Information 2001: Proceedings pp. 87–90. Oxford: Learned Information Europe.

Behrens, S. J. (1994). A conceptual analysis and historical overview of information literacy. *College and Research Libraries*, 55(4), 309–322.

Boekhorst, A. K. (2003). Becoming information literate in The Netherlands. *Library Review*, 52(7), 298–309.

British Film Institute (2000). *Moving images in the classroom: A secondary teacher's guide to using film and television*. London: British Film Institute.

Bruce, C. (2002). *Information literacy as a catalyst for educational change: A background paper*. White Paper prepared for Unesco, the U.S. National Commission on Libraries and Information Science, and the National Forum on Information Literacy. Prague, available at: http://www.nclis.gov/libinter/infolitconf&meet/papers/bruce-fullpaper.pdf.

Bruce, C. (1997). *The seven faces of information literacy*. Adelaide: Auslib Press.

Buckingham, D. (2008). *Youth, identity, and digital media*. Cambridge, MA: MIT Press.

—— (2007a). Digital media literacies: Rethinking media education in the age of the Internet. *Research in Comparative and International Education*, 2(1), 43–55.

—— (2007b). *Beyond technology: Children's learning in the age of digital culture*. Cambridge: Polity.

—— (2006). Defining digital literacy. What do young people need to know about digital media? Digital kompetanse. *Nordic Journal of Digital Literacy*, 1(4), 263–276.

—— (2005a). *The media literacy of children and young people: A review of the research literature*. London: OFCOM.

—— (2005b). Schooling the digital generation: *Popular culture, the new media and the future of education*. London: Institute of Education.

—— (1993a). *Changing literacies: Media education and Modern culture*. London: Tufnell.

—— (1993b). *The development of television literacy: Talk, text and context*. London: University of London.

—— (1993c). *Children talking television: The making of television literacy*. London: Falmer.

—— (2003). *Media education: Literacy, learning, and contemporary culture*. Cambridge: Polity Press.

Buckingham, D., & Willett, R. (2006). *Digital generations: Children, young people, and new media*. Mahwah, NJ: Lawrence Erlbaum Associates.

Cambridge Advanced Learner's Dictionary (2009). Available at http://dictionary.cambridge.org/define.asp?key=46569&dict=CALD.

Cameron, D (2002). Globalization and the teaching of 'communication skills'. In D. Block & D. Cameron, (eds.), *Globalization and language teaching*, pp.67–82. London: Routledge.

Carbo, T. (1997). Mediacy: Knowledge and Skills to Navigate the Information Highway. *International Information and Library Review*, 29, 393–401.

Castells, M. (2000). *The rise of the network society*. Malden, MA: Blackwell.

Catts, R., and Lau, J. (2008). *Towards information literacy indicators*. Paris: Unesco.

Cheetham, G. and Chivers, G. (2000). A new look at competent professional practice. *Journal of European Industrial Training*, 24(7), 374–383.

—— (1998). The reflective (and competent) practitioner: A model of professional competence which seeks to harmonise the reflective practitioner and competence-based approaches. *Journal of European Industrial Training*, 22 (7), 267–276.

Clanchy, M. T. (1993). *From Memory to Written Record: England 1066 – 1307*. Oxford: Blackwell Publishers.

Clifford, G.J. (1984). Buch und lesen: Historical perspectives on literacy and schooling. *Review of Educational Research*, 54(4), 472–500.

Clyne, M. (1994). *Intercultural communication at work: Cultural values in discourse*. Cambridge: Cambridge University Press.

Cope, B.,and Kalantzis, M. (eds.) (2000). *Multiliteracies: literacy learning and the design of social futures*. London: Routledge.

—— (1993). *The Powers of Literacy: a Genre Approach to Teaching Writing*. London: Falmer Press.

Cuban, L. (1993) Computers meet classroom: Classroom wins. *Teachers College Record*, 95(2), pp. 185.

—— (2003). *Oversold and Underused: Computers in the Classroom*. Harvard University Press.

—— (1993). *How teachers taught: Constancy and change in American classrooms 1890–1980*. New York: Longman.

—— (1986). *Teachers and machines: The classroom use of technology since 1920*. New York: Teachers College Press.

De Block, L., and Buckingham, D. (2007). *Global children, global media: Migration, media and childhood*. Basingstoke: Palgrave Macmillan.

deCastell, S., and Luke, A. (1986). Models of literacy in North American schools: Social and historical conditions and consequences. In S. de Castell, A. Luke & K. Egan (eds.), *Literacy, society, and schooling*, pp. 87–109. New York: Cambridge University Press.

Drotner, K., and Livingstone, S. (eds.) (2008). *The international handbook of children, media and culture*. London: Sage.

Eisenstein, E. L. (1979). *The printing press as an agent of change: Communications and cultural transformations in early-modern Europe*. Cambridge: Cambridge University Press.

Eshet-Alkalai, Y. (2005). Thinking skills in the digital era. In C. Haward, J. V. Bottcher, L. Justice, K. Schenk, P. L. Rogers & G. A. Berg (eds.), *Encyclopedia of distance learning*, vol. I, pp. 1840–1845. London: Idea Group Inc.

—— (2004). Digital literacy: A conceptual framework for survival skills in the digital era. *Journal of Educational Multimedia and Hypermedia*, 13(1), 93–106.

Eshet-Alkalai, Y., and Amichai-Hamburger, Y. (2004). Experiments with digital literacy. *Cyber Psychology and Behavior*, 7(4), 425–434.

Eshet-Alkalai, Y., and Geri, N. (2007). Does the medium affect the message? The influence of text representation format on critical thinking. *Human Systems Management*, 26(4), 269–279.

European Commission (2000). *A memorandum on lifelong learning. Brussels:* European Commission.

European Commission's Digital Literacy Review (2008). *e-inclusion Digital Literacy European Commission Working Paper and Recommendations from Digital Literacy*, High-Level Expert Group, Ministerial Conference and Expo 30th November–2nd December 2008 Vienna Austria, available at

http://ec.europa.eu/information_society/eeurope/i2010/docs/digital_literacy/digital_literacy_ review.pdf

Facer, K., Furlong J., Furlong, R., and Sutherland, R. (2003). *Screen play: Children and computing in the home*. London: Routledge Falmer.

Felstead, A., Gallie D., Green F., and Zhou Y. (2007). *Skills at work, 1986 to 2006*, University of Oxford, SKOPE.

Frechette, J. D. (2002). *Developing media literacy in cyberspace: Pedagogy and critical learning for the twenty-first century classroom*. New York:Praeger Publishers.

Freire, P. (1970). *Pedagogy of the oppressed*. New York: Seabury.

Freire, P., and Macedo, D. (1987). *Literacy: Reading the word and the world*. South Hadley, MA:

Bergin and Garvey.

Gallego, M. A., and Hollingsworth, S. (2000). Introduction. The idea of multiple literacies. In M.A. Gallego & S. Hollingsworth (eds.), *What counts as literacy: Challenging the school standard* pp.1–23. New York: Teachers College Press.

Gee, J. P. (2001). Literacies, schools and kinds of people: Educating people in the new capitalism. In M. Kalantzis & B. Cope (eds.), *Transformations in language and learning: Perspectives on multiliteracies*, pp. 81–98.Champaign, IL: Common Ground.

—— (2000). New people in new worlds: Networks, the new capitalism and schools. In B. Cope & M. Kalantzis (eds.), *Multiliteracies: Literacy learning and the design of social futures*, pp. 43–68. London: Routledge.

—— (1996). *Social linguistics and literacies*. London: Taylor & Francis.

—— (1991). *Social linguistics: Ideology in discourses*. London: Falmer Press.

Gee, J. P. (1988). *The legacies of literacy: From Plato to Freire through Harvey Graff. Harvard Educational Review*, 58, 195–212.

Gilster, P. (1997). *Digital Literacy*. New York: Wiley Computer Publishing.

Goody, J. (1987). *The interface between the written and the oral*. Cambridge: Cambridge University Press.

—— (1986). *The logic of writing and the organisation of society*. Cambridge: Cambridge University Press.

—— (Ed.) (1968). *Literacy in traditional societies*. Cambridge: Cambridge University Press.

Goody, J., and Watt, I. (1968). The consequences of literacy. In J. Goody (ed.), *Literacy in traditional societies*, pp. 27–68. Cambridge: Cambridge University Press.

Graff, H. J. (2001). Literacy. In P. S. Boyer (ed.), *The Oxford companion to United States history*. Oxford University Press. Oxford Reference Online, available at http://www.oxfordreference.com/views/ENTRY.html?subview=Main&entry=t119.e0910

—— (1995). *The labyrinths of literacy: Reflections on literacy past and present*. Pittsburgh, PA: University of Pittsburgh Press.

——. (1987). *The legacies of literacy: Continuities and contradictions in Western culture and society*. Bloomington,: Indiana University Press.

——.(1979). *The Literacy myth: Literacy and social structure in the nineteenth century city*. London: Academic Press.

Grafton, A. (2009). *Worlds made by words: Scholarship and community in the modern West*. Cambridge, MA: Harvard University Press.

Gray, W. S. (1956). *The teaching of reading and writing*. Chicago: Unesco and Scott Foresman.

Green, B. (1988). Subject-specific literacy and school learning. *Australian Journal of Education*, 32(2), 156–179.

Green, B., and Bigum, C. (1996). Hypermedia or media hype? New technologies and the future of literacy education. In G. Bull & M. Anstey (eds.), *The literacy lexicon*, pp.193–204. Sydney: Prentice Hall.

Greenfield, P. M. (1984). *Mind and media: The effects of television, video games, and computers*. Cambridge, MA: Harvard University Press.

Gurak, L. J. (2001). *Cyberliteracy: Navigating the internet with awareness*. New Haven, CT: Yale University Press.

Hartley, J. (2002). *Communication, cultural and media studies: The key concepts*. London: Routledge.

Hawisher, G. E., and Selfe, C. L. (2000). Conclusion: Inventing postmodern identities: Hybrid and transgressive literacy practices on the web. In G. E. Hawisher & C. L. Selfe (eds.), *Global literacies and the world-wide web*, pp. 277–289. London: Routledge.

Heath, S. B. (1983). *Ways with words: Language, life and work in communities and classrooms.* Cambridge: Cambridge University Press.

Hillerich, R. (1976). Toward an assessable definition of literacy. *The English Journal*, 65(2), 50-55.

Hirsch, E. D. (1987). *Cultural literacy: What every American needs to know.* Boston: Houghton Mifflin.

Hoffman, M., and Blake, J. (2003). Computer literacy: today and tomorrow. *Journal of Computing Sciences in Colleges*,18(5), 221 - 233.

Hornby, S., and Clarke, Z. (eds.). (2003). *Challenge and change in the information society.* London: Facet Publishing.

Inoue, H., Naito, E., and Koshizuka, M. (1997). Mediacy: What it is? Where to go? *International Information & Library Review*, 29 (3–4), 403–413.

Junge, K., and Hadjivassiliou, K. (2007). What are the EU and member states doing to address digital literacy? *eLearning Papers*, 6, 1887–1542.

Kaestle, C. F. (1991). Studying the history of literacy. In C. F. Kaestle, H. Damon-Moore, L. C. Stedman, K. Tinsley, & W. V. Trollinger, (eds.), *Literacy in the United States: Readers and reading since 1880*, pp. 3–32. New Haven, CT: Yale University Press.

Kajder, S. B. (2007). Bringing new literacies into the content area literacy methods course. *Contemporary Issues in Technology and Teacher Education*, [Online serial], 7(2), available at http://www.citejournal.org/vol7/iss2/general/article3.cfm.

Kalantzis, M., and Cope, B. (2008). *New Learning: Elements of a Science of Education.* Cambridge: Cambridge University Press.

Kellner, D. M. (2002). Technological revolution, multiple literacies, and the restructuring of education. In I. Snyder (ed.), *Silicon literacies: Communication, innovation and education in the electronic age*, pp.154–170. London: Routledge.

Kellner, D. and Share, J. (2007). Critical media literacy: crucial policy choices for a twenty-first-century democracy. *Policy Futures in Education*, 5(1), 59–69.

Kellner, D., and Share, J. (2005).Toward critical media literacy: Core concepts, debates, organizations, and policy. *Discourse: studies in the cultural politics of education*, 26(3), 369–386.

Knobel, M.,and Lankshear, C. (2003). Researching young children's out-of-school literacy practices. In N. Hall, J. Larson & J. Marsh (eds.), *Handbook of early childhood literacy*, pp. 51–65. London: Sage.

Koper, R. (2000). *From change to renewal: Educational technology foundations of electronic learning environments.* Heerlen: Report from the Open University of the Netherlands.

Kress, G. (2003). *Literacy in the new media age.* London: Routledge.

—— (2000). Multimodality, in B. Cope & M. Kalantzis (eds.), *Multiliteracies: Literacy learning and the design of social futures*, pp.182–202. London: Routledge.

——. (1998). Visual and verbal models of representation in electronically mediated communication: the potentials of new forms of text, in I. Snyder (ed.), *Page to Screen: Taking literacy into the electronic* era, pp.53–79. London: Routledge.

Kubey, R. (ed.) (1997). *Media literacy in the information age.* New Brunswick, NJ: Transaction

Publishers.

Lankshear, C., and Knobel, M. (2006). *New literacies: Changing knowledge in the classroom.* London: Open University Press.

—— (1997). Literacies, texts and difference in the electronic age. In C. Lankshear (ed.), *Changing literacies*, pp.133–163, Buckingham: Open University Press.

Lankshear, C., Snyder, I., and Green, B. (2000). *Teachers and technoliteracy: Managing literacy, technology and learning in schools.* St Leonards Australia: Allen & Unwin.

Lerner, D. (1958). *The passing of traditional society.* New York: Free Press.

Leu, D. J. (2000). Literacy and technology: Deictic consequences for literacy education in an information age. In M. L. Kamil, P. Mosenthal, P. D. Pearson, & R. Barr (eds.), *Handbook of reading research*, vol 3, pp. 743–770. Mahwah, NJ: Erlbaum.

Levi-Strauss, C. (1983). *Structural anthropology.* Chicago:University of Chicago Press.

Livingstone, S. (2009). *Children and the internet: Great expectations and challenging realities.* Cambridge: Polity.

—— (2004). Media literacy and the challenge of new information and communication technologies. *The Communication Review*, 7, pp.3–14.

—— (2003). *The changing nature and uses of media literacy.* Available at http://www.lse.ac.uk/collections/media@lse/pdf/Media@lseEWP4_july03.pdf.

—— (2002). *Young people and new media: Childhood and the changing media environment.* London:Sage.

—— (2000). Research report: thoughts on the appeal of 'screen entertainment culture' for British children. In Lees, Tim and Ralph, Sue and Langham Brown, Jo, (eds.) *Is regulation still an option in a digital universe? Papers from the 30th University of Manchester International Broadcasting Symposium, 1999.* Luton: University of Luton Press 43-64

Livingstone, S., Bober, M. and Helsper, E. J. (2005). Active participation or just more information? Young people's take up of opportunities to act and interact on the internet. *Information, Communication and Society*, 8(3), 287–314.

Lotherington, H. (2007). From literacy to multiliteracies in ELT. In C. Davison & J. Cummins (eds.), *Handbook of English language teaching*, pp. 891–905. Berlin: Springer.

Luke, C. (2007). New literacies—new media: mediascapes and infoscapes. In P.Puamau (ed.), *Pacific voices teacher education on the move*, pp. 177–200. The Pride Project Institute of Education University of the South Pacific.

—— (2003a). Critical media and cultural studies in new times, in T. Lavender, B. Tufte, & D. Lemish (eds.), *Global trends in media education*, pp.105–118. New York: Hampton Press.

—— (2003b). New directions in ICT research: Pedagogy, connectivity, multimodality, and interdisciplinarity. *Reading Research Quarterly*, 38(3), 397–403.

—— (2001). New times, new media: Where to media education? *Media International Australia*, 101, 87–100.

—— (2000a). Cyberschooling and technological change: Multiliteracies for new times, in M. Kalantzis & B. Cope (eds.). *Multiliteracies: Literacy learning and the design of social futures*, pp. 69–91. London: Routledge.

—— (2000b). New literacies in teacher education. *Journal of Adolescent and Adult Literacy*, 43(5), 424–435.

—— (1989). *Pedagogy, printing, and protestantism: The discourse on childhood.* Albany: State

University of New York Press.

Luke, A., and Freebody, P. (1997). Shaping the social practices of reading. In S. Muspratt, A. Luke, & P. Freebody (eds.), *Constructing critical literacies: Teaching and learning textual practice*, pp.185–225. St. Leonards, NSW: Allen & Unwin.

Luke C. and Luke, A. (2000). A situated perspective on cultural globalisation. In N. Burbules & C. Torres (eds.), *Globalisation and educational policy*, pp.275–298. New York: Routledge.

Luke, A., Luke C. and Mayer, D. (2000). Redesigning teacher education. *Teaching Education*, 11(1), 1–6.

Markauskaite, L. (2006). Towards an integrated analytical framework of information and communications technology literacy: From intended to implemented and achieved dimensions. *Information research*, 11(3), available at http://informationr.net/ir/11-3/paper252.html.

Martin, A., and Madigan, D. (eds.) 2006. *Digital literacies for learning*. London: Facet Publishing.

Martin, A., and Grudziecki, J. (2006). DigEuLit: Concepts and tools for digital literacy development, *Italics*, 5 (4), available at

http://www.ics.heacacademy.ac.uk/italics/vol12iss4/ martin-gruziecki.pdf

Martin-Jones, M., and Jones, K. (2000). Introduction: Multilingual literacies. In M. Martin-Jones & K. Jones (eds.), *Multilingual literacies*, pp. 1–15. Amsterdam: John Benjamins.

McGarry, K. J. (1994). Definitions and meaning of literacy. In K. Barker & R. Lonsdale (eds.), *Skills for life? The meaning and value of literacy*, 3–17. London: Taylor-Graham.

McGarry, K. J. (1993). *The changing context of information: An introductory analysis*. London: Library Association Publishing.

McLaren, P., and Lankshear, C. (1993). Critical literacy and the postmodern turn. In C. Lankshear, P. McLaren (eds.), *Critical literacy: Politics, praxis, and the postmodern*, pp. 379–421. Albany: State University of New York Press.

McLuhan, M. (1962). *The Gutenberg galaxy: The making of typographic man*. Toronto: University of Toronto Press.

Messaris, P. (1994). *Visual 'literacy': Image, mind and reality*. Boulder, CO: Westview.

Moore, D., and Dwyer, F. (1994). *Visual literacy: A spectrum of visual learning*. Englewood Cliffs, NJ: Educational Technology Publications.

Muir, A., and Oppenheim, C. (2002). National information policy developments worldwide II: Universal access–addressing the digital divide. *Journal of Information Science*, 28(4), 263-273.

Myers, J., Hammett, R., and McKillop, A.M. (1998). Opportunities for critical literacy and pedagogy in student – authored hypermedia. In D. Reinking, M. McKenna, L. Labbo, & R. Kieffer (eds.), *Handbook of literacy and technology: Transformations in a post-typographic world*, pp.63–78.Mahwah. NJ: Lawrence Erlbaum.

—— (2000). *Learning to bridge the digital divide*. Paris: OECD Publishing .

—— (1996). *The knowledge based economy*. Paris: OECD.

OECD (2000). *Literacy in the Information Age, Final Report of The International Adult Literacy Survey*. Paris: OECD Publications Service.

Olson, D. R. (1994). *The world on paper*. Cambridge: Cambridge University Press.

Oxford Dictionary of English. (2005). Oxford: Oxford University Press.

Paul, P. (2006). New literacies, multiple literacies, unlimited literacies: What now, what next, where to? A response to Blue Listerine, parochialism and ASL literacy. *The Journal of Deaf Studies and Deaf Education* 11(3), 382–387.

Pool, C. R. (1997). A new digital literacy: A conversation with Paul Gilster. *Educational Leadership*, 55(3), 6–11.

Poster, M. (2001). *What's the Matter with the internet?* Minneapolis: University of Minnesota.

Poter, J. (2005). *Media literacy*. London: Sage.

Prensky, M. (2001). Digital natives, digital immigrants. *On the Horizon*, 9(5), 1–6.

Reder, S.,and Davila, E. (2005). Context and literacy practices. *Annual Review of Applied Linguistics*, 25, 170–187.

Rosado E., and Bélisle Cl. (2006). Analysing digital literacy frameworks. A European framework for digital literacy (eLearning Programme 2005–2006). Available at http://hal.archives-ouvertes.fr/ docs/00/13/77/79/PDF/ Analysing-Edu-Frameworks.pdf.

Savolainen, R. (2002). Network competence and information seeking on the Internet: From definitions towards a social cognitive model. *Journal of Documentation*, 58(2), 211–226.

Scribner, S., and Cole, M. (1981). *The psychology of literacy*. Cambridge, MA: Harvard University Press.

Selwyn, N. (2004). Reconsidering political and popular understandings of the digital divide. *New Media & Society*, 6(3), 341–362.

Selwyn, N. and Facer, K. (2009). Beyond digital divide: Towards an agenda for change, in E. Ferro, Y. Dwivedi, R. Gil-Garcia, & M.,Williams, (eds.), *Handbook of research on overcoming digital divides: Constructing an equitable and competitive information society*, pp.1–20. Hershey, PA: IGI Global.

—— (2007). *Beyond the digital divide. Rethinking digital inclusion for the 21st century*. Available at www.futurelab.org.uk/ opening education.

Selwyn, N., Gorard, S., and Furlong, J. (2005). *Adult learning in the digital age*. London: Routledge.

Shneiderman, B. (1997). Foreword. In R. Debski, J. Gassin, & M. Smith (eds.), *Language learning through social computing*, pp. v–viii. Melbourne: Applied Linguistics Association of Australia.

Snavely, L., and Cooper N. (1997). The information literacy debate. *The Journal of Academic Librarianship*, 23(1), 9–14.

Snyder, I. (2000). Literacy and technology studies: Past, present and future. *Australian Educational Researcher*, 27(2), 97–119.

Snyder, I. (ed.) (1998a). *Page to screen: Taking literacy into the electronic era*. London: Routledge.

—— (1998b). Beyond the hype: Reassessing hypertext, in I. Snyder (ed.), *Page to screen: Taking literacy into the electronic era*, pp. 125–143. London: Routledge.

Spencer, M. (1986). Emergent literacies: a site for analysis. *Language Arts*, 63(5), 442–453.

Street, B. (2000). Literacy events and literacy practices: Theory and practice in the new literacy studies, In M. Martin-Jones & K. Jones (eds.), *Multilingual literacies*, 17–29. Amsterdam: John Benjamins.

—— (1995). *Social literacies: Critical approaches to literacy in development, ethnography and education*. London: Longman.

—— (ed.) (1993). *Cross-cultural approaches to literacy*. Cambridge UK: Cambridge University Press.

—— (1984). *Literacy in theory and practice*. Cambridge UK: Cambridge University Press.

Stubbings, R., and Brine, A. (2003). Reviewing electronic information literacy training packages. Available in http://www.ics.heacademy.ac.uk/italics/issue1/stubbings/stubabrev.pdf .

Subrahmanyam, K., and Greenfield, P. (2008). Virtual worlds in development: Implications of social networking sites. *Journal of Applied Developmental Psychology*, 29(6), 417–419.

Tapscott, D. (1998). *Growing up digital: The rise of the net generation*. New York: McGraw-Hill.

The New Oxford Dictionary of English (2001). J. Pearsall & P. Hanks (eds.). Oxford: Oxford University Press.

Thomas, R. (2009). Writing, reading, public and private 'literacies': Functional literacy and democratic literacy in Greece. In W. A. Johnson & H. N. Parker (eds.), *Ancient Literacies: The culture of reading in greece and rome*, pp.13–45. Oxford: Oxford University Press.

—— (1998) Literacy. In S. Hornblower & A. Spawforth (eds.) *The Oxford companion to classical civilization*. Oxford University Press, available at: http://www.oxfordreference.com/views/ENTRY.html?subview=Main&entry= t133.e372.

—— (1992). *Literacy and orality in ancient Greece*. Cambridge: Cambridge University Press.

Tsitouridou, M., and Vryzas, K. (2004). The prospect of integrating ICT into the education of young children: The views of Greek early childhood teachers. *European Journal of Teacher Education*, 27(1), pp.29–45.

Tsitouridou, M. and Vryzas, K. (2003). Early childhood teachers' attitudes towards computer and information technology: The case of Greece. *Information Technology in Childhood Education Annual*, 187–207.

Turkle, S. (1995). *Life on the screen: Identity in the age of the internet*. New York: Simon & Schuster.

Tyner, K. (2003). Beyond boxes and wires: Literacy in transition. *Television New Media*, 4(4), 371-388.

—— (1998). *Literacy in a digital world*. Mahwah, NJ: Lawrence Erlbaum.

Unesco (1986). Revised recommendations concerning the international standardization of educational statistics. Adopted by the General Conference at its 20th session, Paris, 27 November 1978.*Unesco's Standard-Setting Instruments* V3, B4. Paris: Unesco.

—— (1965). Statistics of Illiteracy. Paris: Unesco.

Vincent, D. (2003). Literacy literacy. *Interchange*, 34(2–3), 341–347.

—— (2000). *The rise of mass literacy. Reading and writing in modern Europe*. Cambridge: Polity.

Virkus, S. (2003). Information literacy in Europe: A literature review. *Information Research*, 8(4), paper no.159, available at http://informationr.net/ir/8-4/paper159.html

Vryzas, K. (2006). *Communication technologies and development of human society*. Thessaloniki: Vanias (in Greek)

Ware, P., and Warschauer, M. (2005). Hybrid literacy texts and practices in technology-intensive environments. *International Journal of Educational Research*, 43, 432–445.

Warnick, B. (2002). *Critical literacy in a digital era: Technology, rhetoric, and the public interest*. Mahwah, NJ: Lawrence Erlbaum.

Warschauer, M. (2008). Whither the digital divide? in D. L. Kleinman, K. A. Cloud-Hansen, C. Matt, & J. Handesman (eds.), *Controversies in science & technology: From climate to chromosomes*. New Rochelle, NY: Liebert.

—— (2007a). The paradoxical future of digital learning. *Learning Inquiry* 1(1), pp.41–49.

—— (2007b). A teacher's place in the digital divide. *National Society for the Study of Education*

Annual Yearbook,106(2), 147–166.

—— (2006). Literacy and technology: Bridging the divide, in D. Gibbs & K. L. Krauss (eds.), *Cyberlines 2: Languages and cultures of the internet*, pp.163–174. Albert Park, Australia: James Nicholas.

—— (2004). *Technology and social inclusion:Rethinking* the digital divide. Cmabridge, MA: MIT Press.

—— (1999). *Electronic literacies: Language, culture, and power in online education*. Mahwah, NJ: Lawrence Erlbaum.

—— (in press). A literacy approach to the digital divide. In M. A. Pereyra (ed.), *Las mulialfabetizaciones en el espacio digital*. Malaga, Spain: Ediciones Aljibe.

Warschauer, M., Knobel, M., and Stone, M. (2004). Technology and equity in schooling: Deconstructing the digital divide. *Educational Policy*, 18(4), 562–588.

Warschauer, M., and Ware, M. (2008). Learning, change, and power: Competing discourses of technology and literacy. In J. Coiro, M. Knobel, C. Lankshear, & D. J. Leu (eds.), *Handbook of research on new literacies*, pp. 215–240. New York: Lawrence Erlbaum.

Webber, S., and Johnston, B. (2000). Conceptions of information literacy: New perspectives and implications. *Journal of Information Science*, 26 (6). 381–397.

Webber, S., and Johnston, B. (2003). Information literacy in the United Kingdom: a critical review, in C. Basili, (ed.) *Information Literacy in Europe*, pp. 258–283. Rome: Italian National Research Council.

Whitworth, A. (2006). Communicative competence in the information age: Towards a critical theory of information literacy Education. *Communicative Competence in the Information Age*, 5 (1) available at

http://www.ics.heacademy.ac.uk/italics/vol5-1/pdf/Whitworth_final.pdf.

Wilson, L. A. (2001). Information literacy: Fluency across and beyond the university, in B. I. Dewey (ed.), *Library user education: Powerful learning, powerful partnership*, pp.1–17. Lanham, MD: Scarecrow Press, Inc.

Woolf, G. (2009). Literacy or literacies in Rome? In W. A. Johnson, H. N. Parker (eds.), *Ancient Literacies: The culture of reading in Greece and Rome*, pp. 46–68. Oxford: Oxford University Press.

CHAPTER 2

Digital Literacy and the Dark Side of Information: Enlightening the Paradox

David Bawden and Lyn Robinson

Summary

This chapter will briefly review some of the 'pathologies' of information, including information overload, information anxiety, information avoidance, infobesity, inability to assimilate knowledge at a deep level, and the poor use of the 'satisficing' principle. Paradoxically, these seem to be made worse by the success, and the increasing capacity and availability, of systems for communicating and providing information in many formats and media. These may have the effect of leaving us paralysed by the 'paradox of choice'. They have even led some commentators to suggest that they may cause the end of our present form of civilisation.

After examining the reality of some of these issues, we will consider to what extent digital literacy—which we can best understand as a framework of understanding, skills and competences, and perspectives, with meaning and context at its centre—may assist in overcoming them.

The New Information Environment

We now live in the age of the 'digital transition'; the move towards a situation in which most information, whether academic, professional or 'everyday life' information, is available in digital rather than printed form. Beginning in the 1970s, this trend has been greatly extended by the rise of the Internet, and more specifically the World Wide Web, in the 1990s, and latterly by the advent of the social networking tools of Web 2.0. These technical advances have led to a much more rich and complex information environment, with a vastly greater amount of information available, in a greater variety of formats and types of information resource, and accessible through a greater variety of media and communication channels.

These factors are likely to affect people at all stages of their life. Most emphasis has been placed on studying and commenting on them in the contexts of tertiary education and of the workplace; but they are equally relevant to the earlier stages of education, and of lifelong learning.

So far, so good. Quick and simple access to a wide variety of information, usually available at any day and at any time, is self-evidently a great improvement on what has gone before. We may contrast it with the situation of, say 20 years ago, when there were only a very limited set of types of information resources available to any person (usually books, journals or magazines, the mass media, perhaps patents and specialist reports, and some limited computer files), and where there would usually be one and only one obvious source for any particular information request.

This modern, and highly desirable, diversity of provision, however, is typically delivered through a limited number of interfaces: most usually a web browser, whether on a computer screen, a mobile device, an e-book reader etc. The result is a 'homogenisation' of the information, with the look and feel of different resources of the print age—a text book, a newspaper, a hand-written diary entry, a photocopy of a journal article, a printout of a data file, etc.—being largely lost. It is this 'homogenised diversity' of the communication of information which lies at the root of the problems discussed here, as much as the expanded volumes of information which are available. It is sometimes thought, indeed apparently taken for granted, that these problems do not affect the so-called 'digital natives', who have grown up assuming the availability of digital information, but this may be a very mistaken view.

Furthermore, the sheer amount of information, variety of channels, and number of alternative sources now available may lead firstly to an extent of choice which may be a positive hindrance, and may also lead to potentially damaging expectations and behaviours; see Bawden and Robinson (2008) for a fuller review.

Information Problems and Paradoxes

A number of named information problems and issues have been identified, largely stemming from this excess of information (Bawden and Robinson

2008). In large part, these have been identified and discussed on the basis of anecdote and personal opinion, rather than extensive study. But there is now sufficient research and publication, some of which is cited below, to suggest that these are indeed real problems, meriting solution. Whilst, as noted above, most of this has dealt with college students and adults engaged in academic and professional work, other studies have dealt with such issues in other contexts, including school students; see, for recent examples, Lundh and Limberg (2008), Shenton (2008), and Madden, Ford and Miller (2007).

Best known, to the readers of the popular press as well as the academic and professional literature, is the idea that there is just too much information ('TMI') to hand, and easily and quickly accessible. This situation is exacerbated by the multiple formats and channels available for its communication. This has led to the concept of information overload, perhaps the most familiar of the 'information pathologies'; see Eppler and Mengis (2004) and Bawden, Holtham and Courtney (1999) for full discussion.

There is no single generally accepted definition of information overload. The term is usually taken to represent a state of affairs where an individual's efficiency in using information in their work is hampered by the amount of relevant, and potentially useful, information available to them. In library settings, it has sometimes been termed *reference overload*. *Infobesity* is a term increasingly used to denote a situation of personal information overload, particularly if caused by a diet of information, akin to feasting on fast food.

In any of these cases, the information must be of some potential value, or it could simply be ignored, and it must be accessible, or the overload will only be potential, not actual. The feeling of overload is usually associated with a loss of control over the situation, and sometimes with feelings of being overwhelmed. In the extreme, it can lead to damage to health.

It is fair to say that some commentators are sceptical of the whole idea of information overload as a serious issue. They point out that complaints of 'too much information' have been made, in various ways, for hundreds of years, and that people have always found ways to cope. While there may be some validity in this, circumstances very much alter cases. In the fifteenth and sixteenth centuries, the complaint was that printing had made it impossible to keep up with everything that had been written. By the nineteenth century, this had changed to the lament that the communications revolution, with great expansion in the production of books and journals, had made it impossible to keep up with the literature of one's own profession or discipline. Today, the issue is that it is difficult to deal with the specific and necessary information for one's own particular situation. Overload does seem to be a real and pressing issue, promoted in particular by the twin forces of internet information, specifically from the web, and of the universal use of e-mail, now augmented by blogging, internet chat, and similar channels. The fact that many individuals adopt coping strategies, with more or less rationality, does not mean that the problem does not exist.

Various psychological conditions have been described associated with the overloaded state (Bawden and Robinson 2008, Case, Andrews, Johnson and Allard 2005), such as *continuous partial attention*, a focus on being 'in touch' and 'connected' which results in stress, and *attention deficit trait*, a distractability and impatience due to too much mental stimulus. A condition of *cognitive overload*, when information overload is added to multitasking and interruptions, has been recognised, while overload has been noted as a contributor to *technostress* in library settings. Another condition associated with information problems, and in particular to the effect of the mis-use and over-use of e-mail (Camargo 2008) is *burnout*, which leads to feelings of tiredness, frustration and depression, decline in work performance, and subsequent ill-health (Potter 2005).

Information anxiety, a term coined by Saul Wurman, is usually taken to be a condition of stress caused by the inability to access, understand, or make use of necessary information (Wurman 2001). The cause of this may be information overload, or (paradoxically) insufficient information; it may equally be due to poorly organised or presented information, or a variety of other causes, including a lack of understanding of the information environment in which one is working. The rather similar condition of *library anxiety* was recognised and named as far back as 1986, and has been analysed further since then. This is a type of anxiety which leads to a sense of powerlessness when beginning an information search in a library, and in feelings of being lost, unable to find one's way around, and afraid to approach the library staff (Kwon, Ongwuegbuzie and Alexander 2007).

Naturally, people adopt a variety of heuristics to deal with these problems, as they have always done in different information environments; but sadly these solutions, if too simplistic, may lead straight to new problems.

The simple, if brutal, tactic of information avoidance; ignoring relevant information and useful information sources, because there is too much to deal with, is extremely common; see, for example, Case, Andrews, Johnson and Allard (2005). In similar vein, Savolainen (2007) has identified the analogous phenomenon of *information withdrawal*, keeping the number of sources considered to a minimum, as well as more nuanced filtering strategy, with a rapid weeding of material of limited use.

The root cause of many of the problems appears to lie in the '*paradox of choice*'; the observation, in many social and economic settings, that while some choice is good and positive, too much choice leads to indecision and to bad decisions. This phenomenon, known for many years, has recently been drawn to popular attention by Barry Schwartz (2004), and examined most particularly in retail settings, where too many options for purchasing straightforward goods—jam is often cited as an example—leads to the would-be purchaser becoming frustrated, and purchasing randomly, or not at all. The same phenomenon is to be seen in information contexts.

Satisficing is a popular heuristic way of coping, taking just enough information to meet a need, rather than being overwhelmed by all the information available: just enough information is good enough. This form of behaviour, also known as 'bounded rationality', was identified by the economist Herbert Simon (1955). It is a way of making decisions and choices, when the full spectrum of options may not be known, and when it is not feasible to compare fully the benefits of each. In information seeking terms, it implies choices of information sources, and selection of information from within them, so that the information found is good enough, even if not the best available. The theory was popularised fifty years after its appearance by the psychologist Barry Schwartz, who argued that the wide choices available in modern life caused anxiety, and that satisficing was a valid approach, and tended to increase happiness.

The information environment of the early twenty-first century certainly seems to offer the variety of choices to make satisficing a sensible option, and indeed the use of satisficing tactics, and the judgement of what is 'enough information', in information seeking has been investigated by several researchers (see, for example, Mansourian and Ford 2007, and Prabha, Connaway, Olszewski and Jenkins 2007). It is clear that this is a common, if not ubiquitous, way of dealing with a complex information environment. However, it is important to note that satisficing must be carried out rationally; there must be some clear judgement as to why decisions are being taken. If this is not the case—and one must suspect that often it is not—then this behaviour reduces to information avoidance, or a random and contingent selection of sources and material. We may distinguish these two cases as appropriate (good) satisficing and inappropriate (bad) satisficing respectively.

Finally, we might note that the particular success of media and systems based on Web 2.0 tools has led some commentators to speak of this as a problem in itself; for a much-quoted example, see Keen (2007), and analogously for the educational context see Brabazon (2007).

A specific concern is the *loss of identity* inherent in tools which allow anonymity and pseudonimity in their contributors. There are numerous anecdotal accounts of contributors to wikis making false claim to qualification and authority, and of authors of blogs adopting false personas. This makes it particularly difficult to assess the validity of the information presented, and has led some commentators to claim that this aspect of Web 2.0 so attacks the basis of the authority of any recorded information as to amount to the end of Western culture and civilisation. The proliferation of social bookmarking and tagging may also be interpreted as a loss of identity and authority, as subjectivity replaces an objective (albeit imperfect) knowledge organisation through established public taxonomies, thesauri and similar tools.

The mutable nature of Web 2.0 information, even more than that of the older web, leads to issues of *impermanence of information*. If an encyclopaedia, or a textbook, in wiki form can be altered from day to day, or even hour to hour, by any of its users, what meaning can be given to its 'original' or 'final' form? and at what point could, or should, such a resource be archived?

The nature of web 2.0 tools is also alleged to promote an information landscape based on *shallow novelty*. Because the tools allow, and encourage, rapid updating and posting of new material, there emerges an expectation of constant novelty. Because genuinely significant new material is as hard as ever to discover or produce, this expectation can be satisfied only by the re-using of existing material, by linking or re-packaging, or by the generation of shallow and ephemeral material. Furthermore, the nature of the tools themselves—consider RSS feeds and podcasts as example—are well suited to 'soundbites' and 'microchunks' of decontextualised information. Naturally, these are easier and quicker to produce, and to assimilate, than more thoughtful and deeply researched material.

Many concerns about these aspects are tied up with the idea of the 'Google Generation'; those born since the early 1990s, who have not known a world without the ready availability of networked digital information, accessed mainly via search engines. The behaviour of this generation has been much studied, with concerns as to how new and how different it really is; see, for example, Nicholas and Rowlands (2008), and Rowlands et al. (2008).

In order to overcome these problems, the often-quoted solution is to 'take control' of one's information input and processes, and to use information and knowledge resources appropriately and realistically. But in order to do so, it is necessary not merely to have a full set of skills relevant to the current information environment, but also to understand a good deal more about the world of information than was necessary in the past. Crucially, it is also necessary to have the desire to deal with information in this way, and the confidence that this can be done, and is worthwhile. This co-occurrence of skills, understandings and attitudes has been termed 'digital literacy', and it is to this topic that we now turn.

Digital Literacy

The concept of digital literacy, as the term is now generally used, was introduced by Paul Gilster, in his book of the same name (Gilster 1997). The term itself had been used occasionally during the previous decade, though with a more restricted meaning; the ability to deal with hypertextual information (Bawden 2001). Gilster's idea was much broader, and did not involve the enumeration of lists of particular skills, competences or attitudes defining what it is to be digitally literate. Rather, he explained the concept quite generally, as an ability to understand and to use information from a variety of digital sources, and regarded it simply as literacy in the digital age. It is therefore the current form of the traditional idea of literacy per se; the ability to read, write and otherwise deal with information using the technologies and formats of the time. In an 'information society' and a 'knowledge economy', it is plainly an essential life skill. This generic expression of the idea, although it has irritated some commentators, is one of the strengths of Gilster's concept, allowing it to be applied without concern for the sometimes restrictive 'competence lists' which have afflicted some other descriptions of the literacies of information. Indeed, Gilster himself has developed the theme considerably (see, for instance, Gilster 2006).

Despite some continuing inconsistency in the use of the term, we see that several authors, following Paul Gilster, are using 'digital literacy' to denote a broad concept, linking together other relevant literacies, based on computer/ICT competences and skills, but focused on 'softer' skills of information evaluation and knowledge assembly, together with a set of understandings and attitudes (Martin 2006, 2008, Bawden 2008).

This is also referred to by other names, particularly e-literacy and, by some, information literacy. However, the former has not gained popularity, while the latter is strongly associated with various linear models, espoused particularly by the library community (Bawden 2001; Bawden and Robinson 2002; Virkus 2003; Andretta 2005).

These typically see the matter as a series of sequential steps, such as:

- recognising a need for information
- identifying what information is needed
- finding the information
- evaluating the information
- organising the information
- using the information

Variations abound: 'communicating' may be included, for example, while 'deleting' and 'preserving' are given mention by those with a records management perspective. Greater granularity may be included, with 'finding' sometime broken down into sub-processes, such as 'choosing a source', 'retrieving' and 'accessing'.

While this is sometimes a useful concept, particularly in planning training programmes, it is rather too prescriptive, and too limited to a 'library-style' formal information request, to be useful for describing all that is needed in dealing with the modern information environment. Attempts have been made to move away from a strongly linear and sequential approach, by including ideas of non-linear processes in finding and using information (see, for example, Markless and Streatfield 2007). However, it seems that some more flexible and hospitable framework is needed, if the development of any sort of 'literacy' is to be an answer to the information problems discussed above.

Gilster's idea of information literacy, particularly as developed by a number of writers since, seems a suitable candidate. 'Digital literacy' seems an appropriate name, in an age where information comes mainly in this form; though with the caveat that an important part of digital literacy is knowing when to use a non-digital source.

Digital literacy in this sense is a framework for integrating various other literacies and skill-sets, though it does not need to encompass them all; as Martin (2006) puts it, we do not need "one literacy to rule them all". And, while it may be possible to produce lists of the components of digital literacy, and to show how they fit together, it is not sensible to try to reduce it to a finite number of linear stages. Nor is it sensible to suggest that one specific model of digital literacy will be appropriate for all people, or indeed for one person over all their lifetime. Updating of understanding and competence will be necessary, as individual circumstances change, and as changes in the digital information environment bring the need for new fresh understanding and new competences; as Martin (2006) puts it, digital literacy is "a condition, not a threshold".

With these caveats, we might set out four generally agreed components of digital literacy, as agreed by most writers, in this way (Bawden 2008):

1. Underpinnings

- Literacy per se
- Computer / ICT literacy

These 'underpinnings' reflect the rather traditional skills, of which we may now need to regard computer literacy as one, which make up an older idea of literacy, and an ability to function in society. It seems an open question as to whether they should be regarded as a part of digital literacy proper or whether they should be assumed, before digital literacy is grafted on. They are increasingly regarded as simply 'literacy' in educational settings, or under headings such as 'smart working' or 'basic skills' in the workplace (Robinson 2005).

These are the kind of basic skills which are needed in order that a start can be made on avoiding the information problems noted above. If traditional literacy is lacking, then however good the IT skills, information will not be handled well. On the other hand, ICT literacy is essentially in dealing effectively with varied communication channels, e.g., in avoiding the problems due to poor use of e-mail.

2. Background knowledge
- The world of information
- Nature of information resources

This is the kind of knowledge which was assumed of any educated person, in the days when information came as books, newspapers and magazines, academic journals, professional reports, and not much else, and was largely accessed through physical print-on-paper libraries. The well-understood 'publication chain'—from author to archivist, passing through editors, publishers, booksellers, librarians and the rest—lasted as a sensible concept well into the computer age. Now, it is largely meaningless, and there is no clear model to replace it. Nonetheless, attaining as good an understanding of what the new forms of information are, and where they fit into the world of digital information, has to be an essential start in being digitally literate.

This is, of course, the 'good knowledge of the world of information', which we noted above as being essential in avoiding information problems.

3. Central competencies
- Reading and understanding digital and non-digital formats
- Creating and communicating digital information
- Evaluation of information
- Knowledge assembly
- Information literacy
- Media literacy

These are the skills and competences, building on the basic 'underpinnings', without which any claim to digital literacy has to be regarded sceptically. They are a remarkably wide set, and it would be sobering to try to assess to what degree they are possessed in the various countries of the world.

The extent to which they are possessed is a good measure of the extent to which many of the problem described above may be minimised.

4. Attitudes and perspectives
- Independent learning
- Moral / social literacy

These attitudes and perspectives are perhaps what make the link between the new concept of digital literacy, and an older idea of literacy, in vogue over two hundred years ago. It is not enough to have skills and competences, they must be grounded in some moral framework, strongly associated with being an educated, or as our ancestors would have said, a 'lettered', person. They are arguably the most difficult to teach or inculcate of all the components, but they come closest to living up to the meaning of information from 'infomare'; the transforming, structuring force.

They are precisely those qualities which are needed so as to give a person the motivation and mindset to make best use of information, and to avoid being troubled by its paradoxes and problems. They provide the basis for understanding the importance of information, and of 'right dealing' with information resources and communication channels, a swell as the incentive to continually improve one's capabilities.

Taken together, these four components may seem to present a very ambitious set of competences and attitudes to demand of anyone. But this seems likely to be what is needed to cope and to succeed in today's information environment, and to avoid the dark side of information.

Conclusions

We have seen that the very success of information systems and services, in giving quick and easy access to a great amount of information in many forms, has led to a number of information 'paradoxes and problems'.

Some of these may be solved by technical means, though experience suggests, perhaps cynically, that for every problem solved in this way, another is created. Some may be solved by applying simple and pragmatic information behaviours: the familiar topics of time management, desk management, good filing practices and the like are undergoing something of a renaissance under the guise of 'personal information management'.

However, an approach to a full solution is likely to mean the development of a new and wide-ranging set of information-related capabilities. The concept of digital literacy, as outlined here, seems to capture these clearly. Development of digital literacy may be the crucial factor in ensuring that full advantage is taken of the systems now available, and those which will be developed in the future. This may offer the best prospect of minimise the impact of the dark side of information. Who knows, it may even stave off the end of civilisation.

Bibliography

Andretta, A. (2005). *Information literacy: A practitioner's guide*, Oxford: Chandos.

Bawden, D. (2001). Information and digital literacies; a review of concepts. *Journal of Documentation*, 57(2), 218–259.

Bawden, D. (2008), *Origins and concepts of digital literacy*. In C. Lankshear and M. Knobel (eds.)Digital literacies: Concepts, policies and paradoxes. New York: Peter Lang, pp.15–32.

Bawden, D., Holtham, C., and Courtney, N. (1999). Perspectives on information overload. *Aslib Proceedings*, 51(8), 249–255.

Bawden, D., and Robinson, L. (2002). Promoting literacy in a digital age: Approaches to training for information literacy. *Learned Publishing*, 15(4), 297–301.

Bawden, D., and Robinson, L. (2008), The dark side of information: Overload, anxiety and other paradoxes and pathologies. *Journal of Information Science*, XX(X), p. 1–12

Brabazon, T. (2007). *The University of Google: Education in the [post] information age*. Aldershot: Ashgate.

Camargo, M.R. (2008). A grounded theory study of the relationship between e-mail and burnout. *Information Research*, 13(4), paper 383, available from http://InformationR.net/ir/13-4/paper383.html

Case, D.O., Andrews, J.E, Johnson, J. D., and Allard, S.L. (2005). Avoiding versus seeking: The relationship of information seeking to avoidance, blunting, coping, dissonance and related concepts. *Journal of the Medical Library Association*, 93(3), 353–362.

Eppler, M. J., and Mengis, J. (2004). The concept of information overload: A review of literature from organizational science, accounting, marketing, MIS and related disciplines. *Information Society*, 20(5), 325–344

Gilster, P. (1997). *Digital literacy*. New York: Wiley.

Gilster, P. (2006). Digital fusion: Defining the intersection of content and communications. In A. Martin and D. Madigan (eds.), *Digital literacies for learning*, London: Facet Publishing, 42–50.

Keen, A. (2007). *The cult of the amateur: How today's internet is killing our culture*. London: Nicholas Brealey.

Kwon, N., Ongwuegbuzie, A.J., and Alexander, L. (2007), Critical thinking disposition and library anxiety, *College and Research Libraries*, 68(3), 268–278

Lundh, A., and Limberh, L. (2008), Information practices in elementary school. *Libri*, 58(2), 92–101

Madden, A.D., Ford, N. J., and Miller, D. (2007). Information resources used by children at an English secondary school: Perceived and actual levels of usefulness, *Journal of Documentation*, 63(3), 340–358.

Mansourian, Y., and Ford, N. (2007). Search persistence and failure on the Web: A 'bounded rationality' and 'satisficing' analysis. *Journal of Documentation*, 63(5), 680–701

Markless, S., and Streatfield, D. (2007). Three decades of information literacy: Redefining the parameters. In S. Andretta (ed.), *Change and challenge: Information literacy for the 21st century*, Adelaide: Auslib Press.

Martin, A. (2006). Literacies for the digital age. In A. Martin and D. Madigan (eds.), *Digital literacies for learning*. London: Facet Publishing, pp.3–25.

Martin, A. (2008). Digital literacy and the "digital society". In C. Lankshear and M. Knobel (eds.)*Digital literacies: Concepts, policies and paradoxes*. New York: Peter Lang, pages 151–176.

Nicholas, D., and Rowlands, I. (2008), *Digital consumers: Reshaping the information profession*. London: Facet Publishing, 2008, particularly chapters 6 and 7.

Prabha, C., Connaway, L.S., Olszewski, L., and Jenkins, L.R. (2007) What is enough? Satisficing information needs, *Journal of Documentation*, 63(1), 74–89.

Potter, B. (2005). *Overcoming burnout. How to renew enthusiasm for work*, Berkeley CA: Ronin Publishing.

Robinson, L. (2005). Healthcare librarians and learner support: Competences and methods, *Health Information and Libraries Journal*, 22(supplement 2), pp.42–50.

Rowlands, I. et. al, (2008). The Google generation: the information behaviour of the researcher of the future. *Aslib Proceedings*, 60(4), 290–310.

Savolainen, R. (2007). Filtering and withdrawing: Strategies for coping with information overload in everyday contexts, *Journal of Information Science*, 33(5), pp.611–621.

Schwatrz, B. (2004). *The Paradox of choice*, New York NY: Ecco.

Shenton, A.K. (2008). The information seeking problems of English high scholars responding to academic information need. *Library Review*, 57(4), 276–288.

Simon, H. (1955), A behavioral model of rational choice. *Quarterly Journal of Economics*, 69(1), 99–118.

Virkus, S. (2003). Information literacy in Europe: A literature review. *Information Research*, 8(4), paper 159, available from http://informationr.net/ir/8-4/paper159.html

Wurman, R.A. (2001). *Information Anxiety 2*. New York: New Riders Publishers.

CHAPTER 3

Digital Literacy as a Category of Media Competence and Literacy—An Analytical Approach of Concepts and Conditions for Supporting Media Competence at School

Alivisos Sofos

Introduction

The international discussion in the field of education about the knowledge, the aptitudes and the attitudes of students nowadays includes concepts that are synonymous, hyperonymous, partly opposites, and being used as basic categories, e.g. "Literacy", "reading literacy", "mathematics literacy", "scientific literacy", "Information Literacy", "Media-literate", "competence", "Media Literacy", "ICT Literacy", "digital Literacy", "Media Literacy training", "Audiovisual Literacy", "Visual Literacy", "Photography Literacy", "Computer Literacy", "functional Literacy", "ICT Alphabetisierung", "Media competence", " ICT Competencies".

In the sphere of everyday apperception, the above concepts signal a common range of abilities that students and in general the people of the knowledge society and information should possess. On the other hand, through an analytical investigation of the concepts, differentiations are detected concerning the theoretical background, the type of the approach, the educational content, the specific media focused, the partial dimensions they include and their rationalisation.

The realisation that the adoption of concepts depends on scientific approaches and traditions is interesting. Thus, in the Anglo-Saxon countries the term "Media Literacy" is used, in the francophone countries the term "Medienkompetenz" is used and in the Scandinavian countries in everything that has to do with the digital media, the term "Digital competence" is used (Krumsvik, 2008). The two basic concepts used however are, "Competence" and "Literacy" as connecting terms in order to connote a system of knowledge, abilities and attitudes regarding the utilization of the media. This system of aptitudes and abilities constitutes a cultural capital (Buckingham 2005, Sofos 2009) and is different for each individual because it is configured within the social, political and economic framework one lives in. Thus, the social environment affects the potential to use the media, understand the world, and participate in the areas of everyday life.

At this point we should note the fact that the concept of "Literacy" has been a source of conflict as to its appropriateness. The disagreements that have been expressed relate to the fact that as a concept it is very general and inaccurate. Specifically, Schäffer (2006) notes that the connection of "Literacy", which is historically related to abilities and aptitudes in a specific media, namely the written language, with other scientific fields as Mathematics and Science, as well as special means and types of presentation, e.g., picture, movies, computers and internet, is problematic, because it is based on a metaphor which hinders the exact demarcation between the different media, the forms of communication and the particular abilities and aptitudes users should develop. In some cases, the concept of "Literacy" is approached as functional literacy which is being conceived through measurable aptitudes. Sting (2005: 30) also denotes that the concept of "Literacy" with a "neutral and undifferentiated" conception as a starting point lies groundless, especially if one reflects on the complexity of the written language and its labored liaison with media, cultural and social fields of action. Moreover, if one considers the special practices and distinctions (visual, audio, audiovisual) in electronic and digital environments which will be broadened in the future (haptic, olfactory), it becomes obvious that the conception of Literacy which is traditionally directed to the written language is a concept without content. Specific literacies like the "aesthetic" (Dunker 2005) which among others includes as partial categories the "coloring", the "envisation", the "visual", the "manipulation" of "image", or the "cinematic language" with the particular camera shots, the 'montage'/editing etc., as well as specific experiences (among other such harassments in social networks), knowledge and roles cannot become a work task of a written language literacy. The New Media create new functions, e.g., digital substitution of natural objects, e.g., digital board, and have the tendency to "disappear" (i.e., be invisible) from the user's perception, e.g., processors in domestic appliances. All of the above constitute new phenomena which the classic concept of "Literacy" is unable to approach.

Conceptual Approach

In the sections that follow, the two basic concepts of "Competence" and "Literacy" and the term "Digital Literacy" are concisely presented. The first concept is profound (deep, but relatively narrow) because it contains essential features that are common to all similar things (of the same kind) to which it refers. "Competence" is regarded as a phylogenetic and ontogenetic value which characterizes humans, on the basis of which they are able to differentiate, to produce new ideas and solutions and to reflect on everything they have elaborated. The second concept is wide because it contains a multitude of subordinate/subsumed concepts e.g., "Photography Literacy", "Visual Literacy", "Audiovisual Literacy", "Computer Literacy", "ICT Literacy", "digital Literacy". Literacy relates to basic abilities and aptitudes like reading, writing and comprehension that have been mastered in educational settings and constitute the basic condition for the recognition of symbolic signs and the understanding of information. Despite the different approaches to the concepts outlined below, both are related in general to the hermeneutic ability of the individual which is conceptualised as an anthropological dimension (Bollnow 1959). In relation to the utilization of the media in different social areas, the two concepts-approaches contribute to the delimitation of a system of knowledge, abilities, aptitudes, capabilities and attitudes.

From Competence to Media Competence

The notion of competence relates to the "communication aptitude" which constitutes the basic "equipment" (Gehlen 1993) of man upon which social interactions rest. Virtual realities are built upon symbolic interactions that take the form of communicative events or actions. Habermas (1981) connects "competence" with the theory of 'Universalpragmatik' and denotes that human communication is a priori founded on the discourse about objectives and can be conceptualized as communicative action. In the educational area, Baacke (1980) based on Habermas's approach delineates "media competence" as a subcategory of "communicative competence". From this point of view, communicative competence, media competence and competence in social action constitute dimensions of an anthropological picture: man as a competent creature. (Baacke 1999a, 32).

The historical structure of communicative competence is formed actively before the commencement of mother tongue learning through diverse expressive forms and expands to technological forms of expression, e.g., use and development of multimedia virtual environments. Although it is an anthropogenic characteristic it must be noted that communicative competence constitutes in parallel an object of active learning and pursuit, which is further developed. Fertile areas for this kind of development are the family, the kindergarten, the school as well as the overall personal experiences from everyday life. Thus, communicative competence implies that man attains "subjective reality" through speech/language and other forms of expression and that it can divert initial ability through social action. According to Oevermann (1979) man as social subject is "self constructed" i.e. he constructs personal reality and generates cognitive structures. This approach of "interactive constructivism" which is also validated by neurobiology (Spitzer 2002) implies that the preconditions for the production of interactions and abilities on one hand pre-exist outside the subject but on the other hand activate and stimulate the subject's construction achievements/attainments, as well as his/her aptitudes/skills. The subject's basic achievement rests precisely in the internal elaboration procedure, that is, in the interpretation and discussion/elaboration of stimulus from its environment. This presupposes that the subject should possess diverse communicative codes (along with the ones that refer to the New Media), to be able to acknowledge that in interpretations there is "room" for diversity and alternative propositions.

Therefore "media competence" is part of a whole, that is, part of a general "communicative competence" focusing on forms of expression based on technology means of any type (analytical/comprehensive dimension of media competence). This means that the term refers to the primary, first generation (symbolic communication) as well as the secondary, second generation (book, newspaper), to the third generation media (radio, telephone, television) and finally, to interactive media, e.g., computers and the internet.

Media competence is used widely in the francophone scientific area. It is considered as a basic qualification for everybody playing an active role in the process of teaching and learning. The use of the term in question, in numerous contexts and the concomitant attempts to define it, make, obvious the fact that the scientific discourse acknowledges central importance and function to the term of media competence. The term also enjoys a foremost position in research and instruction, in the configuration of theories, in the analysis of practice experiences as well as the development of models and the planning of media educational and/or instructional activities, and can be characterized as a category.

The term media competence is used pro rata of the term critical competence, reflection competence etc. However, the point of reference is not the media but the process operation of competence which refers to the media (Kron and Sofos 2007). What is regarded as "media competence" is the ability of an individual, in relation to the particular sociocultural framework and to a system of diverse knowledge, abilities, aptitudes and tendencies, to utilize the media in order to achieve aims, to fulfill wishes and interests in different social areas of everyday life.

The same abilities basically constitute emanation of the cultural and social action of man. For this exact reason they are directly dependent on the communication and the life world of man (Baacke 1999b, p. 32). Furthermore, the term media competence pertains to two dimensions: (1) the product, namely the result of an action, e.g., the formative or artistic ability, which refers to the visible side of an action ability, and (2) to the process of an action or an activity, e.g., research or critical competence, which refers to the invisible side of the subject's ability to apperceive probable activities with the media. In a pragmatic approach of media competence in education these two dimensions are considered as distinctive, the first being observable attainment (Performance) and the second being a non-observable ability, e.g., conception or internal action (Competence), which in educational practice are frequently complementary, forming the two sides of the same coin. (Kron and Sofos 2007, 91).

The specific abilities that are related to specializations, which are usually measurable and are accompanied by specific criteria, constitute the functional dimension of media competence. In the present educational discussion, mention is made more and more often of the measurement of specific abilities that take the form of aptitudes/skills.

From "Literacy" to "Media Literacy"

Historically, the concept of "Literacy" in English meant familiarity with literature; that is, an individual who is engaged with literature and is well educated. From the 19th century onwards, the concept came to refer to abilities and aptitudes in reading and writing texts while, as the reference below makes evident, the breadth of the definition's interpretation becomes broader and differentiated in particular fields and in different languages.

> For example, in French, alphabétisme and analphabétisme are the terms generally used to designate "literacy" and "illiteracy", while alphabétisation refers to "literacy learning" and is used in France to denote the process of literacy acquisition. Until the early 1980s, the terms analphabétisme (illiteracy) and alphabetisation (literacy learning) were used to refer to what was perceived to be a literacy problem of immigrants. (OECD 2008: 10)

Even though the concept of "Literacy" is doomed to criticism as put forward above, it is frequently used in an institutional level and in educational policy texts in the context of community and information. However, it is probably used for strategic reasons as "lingua franca" for the communication between scientists; it presents itself with diverse nuances and is connected to specific criteria and measurement reports of Media Literacy, e.g., the research titled "Current trends and approaches to media literacy in Europe" which was delivered by the group of experts (Media Literacy Expert Group) for the E.U. in 2007.

The International Adult Literacy Survey (IALS) of OECD defines "Literacy" as

> the ability to understand and employ printed information in daily activities, at home, at work and in the community (OECD 2000, OECD 2008)

This approach implies a pragmatic approach. With the printed texts as benchmarks, the hermeneutic ability is stressed as well as the application of the new knowledge in labour, everyday and private situations.

The concept of "Literacy" is similarly approached by UNESCO as

> the ability to identify, understand, interpret, create, communicate and compute using printed and written materials associated with varying contexts. Literacy involves a continuum of learning in enabling individuals to achieve his or her goals, develop his or her knowledge and potentials, and participate fully in the community and wider society. (UNESCO 2008, 25).

It appears here that the concept of "Literacy" is not confined to the aptitudes of reading and writing. This could be approached as "functional literacy" or "alphabetism" which signifies the ability to apply aptitudes that have been acquired in the context of the process of socialization and education. Therefore, the concept of "Literacy" implies the interpretation, the signification and the discussion of notions and values in a particular social context.

While the concept of "Literacy" was traditionally related to a language code, i.e., the aptitude of reading, writing and understanding in relation to the printed media, the effort to expand the width of the concept in all forms of mediated communication with electronic and digital media is observed.

Specifically the approach of the "Media Literacy Expert Group" that holds an advisory role in the European Union in subjects related to "Media Literacy" and the elaboration of propositions for respective activities defines the term as follows:

Media Literacy may be defined as the ability to access, analyse and evaluate the power of images, sounds and messages which we are now being confronted with on a daily basis and which are an important part of our contemporary culture; as well as to communicate competently using media available, on a personal basis. Media Literacy relates to all media, including television and film, radio and recorded music, print media, the Internet and other new digital communication technologies (Media Literacy Expert Group 2007,13).

The above definition broadens the approach of "Literacy" towards the following:

The concept of "Literacy" is regarded a cultural construction which demarcates abilities and aptitudes in relation to reading, writing and understanding, while it is historically related to the written language and the printed media. The development of electronic media formed alterations and introduced specifications to "Literacy", i.e., "audiovisual literacy" which are related with "reading", "understanding" and rarely–because of high cost of production – with "writing", for example, cinematic texts. As a superjacent term, it includes advanced and specialized categories of abilities and aptitudes which are related to the understanding, the reading and the writing (from understanding to creative aptitudes), different forms of media presentations (text, visual, audiovisual) in a convergent framework. In this way, it operates as an umbrella term which includes aptitudes and categories of literacy, like reading and writing literacy, audiovisual literacy (often referred to as image or visual literacy) and digital or information literacy.

As far as it concerns media as the second connective element, it is noted that these are considered as cultural objectification of communicative processes and includes four dimensions: 1) the tools of communication, i.e., language code, picture, 2) materials, i.e., paper, ink, netting, hardware and software, 3) the social structures and organizations, i.e., publishers, providers, and 4) the media contents which proceed from the correlation of these dimensions (Schmidt 2003; Sofos 2005a). "Media Literacy" refers to the four dimensions mentioned above.

Furthermore, if we also consider the architecture of the media, then we can notice that the term "Media Literacy" refers to a framework of a holistic approach in all media: *First generation*, which do not need supporting technology, (having to do with face-to-face communication); *Second generation*, which presuppose supporting technology only from the side of the author of media contents, that is newspapers, books, journals; *Third generation*, which promote the linear communication and presuppose supporting technology from the side of the receptor of media contents; *Fourth generation*, which operate based on decentralized nets, allow two-way and interactional communication and presuppose supporting technology from both sides (Faulstich 1995).

As far as the application and utilization field of "Media Literacy" is concerned, it is acknowledged that it pertains to all the activities of everyday life (education, labour, information) and integrates contemporary culture, regardless of its particular nature (image, sound, video etc.). Under this point of view, the aptitudes around "Media Literacy" pertain to the *familiarization* with all the existing media (from newspapers to virtual realities), the *access* and the *active* use (digital, interactive television, use of search engine, participation in social nets, utilizing the media for pleasure, information, learning), with understanding and analysis, with the evaluation and the critical approach (understanding of economy and ownership of the Media, awareness on the problems of copyright and safe navigation) and with the application and the creative production or the experimentation (for expression, promotion of ideas and the collaboration with all the media).

Within the framework of the "Media Literacy" approach, the discussion around the term "Multiliteracy" is justified and understood. This term focuses on both the different forms of presentation, which is text types, e.g., television, internet text, and the fact that there is no one static "literacy" but different practices and events of literacy (Kalantzis 2000). Consequently the broadened approach of "Media Literacy" is understood as social validation of the hermeneutic abilities and application aptitudes of the users and conceives "literacy" as an ability of social action and participation in social processes.

Comparably to the terms "mathematics literacy", "scientific literacy", "Media Literacy" can be conceptualized as an aggregation of knowledge, abilities, aptitudes and tendencies connected to the terms of education and erudition (Kössler, 1989). The first term stresses the mental and spiritual refinement of the individual in relation to the media and education. The term media education is conceived as the acquisition of social and ethical attitudes through education and the acquisition of knowledge which people use as a reference point in the historical and social reality they live in order to assess, to adopt a stand and act along with and through the media. In this sense, media education is connected to the individual's media biography and media identity.

Digital Literacy as a Separate/Specific Category of Media Literacy and Media Competence

"Digital Literacy" as a term constitutes a determination which befits the technological and social developments and is related to all the media which can be utilized in digital form. The new term is founded on the phenomenon of multiplication, of the mechanical and digital technology approximation, the globalization and the digitization of data, a fact which is particularly profound in advanced societies. Using McLuhan's (2001) prophetical approaches as a point of reference, which approached media using as a starting point the connection between the form and the different operations the media take on through the different nuances, one can assume here that the digital media constitute a new type of media, which probably cannot be considered as Mass Media (Maletzke 1998). According to Maletzke (1998) and Manovich (2001), while the Mass Media promote the public, technology mediated, indirect and one-way communication, the New Media respectively allow the interpersonal, interactional, direct and two-way communication, calling to question the validity of the Mass Media definition, especially when the New Media do not transport information (primordial material), like the newspaper, the radio or the television but often use the classic media as primordial material and allow access to users and diverse forms of development that were not feasible by the classic media. This development dictates diverse abilities and aptitudes from the user, e.g., "nonlinear reading", the double activation of the user as a "reader-author" of messages, i.e., the Web 2.0 (Kron and Sofos 2003), the ability to navigate in three-dimensional textual and multimedia structures.

Under the angle of the above approach the term, "Digital Literacy" refers to diverse forms of work and function of the Media. The hermeneutic attitude of the individual, the reflective observation of use and the critical analysis of the information, that is the cognitive, the emotional and active interactions which constitute a general anthropological substratum, remain common elements. Hence, "Digital Literacy" can be approached as follows:

> Digital Literacy is the awareness, attitude and ability of individuals to appropriately use digital tools and facilities to identify, access, manage, integrate, evaluate, analyse and synthesize digital resources, construct new knowledge, create media expressions, and communicate with others, in the context of specific life situations, in order to enable constructive social action; and to reflect upon this process (Martin 2006).

According to the above definition, "Digital Literacy" is approached as a system of specific abilities and aptitudes of man in a given society which is characterised by mediated communication and technological advance and refers to different areas of social life (formal education, informal lifelong education, work, leisure time, aspects of everyday life). The influence of the condition "in the context of specific life situations" denotes that the quality of "Digital Literacy" may vary according to the specific life situation of an individual and that it is a lifelong ongoing process which develops along with the evolution of the individual's life situation. Consequently, "Digital Literacy" is broader than basic and formal ICT education and includes basic features/elements that derive from different forms of literacy like visual literacy, information literacy, media literacy. The specific knowledge, abilities and aptitudes mentioned in the definition have a pragmatic character because they are utilized in particular contexts for the organization and implementation of individual projects, the accomplishment of individual goals and the development of one's personality in general. According to Rafferty and Steyaert (2007) these can be determined in three categories of aptitudes: 1) the functional-technological, 2) the structural, and 3) the strategic.

The functional-technological aptitudes are necessary in order to manipulate the New Media. These are not confined to simple psychomotor aptitudes, i.e., mouse movement, but expand to more complicated procedures which require cognitive processes, in order to either utilize specific services or look for information.

The structural aptitudes are connected to the way of organizing and presenting information. They constitute an essential qualification in order for someone to orient towards a multimodal environment, to detect, to acknowledge, to interpret and to edit information. Similarly to the efficient utilization of a book or an encyclopedia, where the user should utilize the contents and the word index, in the digital media one should be able to recognize the structures, e.g., hypertext, navigational schemes, RSS, etc., and develop them appropriately.

The strategic aptitudes refer exactly to the quality and the effective use of contents and of the way of using the digital media; that is, they are connected to the reflective and the critical attitudes of an individual on the application strategies using as a criterion the degree of achievement of the goals that had been set. It is evident that abilities and aptitudes of this kind refer to the classic media.

The above categories of aptitudes are considered important in an institutional and political level, because they compose the individual cultural and educational capital of every modern citizen in the 21st century, since the digital media of communication and information constitute basic factors in education, production, development and labor. From this point of view, it is possible to state that, the potential of participation and active use of digital media constitutes a criterion for today's social exclusion (Sofos 2009).

Concepts of Media Competence, Media Education and Media Literacy

Using the second level of analysis as a reference in which pedagogical dialogue takes place and which refers to the way of systematization and diversification of the partial aspects of "media competence", we can examine the suggestions of certain experts (Baacke 1980; Aufenanger 1999; Tulodziecki 1997; Buckingham 2007), as well as those coming from educational institutions (ISTE 2007, National Curriculum for England, UNESCO). According to Tulodziecki (2007) and to the analysis of the suggestions studied in this research, it is assumed that the classification of these concepts can be made based on five approaches:

Classification According to the Fields of "Media Competence"

According to this classification, points of reference are the thematical areas and the fields which facilitate an overview of "media" in a more general way, taking into consideration, at the same time, its complexity. The suggested approaches have an exemplary character, resulting in the restriction of a large number of criteria (Standards) in this classification.

However, the facts that educators face the challenge of transforming their actions in a media-instructional level and that they are required to contribute to the development of school infrastructure in order to enhance media education act as restricting factors. Examples of such suggestions are the following:

Taking into account the socio-ecological approach, Baacke (1980) points out that the diversified media environment shapes a complex reality, which students have to face. Given the fact that they cannot face this reality, based on their current experience, 'media competence' is perceived as a central test of growth; that is, as an ability of successful existence in the world. From this point of view, the notion of "media competence" is considered as an overlying category of "education" and "literacy". "Media competence" extends beyond the institutional organised action and thinking and it includes cultural fields, where an individual can evolve. "Competence" is seen therefore as an anthropological dimension which characterizes humankind. According to Baacke (1999b), "Media competence" covers the following fields:

1. Media critique: a) analytic, b) reflexive, c) ethical
2. Media studies: a) informative, b) instrumental-qualificational
3. Media (use/consumption) "Mediennutzung": a) receptive/passive, applied, b) interactive, proactive

4. Media design: a) Innovative, b) creative

Tulodziecki (1997) focuses on the integration of the media in the teaching of different cognitive subjects according to the recommendations of Germany's Education Ministers of the Länder (KMK) on the promotion of media education in primary and secondary education. In total, he proposes five categories of media education:

1. Selection and use of media
2. Comprehension and assessment of media productions
3. Production and distribution of media
4. Identification and processing of media influence
5. Identifying and evaluating the conditions of media production

Classification According to the Categories of Educational Activities

This classification refers to suggestions which focus in specific activities perceived as key abilities in information and knowledge society. They are usually formed in institutional frameworks and have a pragmatic orientation corresponding to measurable criteria. In this classification lies the danger that educational activities are applied only with a functional or even a mechanistic way.

The International Society for Technology in Education (ISTE) is an organization focusing on the integration of New Technology in education, and in the context of its work, the National Education Technology Standards (NETS) programme was set up. It consists of experts in the educational sector, aiming to edit standards for the promotion of "competence" in relation to New Technologies in primary and secondary education.

The programme was funded twice by the U.S. Department of Education. In total three suggestions were formed: 1. National Education Technology Standards for Students (NET•S), 2. National Education Technology Standards for Teachers (NET•T), and 3. National Education Technology Standards for Administrators (NET•A). NET•S includes 6 categories of abilities (2007):

1. Creativity and Innovation
2. Communication and Collaboration
3. Research and Information Fluency
4. Critical Thinking, Problem Solving, and Decision Making
5. Digital Citizenship
6. Technology Operations and Concepts

The national curriculum of the subject of ICT of the UK focuses on five fields which contain further subcategories: 1. Capability, 2. Communication and collaboration, 3. Exploring ideas and manipulating information, 4. Impact of technology, 5. Critical evaluation.

It also describes four basic categories of processes with more subcategories for the development of ICT: 1. Finding information, 2. Developing ideas, 3. Communicating information, and 4. Evaluating[1].

The categories of "e-curriculum" which were formed in the process of the programs "Socrates" and "Minerva" programmes (2004) diverge from the basic categories of abilities and skills and turn towards learning activities which develop students' "e-competence" in order for them to function effectively in digital society and take advantage of the possibilities digital instruments offer.

In total, four categories are included: 1. exchanging and sharing information, communication and collaboration, 2. researching, finding out information, 3. Modelling, 4. working practices and attitudes

Classification According to Dimensions and Partial Abilities

These suggestions focus on the dimensions of ability and are founded on theories of personal development, as shown by research. In the context of those suggestions, teachers are requested to make an educational reform in order to specify the educational actions in the framework of the curriculum.

Aufenanger (1999) is based on the anthropological approaches of Baacke. Human "open-ness" ("Unbestimmtheit und Offenheit"), according to the author, lies in (1) the ability to separate from oneself and reflect on oneself, and (2) the ability to understand and use different means and codes of communication, aiming to express different notions and negotiate their interpretation and meaning. It is under this approach that Aufenanger perceives the term "media competence" as the general human ability, which relates to all media, to cope with the challenges of a world whose reality is communicated through the media.

He includes the following categories of abilities: 1. cognitive, 2. moral, 3. social, 4. affective, 5. aesthetic, 6. active. Pöttinger (1997) distinguishes three categories of abilities through an empirical approach: 1. Perception ability, 2. Ability of use, 3. Ability of action.

Structure According to Media and Its Structural Components

This sections offers some propositions which are aimed towards functional abilities in specific media and which edit structural components of the media. This approach has some clear advantages. It does not specify specific subjects, thus allowing educational actions to take into account the interests of students. Furthermore, it does not specify a given corpus of knowledge of an area, thus evading the adhesion to knowledge and activities bound to become outdated.

According to UNESCO (Divina, 2006), media education in general and "media literacy" in particular, are oriented towards a group of basic notions, or basic subjects, which relate directly to the media or certain categories of media. The following four notions are suggested. They present a theoretical framework, which can be applied in all kinds of media:

1. Production (of media content), 2. Language (of the media), 3. The representations (media disperse), and 4. The audience (of media content). It should be noted here that Buckingham (2005) uses exactly the same categories to describe the thematic fields of "Digital Literacy".

An example of media abilities construct based on specific Media is put forward by Spanhel (1999), who presents suggestions on the forming of a curriculum for media education, e.g., basic media, such as images, slides, boards, comics for the fifth grade; television, videos and cinema for the sixth grade; audio media for the seventh grade; printed media, such as newspapers and journals, as well as multimedia for the 8th grade; and CD-Rom, Computers and the Internet for the ninth grade.

Mixed Classification

This classification includes categories of "media competence" classified in more levels. The advantage of this suggestion lies on the unification of those suggestions. Sofos (2005a) proposes a model of classification which includes (A) thematic areas of interest in accordance with Tulodziecki (1997) and Aufenanger (1999) on the horizontal dimension (1. Selection and use of media, 2. Comprehension and assessment of media productions, 3. Production and distribution of media, 4. Identification and processing of media influence 5. Identifying and evaluating the conditions of media production) and (B) aspects of media ability (cognitive, active, communicative, affective, critical) on the vertical dimension. In the intermediate frame, categories of activities relative to different means (classic or new) are included. These means are related to educational and evolutionary activities.

From the above suggestions presented briefly, it is concluded that the suggestions refer to all media, while it is apparent that new media and the special abilities needed for their use have a very important role. In general, different terms are used in order to specify the abilities, competence and approach related to the utilization of media, e.g., Media Competence, Media Literacy, Digital Literacy, i-curriculum, National Education Technology

Standards for Students. It becomes obvious that those are established through a pedagogical and interdisciplinary dialogue, while at the same time they are used indicatively to describe the "new characteristics of modern man". The pluralism of terms is related to the point of reference of researchers, according to their scientific approach, their perception of media and the media-educational approaches, e.g., protective, critical and actionary.

Furthermore, the formation of special categories of abilities and competence shows that the above terms are established in the field of media education, as a particular category of educational goals in relation to the socio-technological and economic developments. In parallel, and depending on the theoretic approach, the terms "media competence", "media literacy" and "Digital Literacy" are perceived as 1. general human ability, 2. educative idea, 3. general educational goal, 4. measurable indicator in empirical research.

Here it is pointed out that educational organisations and committees, which are responsible the educational design and the educational management, or act as consultants, express to a higher degree certain abilities, which have a pragmatic orientation, and focus on functional abilities in conjunction with the demands of the school, labour market, and modern society, but which, have not a mechanistic character, like for example, the aptitudes of ECDL (Weinert 2001). However, the approaches of theory experts focus on comprehensive abilities, knowledge and attitudes and orientate towards the emancipation, autonomy and self-determination of the person, which in the education literature seem to form higher educational goals. Thus, it appears that these terms constitute a structure, which attempts to explain and record phenomena and procedures that cannot be immediately accessed or approached. Therefore, the terms "media competence" and "media literacy" cannot be outlined sufficiently.

Despite the diversifications in the approaches to the terminology, one can discern basic orientations and guidelines:

- Technological: basic knowledge of different kinds of media and services (video, cinema, computers, internet, software) and ability to use them
- Functional: access to services and information, acquisition of data, storage, editing, sharing, communication and collaboration
- Analytical: data identification, understanding of the structural elements of certain media or service, interpretation of information, assessment of information quality

- Critical: critical identification of the producer, of the content and the purpose of media content, structure (organization, production), cultural values and representations that media reflect
- Productive: active shaping of content in order to express oneself, sharing of ideas, collaboration, experiment
- Social-political: identification of the role of media in society, taking advantage of their use for a productive participation in politics, danger of digital gap and social exclusion
- Personal: use of the media for information, personal development, learning, lifelong and distance education, construction of knowledge, communication, collaboration and preservation of democratic rights
- Aesthetic: awareness in the use of media, pleasure, enjoyment and sensation
- Ethical: responsible use in relation to social values, reflection on personal attitudes and on the influences by media contents, consequences on ecology (removal/dumping of old computers/equipment in the countries of third world).

From the point of view of the interpretative paradigm we can come to the conclusion that the expressed dimensions of media abilities have no normative character. They mark the basic abilities, but, at the same time, pinpoint the conditions for the development and support of the abilities for the media. As no individual possesses the full spectrum of necessary abilities, apart from those obtained through experience, it is understood that the development of abilities can be realized through processes of cognitive transformation in the subject itself. If an answer is to be given on how different personal abilities can be shaped, we have to take into account anthropological, cultural and social conditions which influence the procedures of transformation. Furthermore, the quality of the process of transformation, as, e.g., by Piaget (Assimilation, Accommodation, Equilibration), is dependent on the mental and moral level of the development of the person. For this reason we should refer to abilities in the media related to age groups and to the level of development. Using as a point of reference constructive and socio-constructive approaches, it should also be highlighted that the meaning of participation in social interactions is crucial for the cognitive and social development of a person, in combination with the acquisition of media aptitudes.

Finally, the meaning of pedagogical and teaching ability of teachers in media should be emphasized as part of a general professional ability, e.g., 1. ability and efficiency in the area of expertise, 2. ability of teaching transformation, 3. ability of reflection and classification of teaching actions, 4. social ability, meta-communication ability.

Prerequisites of Competence in Media

The formulation of the classification of targets for the promotion of the media ability of learners and teachers implies that the acquisition of the relevant abilities and aptitudes depends on personal progress and output. By examining the pedagogy literature (Philipp, Rolff 1998, Schratz, Steiner - Löffler 1998, Kron and Sofos 2003), it seems that important prerequisites are a series of conditions, which will be presented below in three levels: (1) the macro level, the ability in media is perceived as the ability of action inside the educational system, (2) the micro level, it is perceived as the ability of interpretation, and (3) the personal level as a personal ability.

Conditions at a Macro Level

At this level, during the organization of the school, social, political and economical forces are applied, as well as decisions which affect the abilities of students and teachers in media. Lately, for example, specific abilities in media are introduced, which teachers have to possess in order to use them in their teaching NET-T, 2008). On the other hand, it is known that teachers in school act in a framework of stable and prearranged roles and relations and have developed a corresponding systematic ability and logic of action. In this, phenomena of inhibition and manipulation appear. This fact shows that the development of the ability of teachers in media correlates and is co-defined by the systematic ability, meaning the logic and practices at school. Therefore, it is considered important to have a common basis that is a kind of negotiation of the values and orientation between the educational sub-systems. As, for example, there is a common basis of values between the political and legal system, in order for communication between them to be possible, in the same way there has to be a corresponding common basis between the educational policy and the real organization and function of the school. Through the analysis of school curriculums and organizational structures of the school, it seems that this is not always possible and that the relationship is frequently dysfunctional.

The term "dysfunctional" underlines the structural differences inside a system. At school, for example, there can exist tension if some teachers extend the content of their lessons by the use of New Media, coming thus into conflict with the requirements of the curriculum. In this case, the application of new technology is contradictory to the specified target setting. According to

Parson's (1986) structural and functional approach of the existing school subsystems, like the environment adaptation, the use of educational means and the realization of targets cannot any more exist in harmony (= functionality). The identification of structural solutions, as an answer to this tension, becomes more difficult. In relation to school as a structure, this means that teachers must develop aptitudes in order to cope with the new challenges. Definitively they cannot modify the existing structures but they can make space for the insertion of New Media in the educational action. The development of media aptitude starts with the development of the ability to co-shape the structures as well as a media philosophy, which presupposes the knowledge of institutional references to incorporate digital media in education, the cooperation with external agents for the support of media-based work (media-rich educational activities) and the continuous broadening of educational activities in electronic environments.

Conditions at a Micro Level

The micro level is to do with factors that affect the communication and the social interactions, which are associated directly or indirectly with the media capability.

The formulated categories of targets for the media capability are seen, in the context of education, as forms of socio-cultural norms which are institutionally established. A definition, e.g., of Critical Evaluation, should be interpreted as a guide for action in a specific educational instance and in an authentic working environment. This means that educators should probably transform them in the context of media educational actions. Such educational interactions are considered as cooperative production processes that include partial (sub) actions for negotiation, for example the negotiation of a theme/subject, information search, documentation and evaluation of the results. A key factor is the support of the media capability in the frame of the curriculum. Within this context, the contribution of the educators is crucial, because they are required to recognize connection points (interfaces) in the curriculum for the incorporation of effective media-based projects in teaching.

Moreover, a basic condition for the promotion of media ability in education is the consideration of knowledge as well as the media experiences of students. Considering the principle of teaching which states that inversion and experience constitute the basic sources/references of the intellectual life, it is concluded that the development of the learners' interests constitutes a pedagogical goal and a target/reference point for media-based work. The pedagogical interpretation of this principle leads emphatically to the conclusion that the use of media in education does not automatically lead to a high level of quality or the reinforcement of teaching.

A presupposition is the capability of teachers to utilize the New Media in order to create learning environments with authentic work settings, to negotiate about the subject matter and the working processes, to include the prior knowledge and the experiences of students, etc. (Design and Develop Digital-Age Learning Experiences and Assessments).

Through Mead's (1998) approach of symbolic interaction, interactions are being perceived as a means for the structure of reality, because the participants give meaning and negotiate social actions under specific conditions. Through this procedure, models are being created and established, which constitute a reference point (benchmark) and on which pedagogical actions are based.

Knowledge, experiences and behaviors which are acquired within this framework are transferred to new conditions as well, for example, in media work. In the context of teacher education, teachers are required to evaluate and reflect on current research and professional practice and to search for alternative practices for the utilization of the New Media in the teaching process, in project creation, in the assessment of progress etc. The functional knowledge of New Media constitutes a basic condition for the design and the implementation of media-based actions, but must be farmed within a setting that promotes professional practice with the use of the digital media (NET-T).

Conditions at a Personal Level

At this level, the interest focuses on the personal learning ability and on personal reflection. Learning, as a self regulated process, of a subject presumes that students organize a series of tasks on a cognitive, affective and activity level. The interest is focused on educational activities which support the abilities and aptitudes of students related to access to internet sources; acquisition of experience with different forms of information, e.g., databases, wiki, online dictionaries and the use of electronic sites; learning management systems; collaborative tools for school and informal learning; the active creation of content in different forms, e.g., webpage, presentations and forums. In any case, it is important to understand the value of digital media in school learning, but also in informal and lifelong learning.

Note

1. See http://curriculum.qca.org.uk/key-stages-3-and4/subjects/ict/keystage3/index.aspx ?return=/key-stages-3-and 4/subjects/ict/index.aspx

Bibliography

Aufenanger, S. (1999). Medienpädagogische Projekte – Zielsetzungen und Aufgaben. In: Baacke et al. (Eds.), *Handbuch Medien: Medienkompetenz. Modelle und Projekte* pp. 94–98. Bonn: bpb.

Baacke, D. (1999). *Kommunikation und Kompetenz. Grundlegung einer Didaktik der Kommunikation und ihrer Medien.* München: Juventa.

—— (1980) *Kommunikation und Kompetenz. Grundlegung einer Didaktik der Kommunikation und ihrer Medien.* München: Weinheim.

—— (1999). Medienkompetenz als zentrales Operationsfeld von Projekten. In: Baacke et al. (Eds.), *Handbuch Medien: Medienkompetenz. Modelle und Projekte* pp.137–149. Bonn: bpb.

Bollnow, O. F. (1959). *Existenzphilosophie und Pädagogik. Versuch über unstetige Formen der Erziehung.* 3 Aufl. Stuttgart: Kohlhammer.

Buckingham, D. (2005). *Media Literacy of Children and Young People.* Retrieved on 19-01-2009 from
http://www.ofcom.org.uk/advice/media_literacy/medlitpub/medlitpubrss/ml_children.pdf

Cope, B., Kalantzis, M. (Eds.) (2000). *Multiliteracies: Literacy Learning and the Design of Social Futures.* London: Routledge.

Divina, M. (2006) (ed.). Media Education. Paris: UNESCO. Retrieved on 19-01-2009 from http://portal.unesco.org/ci/en/ev.php-URL_ID=23714&URL_DO=DO_TOPIC&URL_SECTION=201.html

Dunker, L. (2005). Das didaktische Konzept der ästhetischen Alphabetisierung. In: EU-Projekt PeriSCop Comenius 2.1 (Ed.). *Jugend in Europa* pp. 10–17. Frankfurt. a.M. PeriSCop:

Faulstich, W. (Hrsg.) (1995). Grundwissen Medien. 2. Aufl. München: UTB.

Gehlen, A. (1993): *Anthropologische und sozialpsychologische Untersuchungen.* Hamburg: Rowohlt

Habermas, J. (1981). Theorie des kommunikativen Handelns, 2 Bände, Frankfurt/M.: Suhrkamp.

I Curriculum Partnership (2004). Guidelines for Emergent E-competences at Schools. Project: I Curriculum: The Knowledge and Information Skills Needed for Living in the Digital Age. http://promitheas.iacm.forth.gr/i-curriculum/Assets/Docs/Outputs/Guidelines%20Teachers.pdf

ISTE (2007). The ISTE National Educational Technology Standards (NETS•S) and Performance Indicators for Students. Retrieved on 19-01-2009 from http://www.iste.org

Kössler, H. (1989). Bildung und Identität. In: Henning Kössler (Ed.): Identität. Fünf Vorträge pp. 51–65. Erlangen: Univerität Erlangen.

Kron, F., Sofos A. (2003). *Mediendidaktik. Neue Medien in Lehr- und Lernprozessen.* München: Reinhardt.

Kron, F., and Sofos, A. (2007). *The Didactics of Media. New Media in the context of Didactic and Learning Processes* (Διδακτική των Μέσων. Νέα Μέσα στο πλαίσιο Διδακτικών και

Μαθησιακών Διαδικασιών.) Athens: Gutenberg (in Greek).

Krumsvik, R. J., (2008). Situated Learning and Teacher's Digital Competence. *Education and Information Technologies*, 13, pp.279–290.

Maletzke, G. (1998). Kommunikationswissenschaft im Überblick: Grundlagen, Probleme, Perspektiven. Wiesbaden: Verlag für Sozialwissenschaften.

Manovich, Lev. (2001). *The Language of New Media*. Cambridge, MA: MIT Press

Martin, A. (2006). Digital Literacy Needed in an "e-permeated" world—progress report of DigEuLit project. Available on http://www.elearningeuropa.info/

Mead, G. H. (1998): *Geist, Identität und Gesellschaft. Aus der Sicht des Sozialbehaviorismus*. 11. Aufl. Frankfurt/M.: Suhrkamp.

McLuhan, M. (2001). *Understanding Media: The Extension of Man*. New York: Taylor & Francis.

Media Literacy Expert Group (2007). Current Trends and Approaches to Media Literacy in Europe. Barcelona: Universidad Autonoma de Barcelona. Retrieved on 19-01-2009 from: http://ec.europa.eu/avpolicy/media_literacy/docs/studies/study.pdf

OECD (2000). *Literacy in the Information Age: Final Report of the International Adult Literacy Survey*. Ottawa: Statistics Canada.

—— (2008). Adult Literacy. Retrieved on 19-01-2009 from http://www.oecd.org

Oevermann, U. (1979). Sozialisationstheorie. Ansätze zu einer soziologischen Sozialisationstheorie und ihre Konsequenzen für eine allgemeine soziologische Analyse. In: Lüschen, G. (Ed.). *Deutsche Soziologie seit 1945 Entwicklungsrichtungen und Praxisbezug* pp. 143–168 Kölner Zeitschrift für Soziologie und Sozialpsychologie.

Parsons, T. (1986). *Gesellschaften. Evolutionäre und komparative Perspektiven*. 2. Aufl. Frankfurt/M.: Suhrkamp.

Philipp, E., Rolff, H.-G. (1998): *Schulprogramme und Leitbilder entwickeln*. Ein Arbeitsbuch. Weinheim/Basel: Beltz.

Pöttinger, I. (1997): *Lernziel Medienkompetenz. Theoretische Grundlagen und praktische Evaluation anhand eines Hörspielprojekts*, München: KoPäd Verlag

Rafferty, J., & Steyaert, J. (2007). Social Work in a Digital Society. In: M. Lymbery & K. Postle (Eds.), *Social Work: A Companion to Learning*, pp.165–175. Los Angeles: SAGE.

Schäffer, B. (2006). Die Bildung Älterer mit neuen Medien: Zwischen Medienkompetenz, ICT-Literacy und generationsspezifischen Medienpraxiskulturen. In: Bildungsforschung 3 (2006). Available on: http://www.bildungsforschung.org/bildungsforschung/Archiv/2006-02/medien

Schmidt, J. S. (2003). Geschichten & Diskurse. Abschied vom Konstruktivismus. Hamburg

Schratz, M., Steiner-Löffler, U. (1998): *Die lernende Schule. Arbeitsbuch pädagogische Schulentwicklung*. Weinheim/Basel: Beltz.

Sofos, A. (2005a). Theoretische Perspektiven zur Begründung des Medienbegriffs. in: *Pädagogische Rundschau* 59(2005), pp.719–726.

Sofos, A. (2005b): Quid est hoc? The Concepts of Ability and Aptitude Related to the Media in Education (Quid est hoc? Οι Έννοιες της Ικανότητας και της Δεξιότητας που σχετίζεται με τα Μέσα στην Εκπαίδευση). In Hatzidimou D. And Vitsilaki V. (□ds.): *The school in the society of information and multiculturalism* (Το σχολείο στην κοινωνία της πληροφορίας και της πολυπολιτισμικότητας). □□□ International Conference Proceedings, pp.248–254. Rhodes: Kyriakidis Bros (in Greek).

—— (2009). Issues of Social Inequality, Digital Divide, Identity, and Educational Orientation in the Knowledge Society and in the School (Ζητήματα κοινωνικής ανισότητας, ψηφιακού χάσματος, ταυτότητας και παιδαγωγικού προσανατολισμού στην κοινωνία της γνώσης και στο σχολείο), In Prepi and Koufaki (Eds.), Social Inequalitites in Education («Κοινωνικές Ανισότητες και Εκπαίδευση»), Conference Proceedings, Alexandroupolis: University of Thrace (in Greek).

Spanhel, D. (1999). Integrative Medienerziehung in der Hauptschule. Ein Entwicklungsprojekt auf der Grundlage responsiver Evaluation. München: kopaed. Available on http://www.mediacultureonline.de/fileadmin/bibliothek/spanhel_integra/spanhel_integra.pdf

Spitzer, M. (2002). Lernen Gehirnforschung und die Schule des Lebens. Berlin: Spektrum Akademischer Verlag.

Sting, St. (2005). Literacy versus Schriftlichkeit. In: Ecarius, J., Friebertshäuser, B. (Eds.), Literalität, *Bildung und Biographie:Perspektiven der erziehungswissenschaftlichen Biographieforschung.* pp.18–38. Opladen: Verlag Barbara Budrich.

Tulodziecki, G. (1997). Medien in Erziehung und Bildung. Grundlagen und Beispiele einer handlungs- und entwicklungsorientierten Medienpädagogik. 3. Aufl. Bad Heilbrunn: Klinkhardt.

UNESCO (2008). *International Literacy Statistics: A Review of Concepts, Methodology and Current Data.* Montreal: UNESCO.

Weinert, F. E. (2001). Concept of Competence: A Conceptual Clarification. In: D. S. Rychen & L. H. Salganik (Eds.), *Defining and Selecting Key Competencies* pp.45–66. Göttingen, Germany: Hogrefe & Huber.

Xohelis, P. D. (1997). *Introduction in Pedagogy* (Εισαγωγή στην Παιδαγωγική) (6th edition) Thessaloniki: Kyriakidis Bros (in Greek).

PART II

Digital Literacy Practice: The Pursuit of Digital Literacy in the School and the Roles of the Learners, Teachers, and the School Environment

CHAPTER 4

Digital Literacies and Schooling—Knowledge Practices in Transition

Ola Erstad

Introduction

On January 13th 2009, three leading technology companies announced a co-operation aimed at transforming global educational assessment and improving learning outcomes. In the press release it is further stated that:

> At the Learning and Technology World Forum in London, Cisco, Intel and Microsoft unveiled plans to underwrite a multi-sector research project to develop new assessment approaches, methods and technologies for measuring the success of 21st-century teaching and learning in classrooms around the world. During the session, the three companies called upon educational leaders, governments and other corporations to join in the effort.[1]

The initiative was supported by the OECD and IEA, and the ambition is to influence the next versions of the PISA and the TIMSS studies concerning 21st Century Skills.

Such 'future look' initiatives on competence challenges reflect technology developments in our society at large, and arguments for how these technologies will change our education system. As such it is easy to see how digital literacy[2] has grown as a needed response to technological developments —people need skills and competencies in order to use and reflect on the impact of digital media in different settings. Schools play an important role in providing the young with such skills and competencies based on their social mandate of providing all members of our society with the knowledge needed.

At present we deeply need a critical reflection on these same developments. Not to criticize policy initiatives on digital literacy as such, but to better understand what they represent and which implications they might have. The question is to what extent research can give some direction and indication of what digital literacy really is, and an understanding of the implications such literacies might have on the level of social practices.

Three themes will be elaborated in this article. First, there is a need to understand digital literacy in a historic perspective, seeing learning and human development as a mediation between cultural tools and knowledge building. Second, the social practices of using digital media are framed within local literacies, and as an intersection between formal and informal ways of learning. Third, there is a need to become clearer in what is actually new in the way we use digital media compared to older media.

By knowledge practices I understand the activities and events that young people are involved in, in different contexts. The focus of this article is towards schools, but this also relates to other settings of knowledge production such as gaming communities, social networking, and so forth. The key issue is to study knowledge practices using digital technologies, and the possible transitions of such practices in schools.

Conceptions of Technology and Literacy

The interrelationship between technology and literacy is often taken for granted. The book has, for a long time, been the main technological tool used for our conceptions of literacy, or more broadly as the ability to read (to relate to information), and also to write (to use available tools to express oneself). However, as several writers have pointed out, the link between technological developments and human socio-cognitive development has always been close. Within socio-cultural learning theory (see for example Wertsch, 1998; Säljö, 1999) learning and human development is seen as a mediation between cultural tools and knowledge building that changes over time.

During the 1980s several researchers critiqued the traditional conceptions of literacy, pointing out the strong cultural influence and the importance of studying literacy as social practices (Street, 1984; Heath, 1983; Scribner & Cole, 1981). A recent definition that grasps these conceptions is describing literacy as:

> Socially recognized ways of generating, communicating and negotiating meaningful content through the medium of encoded texts within contexts of participation in Discourses (or, as members of Discourses). (Lankshear and Knobel, 2008)

This definition is broad enough to cover different ways of relating to texts and competencies as part of social practices and discourses in different contexts. In this way literacy also includes new social practices that emerge due to technological developments (Lankshear & Knobel, 2008), and in this sense becomes more complex and situated. The definition also implies that literacy is never neutral, but always defined for certain purposes for someone. The digital part of literacy conceptions today is more used as a rhetorical way of looking at changes in the ways we understand literacy due to the development of digital media. It has raised concerns about the skills, knowledge and conceptions needed to function in our societies today and for the future. In this sense digital literacy is an elaboration of concepts of change, development and innovation as implications of new technologies being introduced into our education system (Kozma, 2003).

One aspect that has not been much referred to in later years, with the exception of David Buckingham, is the reference to the debates within media education in schools, where media literacy has been a key term since the 1980s.[3] Both within media education research and in practical experiences in schools, media literacy has been explored as the way young people reflect and understand media on different levels. When the strong push for computers and the Internet in schools started in the mid-1990s, media education debates were marginalized. However, during the last 5–7 years similar questions concerning the ways we relate to and reflect on the new media has started to evolve, but still with little reference to the older media education debates.[4]

One characteristic of the debates on digital literacy during the last decade has been the multi-dimensions of this concept. This is seen in the term multi-literacies by the New London group (Cope & Kalantzis, 2000) and in multi-modality by Kress (2003). These terms are referring to many different forms of literacy (computer literacy, information literacy, Internet literacy, and so forth), and to the combination of different modalities into one text.

The main question we need to ask is to what extent this really represents a new conception of literacy, or just an elaboration of former understandings. And is there something generic about literacy that transcends different modalities like decoding, critical reflection, meta-cognition, and something more specific related to each technology? If, as I have argued for here, literacy is understood as embedded in social practices and thereby changes over time, we might say that digital literacy is just an elaboration and extension of former understandings due to new cultural tools that give us some new possibilities for relating to information and as ways of expression of our own meanings.

This historic perspective, seeing learning and human development as a mediation between cultural tools and knowledge building, shows that many of the expectations towards the implementation of information and communication technologies (ICT) into our schools during the last decade has been naïve in the sense that there is an overoptimistic belief in what the technology can accomplish in itself. My argument is that we need to develop an understanding of media literacy as embedded in the social practices that teachers and students are involved in using technologies and how these practices change over time, partly due to the ways they use these new technologies.

Beyond Typologies and Frameworks

During the last decade several initiatives have been taken for developing typologies and frameworks of digital literacies. The different definitions and conceptions of technology literacy and fluency have often been related to certain frameworks and the development of standards for educational practices. In January 2001, the Educational Testing Service (ETS), in the U.S., assembled a panel to develop a workable framework for ICT Literacy. The outcome was the report Digital Transformation. A Framework for ICT Literacy (ETS, 2002). In this report the panel of experts propose the following definition of what they call ICT literacy, and their rationale for this.

Reflecting the growing importance and ubiquity of new technologies in work, education, and everyday life, the panel defines ICT literacy in the following way:

> ICT literacy is using digital technology, communications tools, and/or networks to access, manage, integrate, evaluate, and create information in order to function in a knowledge society.

The panel's definition reflects the notion of ICT literacy as a continuum, which allows the measurement of various aspects of literacy, from daily life skills to the transformative benefits of ICT proficiency. This definition is also important in that it lists five critical components of ICT literacy. The five components represent a set of skills and knowledge presented in a sequence that suggests increasing cognitive complexity. (ETS 2002: 3)

Several others have further elaborated this definition (Ainley, Fraillon, Freeman & Mendelovits, 2006). The main focus of this definition is on information handling, and as such building on general competencies that are not connected to specific subjects in school or specific contents in subjects. They can be taught and are not only related to what is learned in school settings, but also to situations outside the school.

Similar points are made in the report by the National Research Council (NRC) in the U.S. with the title Being Fluent with Information Technology (1999). Fluency in Information Technology ("FITness") covers three types of knowledge:

i. contemporary skills: "the ability to use particular (and contemporary) hardware or software resources to accomplish information processing tasks." (ibid.: 18) Naturally these skills will change over time as hardware and software evolve.

ii. foundational concepts: "the basic principles and ideas of computers, networks, and information." (ibid.: 2–3) These include computer structure, information systems, networks, modelling, algorithmic thinking and programming, the limitations of IT and its social impact.

iii. intellectual capabilities, which "integrate knowledge specific to information technology with problem domains of personal interest to individuals." (ibid.: 20) These are general thinking skills which might be recognisable in many disciplines, and include sustained reasoning, managing complexity, testing solutions, evaluating information, collaboration, anticipating change and expecting the unexpected.

The concept of fluency used in this report (1999: 9) connotes the ability to reformulate knowledge, to express oneself creatively and appropriately, and to produce and generate information (rather than simply to comprehend it).

Other frameworks have used 'digital competence' as an overall term. One example is the working group on "key competences" of the European Commission 'Education and Training 2010'. This program identifies digital competence as one of the eight domains of key competences, defining it as

> the confident and critical use of Information Society Technologies for work, leisure and communication. (European Commission 2004: 14)

Information society technologies (IST) are defined as

> offering services based on the use of Information and Communication technologies (ICT), the Internet, digital content, electronic media, etc., via for example a personal computer, a mobile telephone, an electronic banking machine, an eBook, digital television, etc. (European Commission 2004: 14)

Digital competence is regarded as consisting of knowledge, skills and attitudes.

Some initiatives are more oriented towards developing standards for teachers in their practices in schools, such as the one made by UNESCO (2008). It is, however, important that such standards do not become static tests, but can relate to technological and cultural change processes.

Building on such standards some countries have now started to develop assessment tools for digital literacy. Some examples are Australia, Norway and ISTE (International Society for Technology in Education) in the US. These have shown some positive results (Ainley, Fraillon, Freeman & Mendelovits, 2006), but needs to be further elaborated and specified to build good tools for such assessment strategies, that are much needed.

In a Norwegian setting such perspectives on typologies and frameworks have become more apparent due to the national curriculum of 2005. Building on former initiatives on ICT within Norwegian education since the mid-1990s, the committee that prepared the new national curriculum proposed to define 'digital competence' alongside reading, writing, numeracy and oral communication as five basic areas of competence that transcends into all subjects and on all levels of compulsory schooling. Later on the Ministry of Education changed the wording of 'competence' into 'skills' because they believed that the concept of 'competence' was too broad (Erstad, 2005). [5] In the White paper, 'Culture for Learning', outlining the new school reform in Norway, 'digital competence' is defined as;

> Digital competence is the sum of simple ICT skills, like being able to read, write and calculate, and more advanced skills that make creative and critical use of digital tools and media possible. ICT skills consist of being able to use software, to search, locate, transform and control information from different digital sources, while the critical and creative ability also needs an ability to evaluate, critical use of sources, interpretation and analysis of digital genres and media forms. In total digital competence can be seen as a very complex competence. (Ministry of Education, 2004, p. 48, my translation)

The important change of this national curriculum is that all teachers are committed to implement and use digital media in learning activities in schools, while they in former plans should or could use such technologies. In the discussions following this curriculum it is a bit unclear to what extent digital competence/literacy is an area of competence alongside the more traditional ones of reading and writing, numeracy and oral skills, or if digital competence/literacy is part of changes within the others, specifically reading and writing. In a Norwegian sense it has also been important to understand competence/literacy as a continuum from skills in using the technology, towards how ICT changes working methods and the knowledge focus of different subject domains, the learning strategies of information seeking and critical evaluation of sources, towards the more general 'Buildung' issues of cultural competence and what it means to be literate in a digital society.

The critical point to be made is that we need to bring the policy agenda and the more normative research arguing for the necessity of digital literacy down to studying knowledge practices, and how digital media create conditions for change and transition within such practices. What is needed is an orientation towards local literacies (Barton & Hamilton, 1998), and also to challenge the taken-for-granted division between formal and informal ways of learning.

Within schools there is a strong orientation towards certain dominating practices, such as teacher-student interactions, the book as a point of orientation and the evaluation system. My argument is that we need more and better research on how digital media create conditions for change of such knowledge practices. In this way we can give substance to our understanding of digital literacy and schooling. This is a critical question in trying to move beyond simple notions of digital literacy on a policy level.

The Relevance of Research

On one level one might conclude that there is a lot of research that could support such a tracing of digital literacy. This can be seen as an elaboration from large scale quantitative research on how young people use digital media, to more qualitative-oriented research on specific activities using such media, for example on fan fiction (Knobel, 1999) or computer gaming (Gee, 2003).

In the following pages I will refer to qualitative data from some projects studying ICT in Norwegian schools that I have been involved in during the last eight years. The quotes are taken from two large scale projects. One project was called PILOT (Project; Innovation in Learning, Organization and Technology), involving 120 schools in 9 regions of Norway over a four year period (2000–2004) (Erstad, 2004). The case description is taken from one of the twelve Norwegian cases of the international SITES M2 study (Kozma, 2003). The methods used were a combination of video recordings and observations at schools, both in classrooms and other spaces at schools, and interviews with students and teachers about their practices.

Conceptions among Teachers and Students

When working with teachers it often becomes evident that teachers' attitudes and convictions towards their own practice is based on former experiences and the teaching culture at the school. As one teacher told us in an interview at the beginning of one of the projects:

> My students learned much more before these new technologies were introduced. I had long experience with teaching and know what works. New teaching methods create chaos.

This is of course something that the students are very aware of and often complain about when we interview them about using ICT in schools and to what extent they are working towards creating student-centred learning environments. As some students expressed:

Student 1: And many teachers are not so good in using PC, so the teaching does not relate to that.

Student 2: They continue with the traditional methods even though...

Interviewer: What do you mean with traditional methods?

Student 2: Using the blackboard and...

Interviewer: Can you describe a typical traditional teaching?

Student 2: When the teacher enters he says close all the computers and get your note-books. Writes everything on the blackboard. Write assignments with pen and pencil.

Student 1: Our teacher in religion is about 70 years old. She does not know much about using the PC.

These kinds of reflections among the students also become evident when the issue of innovation comes up in the interviews. It becomes clear that what is defined as innovative for teachers is not necessarily so for the students. In one of the projects a student sent me the following e-mail:

> Hello! I am a student at a pretty normal school. We have a lot of computers and some other equipment... We also have study time. We are part of the PILOT project... Study time means that we have to sit with a bunch of assignments to work on. This is called innovative by the teachers. I call it old fashioned. It is just the same as it was in primary school, we almost never get time to work on the computer, it is just working with books and not directed towards the future. You have to do something about this! Best regards...

How the teachers conceive using ICT in learning activities and how they think they organize student-centred learning environments is often very different from what the student experience and how they conceive using ICT for learning. For example, about student involvement or increased participation in their own learning the following student comment:

Student: They say 'responsibility for own learning', but I am not sure if that is correct.

Interviewer: What do they mean then?

Student: I don't know, and I am not sure if they know themselves. In one instance it is 'responsibility for own learning', and in the next it is attendance register and follow up of home work. I don't know how much 'responsibility for own learning' that is. It is just like before.You get a mark if you have not done your homework. The thing with 'responsibility for own learning' is just nonsense.

However, we also see examples where there are changes going on in the way the learning environment and knowledge practices are developed and how the student role is defined. In one project the teachers, for example, focused on how they could change different situations in the school setting by using digital portfolios. One aspect of this was the meeting with the parents where the students traditionally were passive, but where they now became the centre of the discussions.

> I experienced that this created a whole new situation for the traditional parents-conference, where the teacher is the active part and student and parents often become passive listeners. Now it was the student who started the whole situation by presenting his work and starting a conversation based on this presentation. I experienced that it became a much more natural communication between equal partners. The parents became very impressed of what they were shown. The conversation flowed much easier and we could really sit much longer than the 45 minutes.

This shows how new technologies might create new conditions for different school activities. However, it is important to be aware of the different understandings of digital literacies that students and teachers have in order to see how it might change knowledge practices in schools.

A case study: 'The Use of Visual Communication Strategies and Project-Oriented Pedagogy'

One interesting development in Norway has been the connection between ICT use and project work (Erstad et al., 2005). The case presented here is from a lower secondary school situated in an area with families of lower socio-economic income. Since the middle of the 1970s, the focus on project-oriented pedagogy has been dominating at this school. Nationally the school is well known for having a long tradition of working with alternative approaches to teaching and learning. Both the principal and teachers at the school explain the impact of computers as a breakthrough for making their pedagogical visions of engaging the students move on and give digital competence direction towards knowledge construction. As such, importance has been given to create learning environments, which implies an extended definition of knowledge, not just as reading and writing. The teachers organize their learning environment within different areas with different activities, such as drama, art and craft and use of local knowledge.

One important aspect of the schools vision on teaching and learning is to create a learning environment where students can become better at what they are already good at. This implies an approach for creating better self-esteem for learning among the students. Time is spent on finding a subject-area where the developmental potential of each student is high. The challenge for the school is then to stimulate this competence in each student, creating better performance and trust in their potential for learning. The school also emphasize's, strongly the need for students to produce knowledge and present for other students. The students are also responsible for teaching other students at certain times, because the school believes that through teaching others is the best way of learning yourself. The students are organized in teams of 40, with a team of 5 teachers. In the projects the students always work in groups of 3 or 4. Teachers and students decide together the main focus of the project themes.

In one project the students made an animation movie on the theme 'the changing features of water'. Even though the basis for the project is natural science, it has an interdisciplinary approach since they use elements from other subjects, like, e.g., English. Each project consists of 4 steps. The first concerns experience, where the students are introduced to different ways of experiencing the theme for the project, for example water, and the students contribute with their own experiences. Then they can search for information on the Internet or talk to experts in the local community, etc. The next step is called the 'tool box', where they sit down and decide which tools they need to complete the tasks in the project. In this particular project it was important to get special training in visual tools like iMovie and the use of digital video cameras. In addition to this, they got training in word processing (Apple Works). The third step is the production phase where the students collect information about particles to make a storyboard to document their project. The last step is presentation for all students, with feedback and discussion. New technology is an important aspect of the three last steps.

The teacher is not always the expert in the choice of technical and creative solutions. As one of the project teachers says:

> I experience that my role changes from being a person that knows it all to become more of a resource person; a person that is more like a pusher, one that sets the framework, a conflict solver, an adjuster. I feel that this role becomes more important. Another situation that you see more of now is that I sit down more together with the students, and that you communicate on the same level and solve the problem through discussions with the students. It is a larger degree of equality when you sit in front of the screen and have to decide on what has suddenly come up. Also that you as a teacher can say that 'this I don't know, this I have to investigate closer', that is very important.

By studying the students' explorative talk when sitting in front of the computer we get an impression that they are very active participants in negotiating different solutions among themselves. Collaboration was an essential element in working with such a knowledge-production focus. By working together the students support each other, even though conflicts may arise. Many argue however, that disagreements with other children serve to highlight alternatives to the child's own point of view. This can foster a student's progress in understanding (Littleton and Light, 1999).

From the students' point of view, the biggest change is that the teachers don't hand them so much information anymore. In relation to the work with the animation movie, the students say:

> *Boy1:* Editing is the most fun thing to work on. Because we do things ourselves, there are no teachers who stand and point and tell you what you should do. You get to choose yourself and sort of what you think is best.
>
> *Girl:* There is sort of no specific assignments, 'now you have to do that', we decide what we should do and how we should do it.'
>
> *Boy2:* The teacher makes us not to give up.
>
> *Girl:* If we need help, then they are available. But if we want to we can do everything ourselves, if we manage to.
>
> *Boy1:* That we do it the right way.
>
> *Girl:* If we need help, they are there for us.
>
> *Boy1:* The teachers do not give us a lot of information, like they used to do in primary school. They give us an assignment, and then we should find the information we need to complete the assignment ourselves.

The use of iMovie can be defined as an effective artifact that gives flexibility and at the same time quality and a professional product. The visual focus has changed how the students relate to their own learning process and it has created a new framework for engaging the students in different subject-oriented activities. It generates creativity and it is an opportunity for experimenting with different solutions and putting together different components of knowledge.

It makes it easier for them to relate to a challenge partly because they can use a broader repertoire of their own competencies, and partly because it focuses their attention more. They have become more independent as a consequence of using such a resource with different options. This stimulates the students' motivation as well as their focus to the academic content. As one of the teachers says:

> The advantage with visual presentation is that the students have to study the material well, if not, they will not be able to create a movie.

The students themselves say they remember more of what they learn, because they have to know the material well to be able to present it to others. The importance of presentation is shown when a student says:

> And if you stand there and you haven't done it good or you don't remember, then...

The social pressure comes from the other students and not so much the teacher explaining what they have found out in their project.

> *Boy1*: It is more practical, so this way we learn more by doing things more than just to sit and write stuff.
>
> *Girl*: I think it is much better. I think I learn more by doing it on the computer than just sit and read about it. When you just sit and read or write then it becomes boring, and then you don't get it in. However, when you have to do something to get it right then you better grasp it.
>
> *Boy2*: You forget things easier when you just sit and read.
>
> *Boy1*: You just read, take a look in the book; write the assignments, without any of it going through the brain.

The students' discussion shows how important it is with assignments that is practical and appears meaningful. Another element is that both well- and poor-performing students benefit from working with the computer this way. Both parents and teachers expressed this. A strong statement came from one of the mothers to a couple of twins in this group:

> My girls are academically weak because they have dyslexia both of them. And during the years in primary school they have all the time struggled with not being able to prove themselves in any subject-oriented way. I think it was incredibly positive for them to come here...to be able to work on computers and film and editing and such things. They have done a bit of that at home before, so they had knowledge that the other students could get from them, and through that they got a higher status in the group. So for them it has been like...I don't know...almost like a new life. It is very important that they gain ownership to their work. I think that is one of the keys to create engagement. For adults it is like this, and I do not think this is different for children.

The project teacher also confirms this when he talks about the same students:

> We have some students who are very weak; they cannot read the watch and have real problems reading and writing. We got a note from their primary school that they were mentally several years behind the others. Then yesterday they worked on e-mail. In fact they were the first to complete the task. Also, that we discover that they are good at visual communication. Suddenly these students come into a learning environment

> where they have experience related to a new tool that becomes available for them without only focusing on reading and writing. But also for the students that are clever and take things fast, this seems to give them more. Also for them it is a growth environment to produce good results.

The two important aspects for changing the learning process for these girls were, firstly, the importance of coming to a school with a much more open and flexible learning environment where they could use their strong competencies (visually) to strengthen their weaker competencies (reading, writing), and, secondly, the digital resources available at the school that support different learning activities among the students in a more flexible way than before. Heterogeneous grouping that is employed in this project has been very positive for the students at this school.

Digital Literacies and School Practices

The important message from the section above is that digital literacy in schools should not be narrowed down to a question of skills in handling the technology, but rather how such technologies gets embedded into educational practices and the mechanisms influencing such practices. In this way we will get a better understanding of the changes in literate practices in schools that the technologies bring about.

The conceptions that teachers and students have towards educational practices on one side and on technology and its use on the other is of key importance in understanding how digital media might have an impact on changes within such practices. In this way such conceptions might open up or close down the way digital literacy is defined as a new way of understanding 'reading' and 'writing' as mediational means in our culture.

The case story presented above takes this a step further in the sense that it shows how one school has developed their literacy practices by opening up to more visual ways of communication, new ways of engaging students in their learning activities, and how students have a broader set of tools in the way they work on specific issues. For the dyslectic girls this way of working has a major impact on their experiences as literate beings in schools.

Based on research on the educational use of digital technologies, we can suggest some categories to specify aspects and elements of digital literacy in school practices. This is not necessarily understood as going from the simple to the more abstract, even though the listing might give this impression, but as different aspects of how we understand young people's use of digital technologies in the learning activities at school. These are listed in Table 4.1. This list is by no means complete, but understood as a step in the direction of breaking down what we mean by digital literacy in school practices. The categories indicate different activities using digital technologies that are of importance in learning activities where competencies in using the technologies are demanded. This works across different media like computer games, social web, specific learning programs and so forth.

This discussion highlights the importance of studying knowledge practices and students' knowledge building (Scardamalia & Bereiter, 2005), and how they change as part of working with digital technologies in schools.

Table 4.1. Aspects of young people's use of digital technologies in the learning activities at school

Basic skills	Be able to open software, sort out and save information on the computer, and other simple skills in using the computer and software
Download	Be able to download different information types from the Internet
Search	Know about and how to get access to information
Navigate	Be able to orient oneself in digital networks, learning strategies in using the Internet
Classify	Be able to organize information according to a certain classification scheme or genre
Integrate	Be able to compare and put together different types of information related to multimodal texts
Evaluate	Be able to judge the quality, relevance, objectivity and usefulness of the information one has found. Critical evaluation of sources
Communicate	Be able to communicate information and express oneself through different mediational means
Cooperate	Be able to take part in netbased interactions of learning, and take advantage of digital technology to cooperate and take part in networks
Create	Be able to produce and create different forms of information as multimodal texts, make web pages, and so forth. Be able to develop something new by using specific tools and software. Remixing existing texts into something new

A Future Look–
Content Creation, Remixing and Education

Digital literacy, or literacies, relates both to changes in the way we learn and relate to information, and to challenges of competencies needed to be a citizen in digital societies. Such literacies are specified by the social practices that people are involved in using digital media in different ways. Such literacies are both building on older literacies, and also representing something new, related to cultural complexities in the way we live our lives.

Much of our perspective on digital media in education has a narrow understanding of the ways we use technologies and how they should be developed in schools. At the same time these initiatives brings forward some important discussions about the life of citizens in societies that are more and more dependent on digital media in every part of social life. How should we in our research efforts try to grasp what aspects of skills, competencies and literacies are important for being a citizen with the necessary knowledge base to take part in our society. This of course also raises some basic questions about the role of schools in our society.

The most important development in later years concerning digital literacy and new technologies is the Web 2.0 and the possibilities this opens up for user-generated content creation. This is important because the user of technology is no longer only a receiver of information, but also a producer of content. This is seen in many phenomena on the web that have grown in later years like MySpace, YouTube, Flicr and Facebook. Some researchers also highlight the concept of remixing (Lessig, 2008; Erstad, 2008) as an expression of how young people now download content from the Internet, edit sound, music and images together in new ways and upload this on sites on the Internet for others to use further on.

This development is an example of how literacy practices change due to technological developments. Young people produce all sorts of texts and share them with each other in new ways. This of course challenges fundamentally how we traditionally think about teacher and student roles, about teacher education, and how we conceive school as a place for information access and knowledge construction. How this will develop in the future remains to be seen. However, based on developments during the last five years it is clear that digital literacies and school practices will have to be conceived in different ways in the future than it has been in the past, especially in the way people learn and how schools provide sites for stimulating knowledge practices among young people.

Notes

1 See www.latwf.org/latest_news-3.html, retrieved 13th February 2009.

2 I use the term digital literacy even though media literacy is a more correct term since literacy is understood across different modalities.

3 See also special issue of the *Journal of Communication*, Winter 1998, on 'media literacy', with contributions from several key researchers in the US and the UK within the field of media education.

4 D. Buckingham and K. Tyner are examples of researchers that have tried to make a point about this lack of connection to former debates.

5 This created a debate in Norway of how to define digital competence, and the danger that teacher defines skills in a narrow sense. It is also interesting how these concepts resonate differently in different languages.

Bibliography

Ainley, J., Fraillon, J., Freeman, C., & Mendelovits, J. (2006). Assessing information and communication technology literacy in schools. *Paper presented at the Annual Meeting of the American Educational Research Association*, San Francisco, April 2006.

Barton, D., & Hamilton, M. (1998). *Local literacies. Reading and writing in one community*. London: Routledge.

Cope, B., & Kalantzis, M. (2000). *Multiliteracies. Literacy learning and the design of social futures*. London: Routledge.

Erstad, O. (2004). *PILOTer for skoleutvikling* (PILOTs for school development). UniPub. Report no. 28. ITU, University of Oslo

—— (2005). *Digital kompetanse i skolen* (Digital literacy in the school). Oslo: University Press.

Erstad, O., Klovstad, V., Kristiansen, T., & Soby, M. (2005). ITU Monitor 2005. *Digital kompetanse i skolen* [ITU Monitor 2005. Digital literacy in the school]. Oslo: The Norwegian University Press.

—— (2008). Trajectories of remixing – digital literacies, media production and schooling. In C. Lankshear & M. Knobel (eds.) Digital literacies: Concepts, Policies and Practices. New York: Peter Lang, pp. 177–202.

ETS (2002). *Digital Transformation: a Framework for ICT Literacy.* Princeton, NJ: Educational Testing Service.

European Commission (2004). Key Competences for lifelong learning: A European reference framework. Directorate-General for Education and Culture (online at http://europa.eu.int/comm/education/policies/2010/doc/basicframe.pdf). (Entered 13th February 2009).

Gee, J. P. (2003). *What video games have to teach us about learning and literacy*. New York: Palgrave Macmillan.

Heath, S.B. (1983). *Ways with words. Language, life, and work in communities and classrooms*. New York: Cambridge University Press.

Knobel, M. (1999). *Everyday Literacies: Students, discourses and social practice*. New York: Peter Lang.

Kozma, R. B. (2003). *Technology, innovation and educational change*. Eugene, OR: International Society for Technology in Education (ISTE).

Kress, G. (2003). *Literacy in the new media age*. London: Routledge.

Lankshear, C. & M. Knobel (eds.) (2008). *Digital literacies. Concepts, Policies and Practices*. New York: Peter Lang.

Lessig, L. (2008). *Remix. Making art and commerce thrive in the hybrid economy*. New York: The Penguin Press.

Littleton, K., & Light, P. (eds.). (1999). *Learning with computers: Analysing productive interaction*. London: Routledge.

Ministry of Education (2004). *The culture for learning*. White Paper. Oslo.

National Research Council Committee on Information Technology Literacy (1999). *Being fluent with information technology*. Washington, DC: National Academy Press .

Scardamalia, M., & Bereiter, C. (2006). Knowledge building: Theory, pedagogy, and technology. In Sawyer, R.K. (ed.) *The Cambridge handbook of the learning sciences*. Cambridge: Cambridge University Press.

Scribner, S., & Cole, M. (1981). *The psychology of literacy*. Cambridge, MA, Harvard University Press.

Street, B. (1984). *Literacy in theory and practice*. Cambridge: Cambridge University Press.

Säljö, R. (1999). Learning as the use of tools: A sociocultural perspective on the human-technology link. In K. Littleton & P. Light (eds.). *Learning with computers: Analysing productive interaction*. London: Routledge, pp.144–161.

United Nations Educational, Scientific and Cultural Organization (UNESCO) (2008). ICT competency standards for teachers. Paris: UNESCO.

Wertsch, J. (1998). *Mind as action*. New York, Oxford University Press.

CHAPTER 5

Web 2.0 and the Digital Divide: What Can Facebook and YouTube Contribute?

Joe Cullen

Introduction: Web 2.0, Learning and Inclusion

Ask any conference audience these days to take part in a 'homologeo'—a public confession—on whether or not they have a 'Facebook' page and it's as likely as not that at least half of them will put their hands up. Of a total estimated global internet audience of 860 million, 580 million participate in some form of social networking. Of these, some 132 million are involved in 'Facebook', and 117 million are active in 'Myspace'.[1] Social networking is fast rivaling television as the main source of digital recreation. According to Atwell (2007), the 9–17 age group spends 9 hours a week social networking compared with 10 hours per week watching TV. A defining feature of the growing ubiquity of these kinds of social networking applications is their increasing use in learning environments. Some sources suggest that as much as 60% of young people working in social networking environments use them for education-related topics, and 50% employ them as a space to discuss schoolwork.[2]

This genre of Web 2.0 or 'social computing' information and communication technologies (ICTs) refers to the range of digital applications that enable interaction, collaboration and sharing between users and which supports or fosters group interaction (Owen et al., 2006).[3] Following Smith (2007), the definition used in this paper envisages Web 2.0 as a set of practices rather than any particular list of tools, i.e., the use of two or more modes of computer-mediated communication that result in 'community formation'. (Vuorikari, 2005; Owen et al., 2006). In principle, this embraces a wide range of platforms, software and tools – including communication tools to handle capture, stor and present of information—including text, audio and video, wikis and blogs—and interactive tools allowing users to communicate in real time (for example, NetPhone, videochat; instant messaging). What is often not well understood is the range of social networking models—particularly pedagogic or learning models—that underpin Web 2.0 tools. These can be interpreted as particular configurations of organisational, institutional, cultural and behavioural modes which serve to realise particular sets of user interactions and, ultimately, communication outcomes. For example, social network services allow people to come together online around shared interests, hobbies, or causes—like dating. Other services—like LinkedIn—enable business networking. Social network search engines use social networks to filter search results, for example 'Friends Reunited'. Commercial social networks form communities around particular consumer or producer interests. Following Redeker (2008).[4] Web 2.0 tools used in learning environments can be broadly classified into the following types:

- Social Networking services—internet- or mobile-device-based social spaces designed to facilitate communication, collaboration and content sharing across networks of contacts. Examples include Facebook and MySpace
- Syndication and notification technologies—a means of directly sending content updates, typically using a feed reader (or aggregator), relying on protocols called RSS (Really Simple Syndication) to list changes
- Weblogs or blogs—online public writing environments, which enable a single author or a group of authors to write and publicly display articles, including visual, audio and video content, as well as features such as links to other blogs, information about the author, and comments from readers
- Wikis—a website that allows users to collaboratively add, remove and otherwise edit and change content, usually text, for example Wikipedia—a collaboratively created online encyclopedia
- Tagging, Social Bookmarking and Folksonomies—these allow recording (bookmarking) of web pages, and tagging with significant words (tags) that describe the pages being recorded, for example del.icio.us
- Media-sharing devices—these store user-contributed media, and allow users to search for and display content, for example YouTube
- Podcasts and Vodcasts—which enable listeners to keep up-to-date with recent audio or video content

- Virtual and immersive environments—these provide users with an online game-like 3D digital environment, for example 'Second Life'
- Online office and discussion applications—these are software packages that replicate desktop applications like Microsoft Office or Open Office and include collaborative editing tools. They typically include interactive Discussion Forums to enable users to share comments
- Web 2.0 Tools for learning—some online collaboration applications are especially tailored for educational purposes. For example Moodle is a free software e-learning platform designed to help educators create online courses

Web 2.0 has significant potential in supporting digital literacy—particularly for 'hard to reach' and excluded groups. On the one hand, social computing applications empower users to produce, publish, share, edit and co-create content, offering them new opportunities for learning and self-realization. But a number of commentators now argue that Web 2.0 tools and collaborative learning approaches are beginning to fundamentally change the nature of the educational enterprise—and of education itself. One perspective that is beginning to gain currency is the idea that the new generation of eLearning will combine social networks with context-based services. Even though formal content will not vanish, modern technology will support user-generated informal content, and teachers will have to adapt to a new role as facilitator instead of a pure information transmitter. Personal learning environments (PLEs) will replace formal educational environments, like the school and the university, so that learning becomes literally 'life-embedded'—part of a seamless process in which there is no separation between, school, home and work.[5] This view owes much to a notion that has come to the fore in recent thinking on learning—the idea that education is now focusing on 'new millennium learners' (NML), and that the future of learning is inextricably bound up with these learners. NML—those born after 1982—are the first generation to grow up surrounded by digital media, and most of their activities dealing with peer-to-peer communication and knowledge management are mediated by these technologies (Pedró, 2006). A number of characteristics are attributed to NMLs. Based on the results of a range of studies, it is claimed they are "hardwired" to simultaneously utilize multiple types of web-based participatory media (Baird & Fisher (2006); they are 'technologically savvy', have grown up with the Web and are "always-on"; they are adept with computers and creative with technology (Olbinger & Olbinger, 2005) and they are highly skilled at multi-tasking (Pedro, 2006). Perhaps more importantly, some commentators are now taking the view that the new learning skills acquired by NMLs have changed cognitive patterns. It is suggested that NML do not think linearly and are less structured than previous generations (McLester, 2007). They gain knowledge by processing discontinued, non-linear information, which changes their learning styles (Pedró, 2006). And, according to OECD (2008), research shows that the exposure to the proliferation of imagery in media has contributed to the selective increases in nonverbal intelligence scores during the past century in industrialised countries. Indeed, a recent OECD study claims that multitasking as a phenomenon will not disappear, but will become the educational mainstream (OECD, 2008).

Given this emerging evidence, it is not surprising that the notion that Web 2.0 is changing the nature of digital literacy is beginning to gain ground. In turn, there is an increasing consensus that Web 2.0 is reducing the 'digital divide', and opening up opportunities for more people—particularly young people—to participate in the 'Knowledge Society'. Current state of the art suggests that the expansion of Web 2.0, coupled with convergence in platforms and devices, has significantly increased the capacity for people to engage in opinion-formation, knowledge creation and decision-making. It is suggested that the emergence of Web 3.0 will continue these trends, taking Lifelong Learning from its traditional 'transmissive' mode, where learners are to a large extent passive consumers of knowledge, to a 'transformative' mode where knowledge is actively co-constructed as part of everyday life.[6] There is a growing body of evidence—albeit drawn mainly from experimental projects—to suggest that Web 2.0 can contribute to positively supporting the needs of excluded groups. In a literature review of current state of the art Redeker (2008) cites numerous examples to support the view that projects using Learning 2.0 strategies have a high potential to re-engage excluded groups in learning. These include initiatives to support learning for young people in hospitals (for example 'Mundo des Estrellas'); the use of Second life to support learning for people with autism and Asperger's Syndrome (for example 'Brigadoon'); initiatives that offer an alternative to traditional education for young people disengaged from classroom learning because of illness, pregnancy, bullying, phobia, travelling, reluctance to learn, disaffection, exclusion ('Notschool') and projects that aim to exploit the advantages of social computing tools to guarantee a representation of minorities through a direct self expression ('Rete G2 seconde generazioni').[7]

However, it is by no means clear what impact Web 2.0 is having on the broader issues around e-accessibility and e-participation. Recent studies show that, despite significant investment by the EU and member states, around 42% of EU citizens are still classified as 'non participants' in the knowledge society (Cullen, 2007). There is evidence (Facer and Furlong; 2005) to suggest that significant numbers of people remain at the margins of the 'knowledge society' and social networking—not least because the complexity and diversity of their lives, and their roles in a 'technologically rich' society, remain poorly understood. There is also increasing concern, and a lack of knowledge, about the roles that new technologies are playing in reinforcing social problems rather than providing opportunities for learning—for example the use of video mobile phones for 'happy slapping'; the glorification on YouTube of knife and gun crime; the use of social networking sites to promote the 'radicalisation' of young people.[8] Another gap in our understanding, which the study aimed to shed light on, is how technologies that on the surface appear to promote greater social interaction and collaboration in Web 2.0 environments can actually engage people in highly individualistic behaviours that undermine learning and citizenship (Cullen 2007; Oysermann, Koon & Kemmelmeier 2002).[9] There is also evidence that they exacerbate existing cultural, educational and social divisions. Danah Boyd (2007), for example, argues that, in the USA, utilization of social networking technologies reflects complex class, status and educational stratifications in American youth: MySpace is the 'spiritual home' for educational drop-outs—for Latino/Hispanic teens, 'burnouts', 'alternative kids', goths, gangstas—Facebook attracts 'upwardly mobile hegemonic teens'.[10]

Moreover, a number of studies have raised issues about whether Web 2.0 is creating additional problems for particular excluded groups, for example people with disabilities; immigrants and people from ethnic minorities. Woodfine et al. (2008) argue that online learning activities raise problems for higher education students with dyslexia and other cognitive disabilities, and Bühler and Fisseler (2007) argue that blogs, wikis and other social computing applications pose additional threats to accessibility for disabled people.[11]

Against this background, this paper reviews the contribution that Web 2.0 is making to digital literacy—and in particular the evidence that social networking is supporting 'e-inclusion'. It looks in particular at some recent studies carried out by the author and fellow researchers, in collaboration with the Institute for Prospective Technological Studies (IPTS), involving an analysis of a database of over 200 examples of the use of Web 2.0 tools and approaches to promote new forms of learning, including initiatives aimed at 'hard to reach' and excluded groups, together with sixteen in-depth case studies of specific examples. [12] [13] [14] The review focuses on three main questions: what does the emerging 'Web 2.0 for Learning' landscape look like? What kinds of new digital literacies and skills are being supported by Web 2.0? What contribution is web 2.0 making to engaging hard to reach and excluded groups in using ICTs?

The Web 2.0 for Learning Landscape

The 'Learning 2.0' database compiled by the Institute for Prospective Technological Studies (IPTS), containing some 237 cases, is probably the largest repository in Europe, if not worldwide, of examples of applications of Web 2.0 used in learning environments. The cases in this database reflect a diverse spectrum of different configurations of scale; target groups; learning and inclusion themes; pedagogic and inclusion models; technological functionalities and 'social networking' models and methods. Analysis of the features of these examples provides a good snapshot of the emerging landscape of Web 2.0 for learning—or 'Learning 2.0'. As figure 5.1 shows, the examples represent a wide range of technology platforms and tools, with virtually all of the different kinds of Web 2.0 tools currently available being used to support learning. A distinguishing feature of the technologies is that they are typically used in combination—with 53% of the cases using more than one kind of Web 2.0 tool. The tools most commonly used are weblogs (41% of cases); social networking tools like Facebook and Myspace (40% of cases); online Discussion Forums (29% of cases) and wikis (29% of cases). Podcasts, vodcasts, 'folksonomies' and tagging and virtual realities are currently less frequently used. Other tools include a wide variety of specialised software tools and applications such as e-Portfolios, Twitter, Ning, Moodle, Skype, LMS, VLEs, Facebook, Elgg, and interactive games.

This suggests that, at least in principle, the European education and training system is beginning to develop the infrastructure to enable radical forms of learning based on collaborative and co-produced knowledge to flourish. This picture is reinforced by the data in figure 5.2, which shows the learning objectives associated with the initiatives. The objectives and related activities to achieve those objectives are diverse. Objectives range from developing new ways of learning using social software tools (68% of all cases), improving the collaboration amongst actors (57%) and increasing the motivation and thus the participation of learners in the Learning 2.0 experience (49%). It is noticeable that digital literacy strategies figure relatively high in the objectives aimed at by Web 2.0 initiatives, with 25% of cases aiming to increase computer skills and 24% aiming to improve accessibility to learning. As with the adoption of Web 2.0 technologies themselves, the emerging Learning 2.0 landscape is characterized by its multi-dimensionality. Almost 90% of all cases are addressing multiple objectives through the application of Web 2.0 applications in learning and teaching in education and training.

However, it would be premature to suggest that Web 2.0 is precipitating radical changes in the European education and training infrastructure itself. As figure 5.3 shows, conventional learning settings still dominate the Learning 2.0 landscape. Some 40% of cases involve teaching in universities and similar higher education establishments; 39% of initiatives are located in secondary schools and

27% in primary schools. This means that Web 2.0 has some way to go before it can claim to be making real inroads into expanding accessibility for a much broader spectrum of learners than is currently the case–particularly for the hard to reach and adult learners; the long-term unemployed; women with families and other 'marginalised' social groups, who fall outside the orbit of formal education, learners, who work within the education and training 'establishment'.

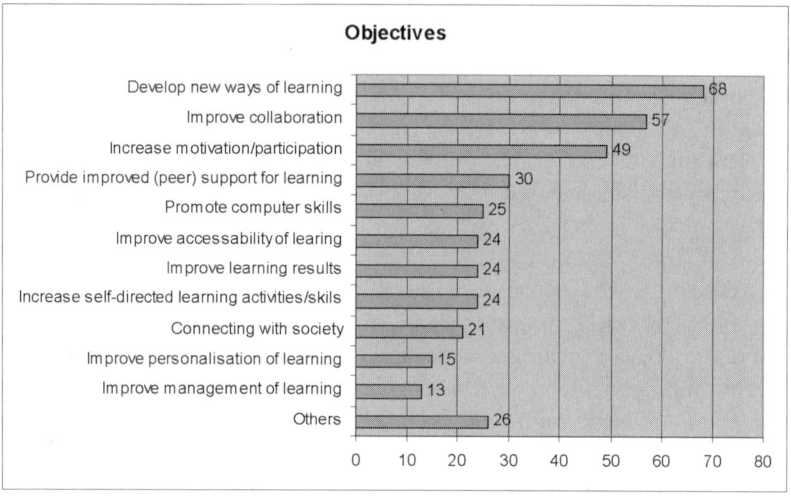

Figure 5.1: Web 2.0 tools used in learning environments

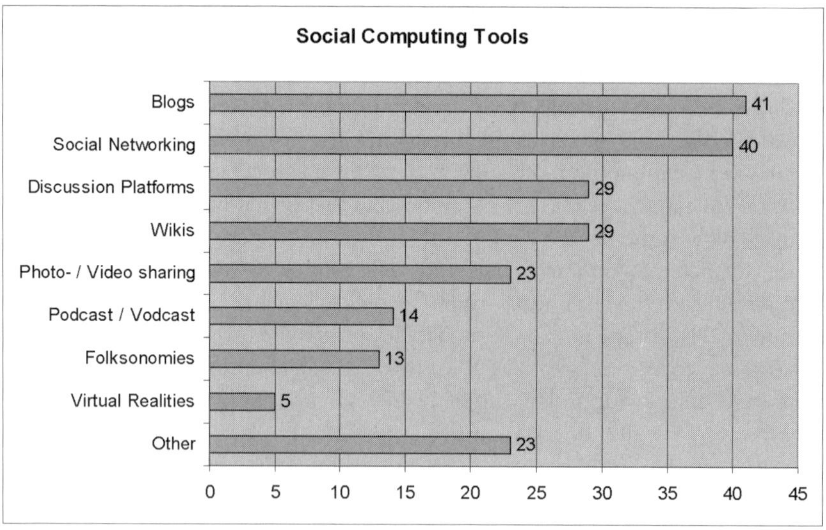

Figure 5.2: Learning objectives of Web 2.0 initiatives

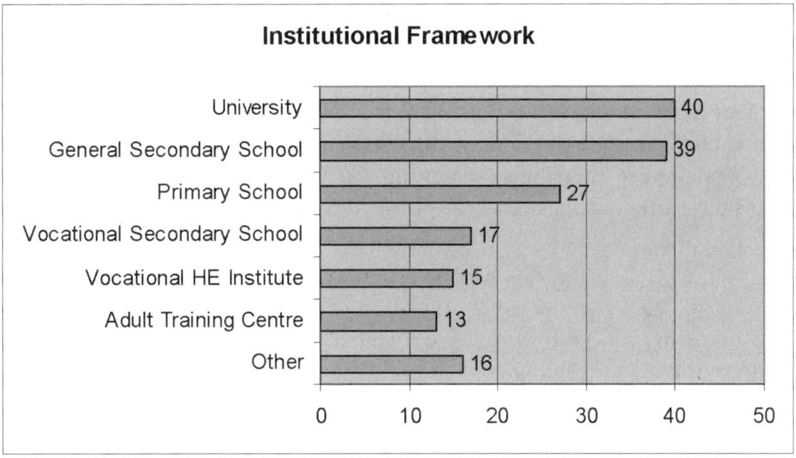

Figure 5.3: Institutional settings for Learning 2.0

Some 78% of cases target learners in formal education; 39% involve teachers and trainers, and only 12% involve citizens or adult learners. As a result, Web 2.0 is primarily targeted at the younger age groups. Around 20% of the cases in the IPTS database focus on users of primary school age; over 40% involve learners in the 12 to 18 age group—those mainly in secondary schools—and over 50% in the 19 to 24 age group—mainly those in higher education. These results suggest that Web 2.0 is currently failing to address the main structural dynamics that are constraining participation in the Knowledge Society for two particularly significant groups—adult citizens generally and older people particularly, since many studies show, and current EU policy recognizes, that these groups constitute key segments of the digitally excluded.[15] In turn, other hard to reach and excluded groups—disadvantaged groups; ethnic minorities; people with disabilities and people with learning difficulties—are relatively under-represented in the Learning 2.0 landscape.

These key features of the Web 2.0 tools and approaches currently being used to support new forms of learning reinforce an overall impression of an emerging, and as yet embryonic technological and socio-cultural process that is un-coordinated, fragmented and only tenuously tied to key policy and political priorities. In an attempt to gain a clearer picture of the Learning 2.0 landscape as a whole, part of the work carried out on analyzing the IPTS database involved a cluster analysis of the cases in order to establish whether it was possible to develop a typology of Learning 2.0 applications. However, the analysis failed to identify a clear-cut typology of Learning 2.0 initiatives. Although the analysis came up with five clusters—or broad groupings of cases with similar characteristics, none of these clusters stood out in terms of distinctive characteristics that distinguished it clearly from the other clusters. This result paints a picture of a highly amorphous and undifferentiated terrain. As noted above, many of the Learning 2.0 examples in the database use several Web 2.0 tools; have a number of objectives; serve more than one user group and involve a range of outputs. Indeed—47% of the cases involve more than one age group; 40% involve more than one user group; 86% have multiple objectives; 53% use several kinds of Learning 2.0 tools; 70% involve more than one type of social networking activity and 34% combine a range of outputs. On the other hand, the Web 2.0 initiatives heavily over-represent formal learning settings and younger age groups—which makes it difficult to distinguish emerging trends involving new and innovative forms of learning and supporting the engagement of hard to reach and excluded groups.

Table 5.1. Target groups for Learning 2.0

	N	% Cases
Learners in Formal Education	184	78
Teachers & Trainers	92	39
External Experts	34	14
General Public	29	12
Adult Learners	26	11
Parents & Other Third Parties	22	9
Workers	20	8
Disadvantaged People	20	8
Ethnic Minorities	18	8
People with Disabilities	15	6
Unemployed	11	5
People with Learning Difficulties	11	5
Early School Leavers	8	3
Others	20	8

This is not to suggest that new, innovative and effective learning approaches using Web 2.0 technologies are completely absent. In fact the studies identified a number of promising examples of new learning innovations involving social computing—several utilizing media-rich environments to create highly innovative learning spaces which encourage the acquisition and use of new digital competences. One example is SecondReiff—a 3D space in the virtual world SecondLife for combining real and virtual learning in studies of architecture in the higher education sector. Another example—aimed specifically at supporting e-inclusion—is Schome Park. Initially aimed at 'gifted' students who were underperforming in school—including students with autism, this initiative expanded its target population to include students from socially disadvantaged or ethnic minority backgrounds who are currently underrepresented in education. Schome explores the potential and pitfalls of 'Teenage Second Life' as a learning platform. It uses an 'open pedagogy' model based on collaborative learning, incorporating Second Life; Machinima; blogs and wikis to create new and empowered roles for students, who play an active role alongside professional educators in co-producing learning content. A key feature of these new learning approaches, utilising Web 2.0 technologies, is that they change in sometimes quite radical ways traditional teacher-learner roles. For example, LeMill develops a web-service for exchange of national learning repositories and materials in the framework of the Calibrate project. The Calibrate project, starting in 2005, is advancing the idea of free and open learning resources and international transfer of online learning material. LeMill follows an open grassroot approach whereby teachers can create learning material that they can use and share with each other. Collaborative development of learning material is possible. Similarly, MOSEP, 'More self-esteem with my e-portfolio'—targets early school leavers by improving their own digital competences as well as the skills and qualifications of their teachers and career counsellors. It integrates Wiki, Moodle, FlashMeeting, blogs, Skype, bookmarking, tagging, RSS feeds, FlickR, SlideShare to provide a suite of media-rich learning tools—but more importantly this creates an enabling environment to support an innovative pedagogic approach that involves tutors as 'learning companions' to support self-organised and self-directed learning for end users.

These innovative media-rich environments have the potential to support inclusion primarily because they provide opportunities to apply less restrictive learning approaches and methods, ones that actively support learners in developing their own learning environments and materials, and because they can empower the excluded. Those cases that were specifically aimed at 'hard to reach' and excluded groups reflect a spectrum of target users, technical platforms and Web 2.0 configurations, learning and inclusion settings and scenarios and objectives. A wide range of Web 2.0 tools are currently being used to support inclusion in these examples, including social networking tools, through wikis, blogs and podcasts through to virtual environments (Second Life), media sharing (mainly YouTube) and syndication tools (RSS feeds). The two groups of tools most frequently used are social networking and on-line office tools, mainly interactive Discussion Forums. However, all of the cases involve combinations of different Web 2.0 tools. The cases represent both 'low tech' environments and media-rich environments. But what is innovative about the cases presented is not primarily their use of 'technical artefacts' but how these technologies support new forms of learning and social relations. For example, Notschool is an alternative on-line school for 'drop-outs' and young people who do not function well in a conventional learning environment—including students with phobias, students from inner city areas with high crime and other social pathologies. The technology platform and tools used in Notschool are relatively basic—essentially involving an asynchronous learning platform using 'Firstclass'. However, this form of social networking supports a novel constructivist pedagogic model which involves students as 'researchers', who actively collaborate with 'mentors', 'experts' and fellow learners (buddies) to promote a democratic, inclusive and highly effective learning environment. Learning materials are collaborative and peer-produced, and the initiative has developed 150 courses blending traditional with unconventional learning.

Two learning themes are common across all cases: supporting creating and sharing knowledge and promoting collaboration and interaction. A common objective across all cases is to promote accessibility to learning. Innovative learning approaches using Web 2.0 are being promoted across different educational institutional settings encompassing formal, non-formal and informal learning, and involving secondary schools, higher education, work-based and adult learners. A wide range of excluded groups are involved—including young people in hospitals with chronic and long term illnesses; people with disabilities; young people at risk of offending; school 'drop outs' and early school leavers; unemployed; ethnic minorities; older people.

The Contribution of Web 2.0 to Digital Literacy and Inclusion

As noted above, the 'Learning 2.0' landscape is embryonic, and many of the current innovations using Web 2.0 tools and approaches are used in traditional learning settings, involving 'mainstream' target groups. Indeed, there are not many examples of 'radical' technological advances being used to support inclusion, for example signs of a movement to 'Web 3.0' and semantic nets, but examples of 'higher end' and media-rich applications using virtual worlds and interactive games can be identified, including the use of 'Second Life' and avatars and interactive games.

In this context, it is difficult to draw evidence-based conclusions about the impacts for learning, digital literacy and inclusion associated with these new approaches. However, on the basis of in-depth analysis of a number of indicative examples of these new approaches, it is possible to identify some emerging trends. Much of the innovation in Learning 2.0 applications for inclusion focuses on the integration of tools and approaches, mostly in blended e-learning environments. An example is 'BREAKOUT', which uses a combination of Web 2.0 and drama workshops to promote 'lifeswapping' in offending prevention for young people—enabling young people at risk of offending and drug misuse to step into the shoes of inmates on 'Death Row' in San Quentin Prison, California, to explore themes about choices and how crime and drugs can limit young people's capacity to make the best use of their talents. Many examples of pedagogic innovation like that of BREAKOUT could be identified—particularly new 'shared' roles in the educational enterprise based on the co-production of knowledge, using an 'open pedagogy' model. Within these new learning environments, the evidence suggests that Web 2.0 can expand learning horizons and engage learners in co-producing rich content environments. The main learning innovations associated with these new environments focus on promoting new ways of collaborative creation, identification, aggregation and exchange of learning content and metadata. Web 2.0 tools also support more personalized and learner-centred environments and individual documentation of competencies. A key feature of these emerging 'Learning 2.0' environments is the positive effects they have on motivation to learn—by supporting active, joyful, discovery-based learning approaches and enhancing the learner's sense of ownership of produced content.

This factor is crucial within the context of strategies aimed at addressing issues associated with hard to reach and excluded groups. Success is associated with the innovative integration and packaging of Web 2.0 tools to create learning environments that are interesting, fun, supportive and which open up spaces to develop creativity and collaboration for excluded groups who find it difficult to flourish in conventional learning environments. 'High-end' technologies support inclusion through promoting empowerment; self-esteem; confidence-building. But equal success can be achieved using low-tech strategies. The key to success lies in implementing a close fit between user needs; pedagogic models chosen and technical strategies adopted. Commitment and motivation at the 'human interface' level is necessary for success. In almost every case, positive learning and inclusion outcomes were linked to the active engagement of a dedicated staff of monitors and coordinators responsible for facilitating and encouraging engagement in project activities.

Overall, the studies show that Learning 2.0 environments involving novel forms of learning like 'open pedagogy' open up opportunities for the 'hard to teach' to engage in creative and self-paced learning. 'Open pedagogy' approaches involving collaborative, co-productive and more 'equal' roles between 'teacher' and 'learner than hitherto implemented are both possible and made more effective by social networking technologies and social networking environments. However, these environments are not suitable in all cases. Key mediating factors in realizing successful learning and inclusion outcomes within these Learning 2.0 environments are: existing levels of basic digital literacy; the cultural and social 'mix' of participating learners; the presence and quality of support available for other sources—for example family and peers. Existing power dynamics—for example those between computer-literate and non-literate—can not only reduce the positive impacts of Learning 2.0 for users but can increase social exclusion for the vulnerable. In addition, accrediting the learning achievements associated with delivering innovative education and training in unconventional settings causes problems in a world of prevailing educational standards, and there is a need for more effort, perhaps drawing on experiences gained in the accreditation of prior learning (APL) domain, to develop accreditation and standards procedures and protocols for Learning 2.0 that can help bridge gaps between it and the conventional education establishment.

The main success factors that can be identified in supporting positive learning and inclusion outcomes include: appropriate and context-relevant integration of the tools; well structured online environments respecting the needs of the different target groups; adequate and stable technical infrastructure; support by institutional management and an open and flexible organizational culture. Organizational buy-in—particular from professionals and senior management—is crucial for success. In addition, strong partnerships, combined with necessary levels of sustainable funding, are crucial in supporting the success of Learning 2.0 initiatives. There is a need for further research to gather the evidence on cost-effectiveness of Learning 2.0 in order to feed into both future business models and policy initiatives designed to promote its further development. This work also needs to consider how low-cost solutions and open-source technologies can contribute to developing Learning 2.0.

All of the examples analysed experienced challenges of different kinds and with varying degrees of severity. The main barriers to positive inclusion encompass five main elements: technical issues; motivation and engagement issues; organisational issues; digital skills issues and finance and funding issues. A divide still exists between formal and informal learning settings. 'Alternative' scenarios using 'open pedagogy' approaches create challenges in terms of recognition of learning achievements and their accreditation. Existing power structures are still resistant to change and equality. For example, the studies identified cases where users who were already computer-literate tended to 'colonise' new initiatives, creating tensions between less literate users, and newcomers. Funding and sustainability issues are a problem across many of the case's studied. Challenges are posed by costs and rapid obsolescence factors where high-tech solutions and content are involved, and some technical problems were identified with 'higher-end' and media-rich tools (for example interoperability issues). Organisational problems mainly concern the changes to organizational culture that are associated with the introduction of Web 2.0—particularly since it radically changes the teacher-student relationship from a 'transmissive' to a 'co-production' mode. Other institutional problems relate to changes in the organisational culture of the educational enterprise associated with the introduction of new types of learning and teaching role.

Whether Web 2.0 is supporting the emergence of new kinds of digital skills is difficult to judge. The evidence of how Learning 2.0 initiatives contribute to developing and supporting 'basic' digital literacy; 'higher level' e-skills; other kinds of skills (for example social interaction; citizenship) and opening up labour market opportunities is patchy and inconclusive. Though there is evidence to suggest that Learning 2.0 initiatives do support the acquisition of basic ICT skills, the depth and quality of the skills learned varies significantly and depends on factors like whether digital literacy is a primary or secondary objective; users' existing level of digital literacy; the governance structures and 'power dynamics' in the initiative; the availability and quality of mentors and tutors. There is convincing evidence that engaging students in a rich immersive Web 2.0 environment has positive outcomes in terms of developing higher level e-skills.

There is strong evidence that Learning 2.0 tools are associated with positive outcomes in developing 'soft skills'—both personal, like self-confidence—and social—like team-working and time management. The studies found no conclusive evidence of negative impacts—for example increased social isolation—associated with participation in Learning 2.0 environments. However,there were some indications that existing 'skills gaps' amongst learners in Web 2.0-rich environments could contribute to increasing skills gaps between students who are computer-literate and students who are not and, in turn, contributing to further feelings of exclusion from learning.

Learning 2.0 also supports e-skills outcomes for intermediaries and supports development of organisational capacity by broadening the skills and knowledge base. For example MOSEP[16] contributed to the professional development of the participating teachers. However, there is no real evidence of a 'downstream' contribution to labour market mobility associated with Learning 2.0 initiatives. The contribution of Web 2.0 to increasing job opportunities—particularly for excluded groups—appears to be determined more by local labour market conditions than the new skills acquired.

There is some evidence that Learning 2.0 is beginning to realise examples of radical new educational structures and environments, focusing on a combination of social networking technologies and 'open pedagogy'. These are linked in turn to the emergence of new forms of 'producer-consumer' relationships based on co-production of knowledge and content that are beginning to change how the educational enterprise operates. New roles—for example 'learning companions'—are being created. However, as noted above, these trends are isolated and embryonic and have to be set against the continuing dominance of mainstream education. What is less clear is how these new forms of 'knowledge relationships' will evolve. There is a growing groundswell of opinion that is beginning to raise concerns about the increasing intrusion of social computing into social, economic and cultural life. It is argued that the business model used by Facebook is predicated on an underlying 'free market' ideology that runs counter to the traditions of liberal-humanist education. In a recent newspaper article, Tom Hodgkinson points out that Facebook's funding platform; its expansion strategy and its vision of the future are rooted in a particular kind of neo-conservative liberalism.[17] Facebook has strong links not only to on-line consumer platforms that are beginning to dominate global patterns of consumerism—like Pay-Pal and e-Bay—but also to political institutions, such as the *Stanford Review* and 'Vanguard.org' that support conservative values, the free market and limited government as 'the best means to bring hope and ever-increasing opportunity to everyone'. New business alliances that are currently developing will link Facebook with global brands like Blockbuster, Sony and Coca-Cola. Meanwhile, Facebook is increasingly becoming the platform of choice for e-learning platforms that are seeking to embed social computing and social bookmarking technologies in learning provision. These developments raise crucial issues for education, and its role in promoting an inclusive, participative democracy and there is a pressing need for research into the implications of these emerging alliances and relationships between educational enterprises and the new social computing global institutions.

Notes

1 Source: comScore Inc, 2008

2 Source: Childnet International, 2008

3 Owen, Martin, Lyndsay Grant, Steve Sayers, and Keri Facer (2006). Social software and learning. Futurelab Opening Education Reports, 2006

4 Redeker, C. (2008) 'Learning 2.0: The impact of Web 2.0 Innovations on Education and Training in Europe, IPTS, Seville

5 See for example Graham Attwell (2008) http://www.checkpoint-elearning.com/article/5655.html

6 Nova Spivak: What is the Semantic Web, Actually? http://www.deitel.com

7 Redeker, C (2008) '*Learning 2.0: The impact of Web 2.0 Innovations on Education and Training in Europe*, IPTS, Seville

8 Young People, New Technologies and Political Engagement, Institute of Advanced Studies, University of Surrey, 2007; URL: http://www.ias.surrey.ac.uk/workshops/young/index.php

9 Oysermann, D., Koon H.- M. & Kemmelmeier, M. (2002). Rethinking individualism and collectivism: evaluation of theoretical assumptions and meta analysis. *Psychological Bulletin*, 2002, 128, 3–72

10 Boyd, D (2007). Viewing American class divisions through Facebook and MySpace.

11 Woodfine, B. P., M. Baptista Nunes and D.J. Wright (2008). "Text-based synchronous e-learning and dyslexia: Not necessarily the perfect match!", Computers & Education, 50 (3) (2008), 703–717

12 Fischer, T. W. Kugemann and S. Held (2009). Final Report on Good Practices for Learning 2.0, IPTS, Seville

13 Cullen, J., C. Cullen, D. Hayward, V. Maes (2009). Final Report on the potential of Learning 2.0 for groups at risk of exclusion, IPTS, Seville

14 Fischer, T., J. Cullen, T. Kretchmer, S. Held (2009). Report on the Landscape of Learning 2.0, IPTS, Seville

15 See for example the European Commission's Action Plan on "Ageing well in the Information Society"

16 'More Self-Esteem with my E-Portfolio' – MOSEP European project, www.mosep.org/

17 *The Guardian*, Monday 14 January 2008.

Bibliography

Attwell, Graham (2007). *Web 2.0 and the changing ways we are using computers for learning: what are the implications for pedagogy and curriculum?*

Attwell, Elferink Graham and Raymond (2007). Developing an architecture of participation, *Proceedings of the International Conference of "Interactive computer aided learning ICL2007: EPortofolio and Quality in e-Learning (2007)*; available at: http://telearn.noe-kaleidoscope.org/warehouse/111_Final_Paper_(001655v1).pdf

Baird, Derek E. and Fisher, Mercedes (2006). neomillennial user experience design strategies: Utilizing social networking media to support 'always on' learning styles. *Journal of Educational Technology Systems* 34, pp.5–32.

Boyd, D (2007). *Viewing American class divisions through Facebook and MySpace.*

Cullen, J., C. Cullen, D. Hayward, V. Maes (2009). *Final report on the potential of Learning 2.0 for groups at risk of exclusion*, IPTS, Seville.

Bühler, C., and Fisseler B. (2007). Accessible E-Learning and Educational Technology - Extending Learning Opportunities for People with Disabilities. *Proceedings of the International Conference of "Interactive* computer aided learning" ICL2007: EPortofolio and Quality in e-Learning (2007), available at:

http://telearn.noe-kaleidoscope.org/warehouse/242_Final_Paper_(001725v1).pdf

Cullen, J., Hadjivassiliou, K., Junge, K., Fischer, T. (2007). *Status of e-Inclusion measurement, analysis and approaches for improvement* e-Inclusion Handbook Version 2. Tavistock Institute.

Facer, K., Furlong, J., Furlong, R. and Sutherland, R. (2003). *Screenplay: Children and computing in the home*. London: Routledge.

Fischer, T., J. Cullen, T. Kretchmer, S. Held (2009). *Report on the landscape of learning 2.0*, IPTS, Seville

Fischer, T, W Kugemann and S Held (2009) Final *Report on Good Practices for Learning 2.0*, IPTS, Seville

McLester, Susan (2007). Technology Literacy and the MySpace Generation: They're Not Asking Permission. *Technology & Learning*, 27 (2007), 16–22.

Oblinger, Diana G., & James L (2005). *Educating the net generation*. Educause e-books, 2005.

http://www.educause.edu/ir/library/pdf/pub7101.pdf.

OECD (2007a). Participative web and user-created content. Web 2.0, wikis and social networking.

http://213.253.134.43/oecd/pdfs/browseit/9307031E.PDF.

—— (2008) http://www.oecd.org/dataoecd/39/51/40554230.pdf.

Owen, Martin, Lyndsay Grant, Steve Sayers, and Keri Facer (2006). *Social software and learning. Futurelab Opening Education Reports*, 2006

Owen, Martin, Lyndsay Grant, Steve Sayers, and Keri Facer (2006). *Social software and learning. Futurelab Opening Education Reports*, 2006.

http://www.futurelab.org.uk/resources/documents/opening_education/Social_Software_report.pdf

Oysermann, D., Koon H. M. & Kemmelmeier, M. (2002). Rethinking individualism and collectivism: evaluation of theoretical assumptions and meta analysis. *In Psychological Bulletin*, 2002, 128, 3–72.

Pedró, Francesc (2006). The new millennium learners: challenging our views on ICT and learning. OECD-CERI, 2006, http://www.oecd.org/dataoecd/1/1/38358359.pdf.

Redeker, C (2008). *Learning 2.0: The impact of Web 2.0 Innovations on Education and Training in Europe*, IPTS, Seville.

Smith, D. M. (2007). *Key Issues for Web 2.0 and Consumerization*. Gartner Research report.

Vuorikari, Riina (2005). *Can personal digital knowledge artefacts' management and social networks enhance learning? Insight Innovation* Brief, Sept., 2005,

http://www.eun.org/.../social_networks_learning_vuorikari_9_2005_insight.pdf.

Woodfine, B. P., M. Baptista Nunes, and D.J. Wright (2008). Text-based synchronous e-learning and dyslexia: Not necessarily the perfect match!. *Computers & Education*, 50 (3) 703–717.

CHAPTER 6

Real Purpose, Real Audience and Real Value: Researching Contributions of Digital Literacy to Learning

Don Passey

Introduction: The Scope and Focus of This Chapter

This chapter looks at outcomes of learning activities when pupils use digital and media literacy capabilities. Technologies continue to change and to be developed; technologies continue to diverge, whilst connectivity continues to converge, so the continuous monitoring of what might constitute capabilities of digital literacy and what might arise from evaluations of leading-edge digital literacy activities is an important need. Recent studies have indicated that access to ranges of technologies by young people is generally high, but using technologies is often occurring more frequently outside schools than it is inside schools. Across a range of different groups of young people, different technologies are being used and selected for different purposes. For learning purposes, desktop technologies are often selected and used, but often for information-seeking purposes. Evidence indicates that young people are not necessarily developing digital and media literacy practices outside schools that will easily allow them to be involved in important and productive learning endeavours. There is a real need to consider how young people who have high levels of technological access ('digital natives') can be supported so that they can become 'learning natives'. To do this effectively, it will be important to identify which aspects of learning should be focuses for uses of digital literacy. Digital literacy practices and their applications to learning have been related in some studies not just to enhancements in certain areas of subject attainment, but also to enhancements in terms of wider achievements. Aspects of digital and media literacy use offer a wide range of potential affordances, potentially supporting a wide range of different aspects of learning; it is important that we can identify benefits arising from specific applications or affordances, if we are to guide learners, teachers and parents effectively. It is becoming increasingly recognised that the selection of digital literacy practices and uses can be different for different groups of young people, including differences according to gender. Two exemplars of practice are explored within this chapter to illustrate the specific affordances, outcomes and impacts that can arise in those learning activities (both involving pupils with different features of digital and media literacy). It is clear that the relationship of affordances, outcomes and impacts to specific activities needs to be identified clearly in the future to allow a movement away from concepts concerned with generalising affordances and impacts arising towards a deeper understanding of the identification of specific groups of young people who can benefit in more specific ways. The exploration offered here is largely United Kingdom (UK) focused, but recognises that the identification of exemplars of practice in helping 'digital natives' to become 'learning natives' should not be limited to a single national focus.

The Shifting Nature of Digital Literacy and Impacting Factors

Digital literacy can be described as a set of skills, but, because of the technological landscape in which we live, the practices described within any definitions of digital and media literacy clearly expand and shift over quite short periods of time. The time periods involved are likely to be quite short, as technological changes happen frequently, within periods of time that are no longer than about 18 months (see Passey 1999). Fundamental changes in technology mean that details concerned with features of digital and media literacy are likely to shift; that shift might mean that some features become easier or redundant, while others are enhanced or arise anew. In general, digital and media literacy will cover an increasing range of practices, but at any one time, for any one purpose, individuals will be likely to select a subset of the entire range of all possible practices in order to carry out one or more specific activities. However, overall, there are a number of features that are likely to determine an individual's digital or media literacy. The key features depend on:

- Access to hardware (and while the hardware is becoming increasingly diverse, individual technologies are also becoming more specific in terms of their applications for use).

- Access to resources (which is becoming increasingly more convergent in some respects, as this feature often depends upon web access).
- Opportunities to use hardware and resources (and these will cover social settings as well as learning and professional settings).
- Existing skills and willingness to adapt to new needs (based on the sorts of priorities of need that an individual has, as well as any focal interests).
- Purposes for using hardware and resources (educationally, but importantly, also socially).
- Audience focus for uses of hardware and resources (increasingly made possible and accessible through applications concerned with online social networking).

Current Levels of Access to Technologies

In a recent report from a study exploring uses of Web 2.0 technologies by young people 11 to 16 years of age, Luckin et al. (2008) concluded that:

- Access to computers and the internet at home was very high (98.4% of the total sample had access to a laptop, a desktop computer or to both, and 96.6% had access to the internet).
- Virtually all schools were found to have a few individuals who reported lack of access (although it was noted that only a minority had their own laptop or desktop computer, while for most the computer was a family resource). It was also reported that such shared access to a computer might help in achieving parental involvement in school activities.
- From the total sample of respondents, 90% used email or instant messaging out of school. By contrast to high levels of use outside schools, learners experienced rather little computer activity in school.

These results indicate that many young people have access to technologies outside school (and often this is shared access outside school, as well as inside school), and that they use these technologies more than they do inside school. This report is not alone in reporting those findings; levels of technology access and use by young people are generally recognised as being high, often associated with their having time to 'play with the devices', leading often to highly dextrous use of some facilities, so that young people are described as being 'digital natives' with regard to uses of technologies (see Prensky, 2007).

Current Access Levels at Home and in School

In terms of considering access and uses of technologies inside and outside school, the report looking at uses of Web 2.0 technology by young people 11 to 16 years of age (Luckin et al., 2008), said that:

- Learners spent, on average, more time working on schoolwork on a computer outside school than they did at school (34% of all learners estimated that they spent only an hour each week using a computer at school).
- Collaborative activity was similarly higher outside school, as were file-sharing activities such as picture sharing, video sharing and music downloading.

The picture that is evoked, of high levels of use and access outside school, but more confined inside school, is not necessarily restricted to those groups of young people who might be expected to have such high levels of technology (associated perhaps with higher socio-economic population categories, or those in employment, for example). Young people who are not in education, employment or training (NEET) have been found in one study to have access to technologies that are generally (and perhaps surprisingly) high (reported recently by Passey, Williams and Rogers, 2008). Findings from this study showed that on the whole, technologies were used by this group of 16- to 18-year-old young people for communication purposes more than for information purposes. Certain technologies tended to be used for more specific purposes; desktop and laptop computers were used more for purposes concerned with learning (perhaps because computers and laptops were seen as workplace or education tools rather than as personal tools).

Interviews conducted as a part of the study, with a range of young people who were NEET, mainly 16 to 18 years of age (although one was 20 years of age), provided evidence of the forms and levels of access and uses made of technologies. In total, 35 young people were interviewed (18 girls and 17 boys). From this sample, a surprisingly large number accessed the internet, and had access to a desktop, laptop or portable computer. It was also surprising to find that very few young people reported using desktop or laptop computers with others (friends or family), while they reported using televisions, games machines and mobile telephones commonly with others around them (friends or family). Relatively few young people accessed the internet with others. It was also surprising to find that few of the young people used computers and internet access for playing games. Indeed, computers and internet access were reported to be used more for aspects concerned with education and employment than they were for playing games. Levels of access to different technologies are shown in Figure 6.1.

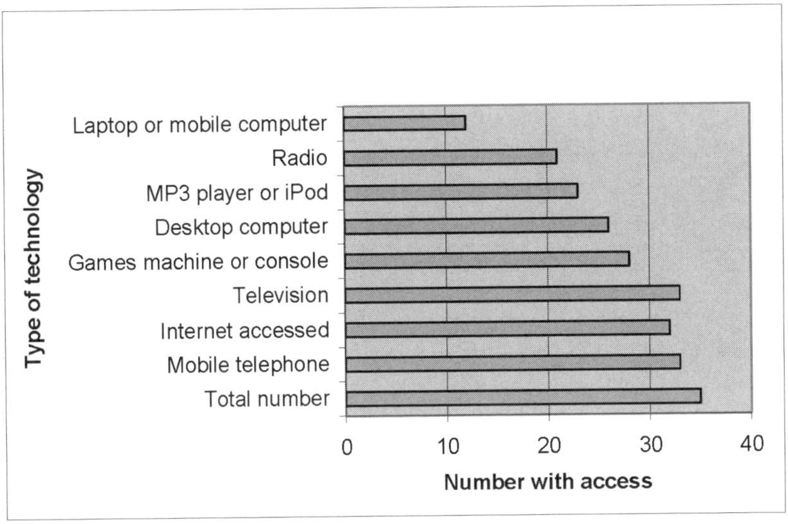

Figure 6.1: Access to technologies by young people interviewed (n=35)
(Source: Passey, Williams and Rogers, 2008)

It is clear from these findings that digital and media literacy are concerned often with using a very wide range of technologies for any one individual. Across the 35 young people interviewed, it is clear that many had access to perhaps 5 different technologies. The most commonly accessible technology was the mobile telephone; young people reported that they used these widely, wherever they were, when they were on their own or with friends or family. Different ways in which the mobile technology was used are shown in Figure 6.2.

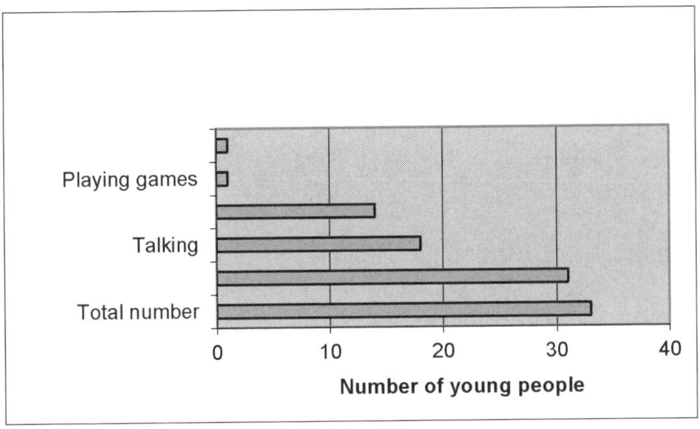

Figure 6.2: Uses of mobile telephones by young people interviewed (n=33)
(Source: Passey, Williams and Rogers, 2008)

These results indicate that the young people were involved to a far greater extent in texting, talking and playing music on mobile telephones than they were involved in activities that might be considered to relate to direct forms of 'learning'. A questionnaire survey run across all careers centres in one region provided more specific evidence about uses of technologies for purposes of direct learning. Questionnaire responses were gathered from, in total, 305 young people. The young people were asked which technologies they had, what they used them for, where, and who with. Their responses are shown in Table 6.1.

Those items where there were about two-thirds or more responses are shaded in grey. It is clear from these responses that technologies are popular with these young people, and that many young people own or have access to more than one form of technology (indeed, on average, each young person has access to between four and five of these forms of technology). In order of decreasing popularity, the technologies owned or accessed by these young people are:

- Mobile telephones (mainly used for texting, talking, and music, both outside and at home, on their own and with friends).
- Television (mainly used for music, video, but also often for learning, at home, on their own or with friends).
- Computers with internet (mainly used for music, finding things, email and learning, at home, school, college or home, on their own or with friends).
- Games machines (used for music, at home, on their own and with friends).
- Radio (used for music, at home, on their own and with friends).
- MP3 or iPods (used for music, at home and out, on their own and with friends).
- Laptops or palmtops (used for music, finding things, video, email, talking and learning, at home, with friends and on their own).
- The uses of these technologies, as reported by the young people, offer ideas about the elements that make up their digital literacies:
- Accessing, copying, manipulating and playing music on mobile telephones, computers with internet access, games machines, television, radio, mp3 players or iPods.
- Accessing, copying, manipulating and playing videos on mobile telephones, computers with internet access, games machines, television, mp3 players or iPods.
- Creating, reading and responding to texts on mobile telephones and computers with internet access.

Technology	Have one	What it is used for							Where it is used			Who with	
		Music	Video	Texts	Talk	Email	Learning	Finding things	School, college, work	Home	Out	On my own	With friends, family
Mobile phone	279	213	153	256	262	22	19	59	99	227	247	211	207
Computer with internet	204	185	127	77	137	181	156	190	124	180	26	147	129
Laptop or palmtop	84	67	52	29	52	59	50	64	40	67	17	51	54
Games machine	201	74	60	6	15	4	25	14	7	140	20	123	125
Television	278	181	188	2	5	2	109	60	32	217	28	186	192
Radio	202	170	6	1	4	1	30	20	15	113	29	105	86
MP3 or iPod	196	187	67	5	3	3	15	7	58	115	135	135	86
Totals	1444	1077	653	376	478	272	404	414	375	1059	502	958	879

Table 6.1: Uses of technologies reported by young people who are NEET (n=305) (Source: Passey, Williams and Rogers 2008)

- Talking via mobile telephones and computers with internet access.
- Creating, reading and responding to emails on mobile telephones and computers with internet access.
- Accessing and using learning resources on computers with internet access, the television and the radio.
- Findings things on mobile telephones, computers with internet access, games machines, television, radio, mp3 players or iPods.
- Sharing and exchanging ideas with friends and family members.
- Practising and developing uses at home, as well as in other locations.

A key question to ask, perhaps, is whether this range of digital literacies matches those that are needed to support young people in learning endeavours. If so, a second key question to ask is whether young people apply these digital literacies to learning situations. Following on from this, a third key question to ask is whether these digital literacies lead to any specific enhancements in learning, or whether they offer some affordances that cannot be provided in any other ways. What is clear from the list above is that the young people apply their digital literacy to uses of these technologies because they believe they offer real audience, real purpose and real value; how far are these beliefs held by these young people, in terms of learning as well as in terms of social endeavours?

Digital Access Related to Attainment and Achievement

The relationship between uses of technologies and enhanced attainment is becoming increasingly recognised and reported. Somekh et al. (2007), in a recent report on uses of technologies by pupils inside and outside school, concluded that:

- Students at all levels (across the 7- to 16- year age range) reported some use of home computing for their homework. Students 14 to 16 years of age, in particular, reported that they regularly used computers in their work at home.
- At the primary level (7 to 11 years of age), it was found that children were less well equipped than secondary students to take advantage of home-school links given their relatively poorer levels of home resources.
- As technology was embedded, schools' national test outcomes improved beyond expectations, although the impact of ICT on attainment levels was greater for primary schools than for secondary schools.

It is clear from these findings that digital access, literacy and attainment enhancement are likely to be linked in certain ways to age groupings. In other studies (Harrison et al., 2002, for example), digital access, literacy and attainment enhancements were linked to subject focus as well as to age groupings.

These studies (and others) have identified enhancements in terms of subject attainment levels, while other studies have identified wider outcomes, in terms of achievements beyond subject attainment enhancements. Luckin et al. (2008), reported that achievements could be categorised through a range of types of activity that could be identified—readers, gamers, file-sharers, communicators and newscasters (in terms of sharing experiences through social networking sites). The authors indicated that amongst their study participants, relatively few learners were:

> engaging in more sophisticated Web 2.0 activities such as producing and publishing their own content for wider consumption

and that:

> In order to be motivated to publish content, learners must perceive that publication carries utility for the self or important others. In addition, learners may lack the technical knowledge and skills needed to publish content online

These findings, in common with others indicated previously, highlight the fact that 'sophisticated' activities are often associated with learning affordances, but that young people either do not possess these abilities, or they do not exercise them.

Crook and Harrison (2008), in their study of Web 2.0 technologies, showed that digital literacies used and developed outside school could be rather different for different gender groups (shown in Figure 6.3). Their findings indicate that girls spend more time out of school typing, reading and on social networking sites, while boys spend more time out of school on general browsing and games. Differences such as these are clearly important when considering how to most appropriately develop digital literacy techniques and their applications.

The report by Luckin et al. (2008), indicated the important role of schools in making a difference to the abilities or application of young people with respect to digital literacies and learning:

> While the data shows that learners have the potential to be critical consumers of information on the internet, they are selective in applying that criticality. It emerged from participant reports in focus groups that copying and pasting information from the internet was extremely common at the schools in this sample. Examples of more sophisticated learning activities were found when the school had engaged learners appropriately.

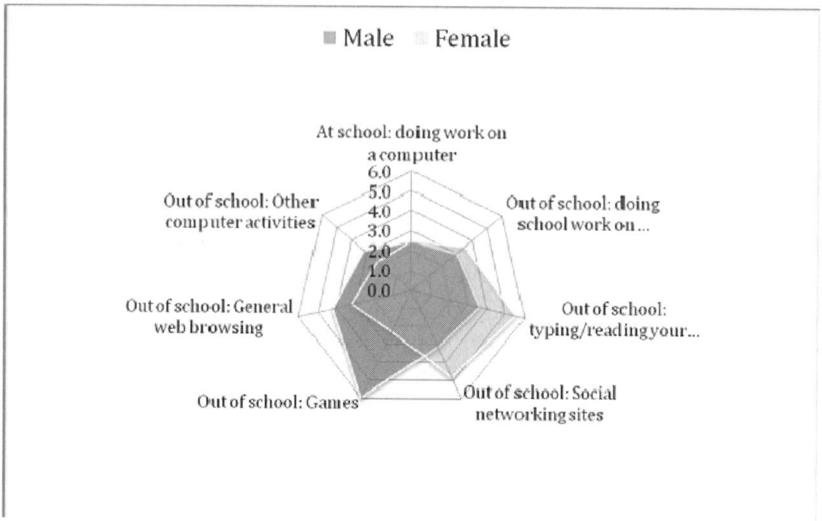

* All values except time spent in school using computer for school work are significantly different between genders.
Normative sample only.

Figure 6.3: Chart showing average time in hours spent each week by gender on selected computer-related activities* (Source: Crook and Harrison, 2008)

It is clear, from the range of evidence offered here, that 'digital natives' are not 'learning natives'; if the development of 'learning natives' is an important concept (and from the perspective of encouraging independent learning, or from the perspective of supporting learning in settings beyond a school building, it could be argued that it is), then there is a need to consider those elements of digital and media literacy that should be included in learner development opportunities, to ensure that important aspects of learning can be achieved and undertaken.

What Should Digital Literacy Seek to Support in Terms of Learning?

An alternative approach (or direction), is to ask, if digital and media literacy are to be used by young people to support learning, then exactly what forms or aspects of learning should the digital or media literacies be focused on? The educational research literature highlights the critical importance of a number of certain aspects of learning, all of which should be accommodated appropriately when students are involved in learning activities, to allow learners to become increasingly expert in their learning. Key aspects include:

- Making learning real or 'authentic' (see McFarlane, 1997).
- Allowing or supporting discussion (see Vygotsky, 1962; Pask, 1975; Mercer and Littleton, 2007).
- Using technologies to support focal aspects of cognition, such as analysis, synthesis, evaluation, creativity, concept formation (see Passey and Rogers, 2004).
- A focus on the transfer of learning (see Bransford et al., 2000).
- Covering multimodal aspects of literacy (see Kress, 2005).
- Using media creatively to express and communicate ideas, information and opinions (see Euro MediaLiteracy, 2008).

If these are the forms of learning that should be supported (no matter which media are involved), then it is important to identify whether these forms of learning can be supported by aspects of digital and media literacy, and which learners gain from these (and under what circumstances). It is not unreasonable to believe that different forms of technologies, different learners, and different activities will lead to different and specific outcomes. Evaluation of digital and media literacy activities, outcomes and affordances, therefore, is likely to present a range of challenges, and will require a focus that will allow specific impacts to be identified. Two exemplars of activities that involve young people in using digital literacy capabilities are selected here to illustrate both the need to evaluate each selected case in its own right, and to illustrate that each activity can afford recognisable learning impacts.

Using an Online Discussion and Mentoring System

Many students now have access to virtual learning environments (VLEs). Some of these systems provide access to online discussion and mentoring facilities. One such system, which has been established in practice for some years, has provided access for a wide range of learners across two local authorities (LAs) in England. In total, 22,000 learners aged 14 to 19 years were registered to use the Virtual Workspace online mentoring system across the two LAs in 2006. This system provided a mentoring service, which included: live communication with human mentors from 8am to 8pm on weekdays; a bank of over 4,500 interactive learning materials supporting the 14–19 curriculum; a range of communication channels, including messaging, discussion forums and chat rooms; online assignment management and storage of work and interest materials; Online Communities, encouraging collaboration between learners and teachers across schools and colleges; and an incentive scheme for learners, offering real rewards.

A study was commissioned to look at the uses made of the system and its outcomes (reported in Passey, 2007). One of the early areas of interest, which arose from interviews with teachers, was the perceived positive impact of discussion and mentoring facilities on reticent or quiet learners in classrooms (termed 'shy' learners for the purposes of the study). Teachers reported often that such young people appeared to be more involved in online discussions, and appeared to be gaining from their involvement. To identify whether this might be the case for these learners, the study involved students completing an online questionnaire. The questionnaire asked learners to indicate whether they would regard themselves as being 'shy in terms of discussing ideas in class'. Table 6.2 shows the comparative responses of all boys, 'shy' boys, all girls and 'shy' girls. When self-reported 'shy' boys' and 'shy' girls' responses were considered, most 'shy' boys and girls (more than 60%) reported that they would like to see more use of the system, they felt the system was safe and secure, they liked the points system, the system had helped them with their school work, had allowed them to share ideas with other learners, they thought discussing points with other learners allowed them to learn better, the system had helped them with coursework or assignments, and had allowed them to maintain contact with other learners to support their work.

By comparing the responses of 'shy' learners to all learners in that group, those cases where there was at least a difference of 8% were highlighted. For these instances, a Chi-squared test of goodness of fit was used to identify any statistically significant difference between the two sets. By comparing the responses of 'shy' boys with all boys, the percentage of responses from 'shy' boys was higher (by at least a difference of 8%) in their reports about: being more involved in learning than might have been the case otherwise (16% difference, $\chi2= 22.96$, $p<0.005$); discussion of work outside the classroom (14% difference, $\chi2= 12.98$, $p<0.005$); allowing ideas to be expressed when this might not happen in class (13% difference, $\chi2= 13.16$, $p<0.005$); helping to understand teachers more (9% difference, $\chi2= 8.99$, $p<0.005$); helping with coursework or assignments (9% difference, $\chi2= 6.27$, $p<0.05$); mentors helping personally (9% difference, $\chi2= 6.36$, $p<0.05$); and wanting to see more use of the system (8% difference, $\chi2= 5.97$, $p<0.05$). By comparing the responses of 'shy' girls with all girls, the percentage of responses from 'shy' girls was higher (by at least a difference of 8%) in their reports about: allowing ideas to be expressed when this might not happen in class (9% difference, $\chi2= 13.64$, $p<0.005$); and being more involved in learning than might have been the case otherwise (8% difference, $\chi2= 11.54$, $p<0.005$). In all the instances highlighted, statistically significant differences were shown between the 'shy' group and the group of all learners (and it should be noted that in all cases where the statistics are quoted, df=1).

Table 6.2: A comparison of percentage responses by all boys (n=533), shy boys (n=179), all girls (n=953) and shy girls (n=412) (Source: Passey, 2007)

Question	Yes % boys	Yes % shy boys	Yes % girls	Yes % shy girls
1. Have you been given sufficient training and encouragement to use the system?	52	53	44	44
2. Do most of the teachers in your school encourage you to use Virtual Workspace?	36	39	38	40
3. Do teachers suggest you use other online systems, such as a school intranet?	38	39	46	47
4. Has Virtual Workspace helped you with your school work?	62	67	56	58
5. Do you use the Communities area most?	30	32	25	28
6. Has Virtual Workspace helped with revision?	34	40	31	33
7. Has it helped with discussion of work outside the classroom?	42	56	36	38
8. Have you used it to keep contact or do work when you have been absent from school?	43	49	46	49
9. Has it allowed you to maintain contact with other students to support your work?	59	64	62	63
10. Has it allowed you to share ideas with other students?	63	67	65	66
11. Do you think discussing points with other students allows you to learn better?	63	67	64	67
12. Has it allowed you to express your ideas when you might not do this in class?	43	56	44	53
13. Would you say you are a shy person in terms of discussing your ideas in class?	34	100	44	100
14. Have you been more involved in learning than you might otherwise have been?	29	45	25	33
15. Has it helped you to make more contact with your teacher(s)?	34	36	30	32
16. Has it helped you to understand your teacher(s) more?	22	31	17	23
17. Has the polling system helped you with certain topics?	32	37	28	32
18. Has Virtual Workspace helped with coursework or assignments?	57	66	57	61
19. Has it helped you to access lesson resources outside the classroom?	58	63	56	60
20. Do you feel the system is safe and secure?	79	83	82	83
21. Have you contacted the online mentors?	38	44	32	32
22. Have mentors helped you personally?	27	36	25	24
23. Would you like to see more use of Virtual Workspace?	76	84	77	82
24. Do you like the points system?	75	81	79	83

The system, according to learner feedback (and supported by interview evidence from a number of teachers), was being used to support the involvement and learning needs of 'shy' learners. There appeared to be a particular emphasis of use by 'shy' boys (even though there were fewer of these that self-reported as being 'shy'), but the potential impacts on both groups were potentially important. It should be noted here that 'shy' was likely to encompass at least three different groups of learners: those who were naturally reticent in terms of limiting the giving of their ideas in classrooms; those who found it difficult for emotional or social reasons to engage in a classroom learning environment; and those who did not want to be seen by others as being engaged or interested in the topic or lesson. In all these cases, online discussion and mentoring was providing opportunities for social involvement that would be unlikely to occur otherwise.

Creating News Stories for Broadcast

The second example focuses on a quite different technology. In this case, young people needed to create news stories. This example comes from a BBC News project, which involved a large number of schools across the UK. The BBC News has run this School Report project for the last two years. The project has enabled young people of secondary school age to develop practice in, to identify, and to create news reports in a form that could be broadcast. As the BBC News School Report web-site states:

> BBC News School Report gives 12 and 13-year-olds from UK schools the chance to make their own video, audio or text-based news at school and to broadcast it for real. While the project is devised for this age group, students aged 11 to 14 may also take part. Using lesson plans and materials from this website, and with support from BBC staff, teachers help students develop their journalistic skills and become School Reporters (BBC News, School Report, 2008)

Outcomes arising from those schools and city learning centres (CLCs) involved in the north-west of England (reported in Passey, 2008), indicated the very wide range of news reports that students created. The news reports were categorised broadly according to topic, and the numbers of news stories in each category is shown in Table 6.3.

There were seven topics that were selected by students more often than others (these are shaded in grey in Table 6.3). Other topics not coloured were involved at rather lower levels. From this topic list, taking those categories where reports were commonly involved, students were clearly concerned about a range of important societal and social issues. An important point to consider in terms of these topic areas is the provision of any opportunity that might be offered in schools (or indeed, outside schools), for students to identify and select these topics, and to offer their ideas, generating and providing levels of 'student voice' that are accessible to a wider audience. It seems highly likely that students would not, using other forms of activity, be able to provide their ideas, views and perspectives on this range of highly relevant and important topics in the same way, especially in terms of audience (real audience). There is a clear link here between topics selected and issues raised within the 'Every Child Matters' document (2003), and the Youth Media Education recommendations addressed to the United Nations Educational Scientific and Cultural Organization (UNESCO) in Seville (2002), which stated that Media Education should be regarded as a part of:

> the basic entitlement of every citizen, in every country in the world, to freedom of expression,

ensuring that young people can:

> Select appropriate media for communicating youngsters' own messages or stories and for reaching their intended audience

Teachers felt that the project led to significant outcomes for their students. Even though some teachers responding through online questionnaires were critical of some organisational aspects of the project, they all, without exception, were able to identify crucial educational outcomes for their students. These outcomes are categorised and shown in Table 6.4.

Many teachers found it difficult to identify specific outcomes (as they felt individual students had gained in different ways), although a number indicated that very many focal learning outcomes (in terms of those identified as important by the educational research literature), had been attained as a consequence of student involvement. For example, one teacher said:

> Most of the outcomes stated on the pdf documents linking the project to curriculum areas [accessible from the web-site] were met. In addition there have been many notable achievements and in general I, and other people have noticed, improved confidence, self-esteem, maturity, team working skills, improved speaking and listening skills, enquiry and questioning skills and lots more. Every child taking part has gained something very individual from this project and it has enhanced both their school work and personal skills dramatically.

Table 6.3: Numbers of school reports categorised by broad topics (Source: Passey, 2008)

Topic	Frequency
Safety and comfort (such as bullying, crime, racism)	22
Education and school issues (such as closures or buildings)	20
Health (including healthy eating)	20
Sports (including school sports events)	18
Entertainment (including entertainment in schools and exhibitions)	16
Current news stories about individuals (such as Sophie Lancaster)	15
Citizenship, finance, current issues and concerns (such as the Budget, climate change or poverty)	13
Science and technology	7
Weather	7
International issues (such as riots)	6
Forms of communication (such as mobile telephones)	4
Shops and shopping	4
Local recreation and living	3
Traffic and transport	3
What's on	3
Feature programmes (such as Question Time)	1
Historic disasters	1
Languages	1

There were some specific areas of skills that teachers noted as being supported by this project. One teacher pointed to the enhancement of confidence, saying:

> It definitely boosts the confidence of our shy students and made our not so shy students even bolder!

The impact of the 'real' situation was highlighted by one teacher:

> All can be gained in other ways but the end result of this is much more real to them

Table 6.4: Educational outcomes reported by teachers (Source: Passey, 2008)

Educational outcome reported	Frequency
Working well with others (outside their social circle)	11
Confidence	6
Multimedia skills	6
More enlightened about the news and journalism	6
Well motivated or interested	5
Reading	4
Working to deadlines	4

Educational outcome reported	Frequency
Gathering evidence to explore an open topic	4
Interviewing techniques	4
Improved speaking and listening skills	4
Independent learning	3
Writing without bias	3
Script writing	3
Communication skills	2
Organisational and planning skills	2
Education outside the classroom	2
Writing for different audiences	2
Interest in journalism as a career	2
Ownership of task	1
Topic knowledge	1
Watched news more	1
Maturity	1
Presenting skills	1

Another teacher indicated some of the very real attributes that can be gained from this 'real' situation that may not arise easily in school environments:

> Too often at school deadlines are flexible and excuses are accepted, there was no room for this at News Day. Working with pupils from other schools and other year groups kept the pupils on their toes. When I evaluated the day with them their first reactions were focused on the people in their groups. Most of them had very positive experiences and those who found it more difficult to work with their group learnt a lot about the true meaning of working as a team and persevering with people you don't naturally get on with

Students were asked about the main challenges they felt they faced when undertaking this project. It was clear from their responses in interviews (shown in Table 6.5), that the meeting of deadlines and finding out correct details about a story were two key areas felt to be particularly challenging (but in a positive, and not in a negative, way).

Table 6.5: Student responses about main challenges they faced (Source: Passey, 2008)

Main challenges	Frequency
Meeting deadlines	21
Finding out correct details on the day	17
Lot to do to get right	9

Main challenges	Frequency
Writing a story to make it interesting	7
Putting things together in time	4
Being on camera	3
Trying to accommodate opinion	3
Technical problems	3
Taking pictures	2

When students were asked about what they felt they had gained most from the project, their responses (shown in Table 6.6) related well to the gains reported by teachers and CLC managers. The main gains reported by students were the acquisition of new skills (such as technical skills), working better in teams and listening more to each other, and gains in confidence (including confidence gains when presenting in front of a camera).

Teachers indicated in a number of cases that students were becoming more 'news aware', were watching the news more, and gaining interest in some cases in taking up a career in media or journalism. This picture was supported by responses from students (shown in Table 6.7), and indeed, in 18 cases out of the 35, students indicated that they would like to work in the future in the media in some way.

Findings from this study indicate that a wide range of affordances, outcomes and impacts can arise from activities that require young people to use digital and media literacy capabilities. However, it also points to the fact that individual young people are likely to be gaining in specific ways. The fact that activities involving digital and media literacy can lead to positive learning outcomes is clear; exactly which learning outcomes arise for which groups of learners is less clear, yet this type of evidence is clearly required if more specific and effective support for different groups of learners is to be set up.

Table 6.6: Student responses about main gains arising (Source: Passey, 2008)

Main gains	Frequency
New skills (including technical skills)	22
Team working and listening	13
Confidence (generally as well as in front of the camera)	12
More involved in news and what it involves	8
How to be a journalist or reporter	7
Not an easy process, especially finding information	5
Meeting deadlines and being organised better	5
Ideas for the future	5
How to put a story together	1
Meeting new people	1

Table 6.7: Student responses about their long-term goals (Source: Passey, 2008)

Ideas for the future	Frequency
Work/course in the media	5
Like to do news casting	4
Become a journalist/do a journalist course	4
Like English more, see the relevance more	4
Become a journalist/photographer	3
Work together more	3
Do the school newspaper in future	1
Think about becoming a reporter	1
Become a scriptwriter	1
Changed views on the news	1
Not sure	8

Conclusions

It is clear that ranges of technologies accessible to young people, and the associated digital literacy required to use these technologies for social as well as for learning purposes, are shifting dramatically and quickly. It is also clear that key learning needs are likely to be met by appropriate use of activities that involve ranges of digital literacy skills. While uses of technologies by young people outside school, and for social purposes, are more advanced than uses of technologies for educational uses or inside school, there remains the question of how the fundamentally important affordances can be effectively supported in schools and through appropriate school activities. Some activities involving uses of digital resources (the two exemplars described in this chapter), have been shown to provide specific learning affordances for individuals, but that a wide range of many affordances are likely to arise as a consequence of the activities. It is clear that a greater research focus is needed to identify useful and effective exemplars of activities that involve the uses of digital and media literacy skills, and that the affordances arising from these specific activities need to be carefully and specifically identified. Once a range of useful activities was been identified and is accessible, and when specific affordances have been identified, then more focused teacher support could be put in place to integrate practice of a range of activities where affordances are already recognised. In parallel, and taking the context outside schools inside consideration, these findings should also be generated in ways that will allow a greater focus on appropriate student and parent support to enhance educational as well as social outcomes.

Bibliography

BBC News (2008). School Report. Accessibleat:http://news.bbc.co.uk/1/hi/school_report/default.stm

Bransford, J. D., Brown, A. L., and Cocking, R. R. (eds.) (2000). *How people learn: Brain, mind, experience, and school.* Washington, DC: National Academy Press.

Crook, C., and Harrison, C. (2008). *Web 2.0 technologies for learning at key stages 3 and 4: Summary report.* Coventry: Becta.

EuroMediaLiteracy (2008). *The European charter for media literacy.* Accessed at: http://www.euromedialiteracy.eu/?Pg=charter&id=3

Green Paper (2003). *Every Child Matters.* The Stationery Office: Norwich.

Harrison, C., Comber, C., Fisher, T., Haw, K., Lewin, C., Lunzer, E., McFarlane, A., Mavers, D., Scrimshaw, P., Somekh, B., and Watling, R. (2002). ICT in *schools research and evaluation series no. 7 – The impact of information and communication technologies on pupil learning and attainment.* London: DfES.

Kress, G. (2005). Communication now and in the future. Paper for the English 21 curriculum consultation project. London: QCA. Accessible at http://www.qca.org.uk/libraryAssets/media/12292_commun_now_and_in_the_future.pdf

Luckin, R., Logan, K., Clark, W., Graber, R., Oliver, M., and Mee, A. (2008). *Learners' use of Web 2.0 technologies in and out of school in key stages 3 and 4.* Becta: Coventry.

McFarlane, A. (ed.) (1997). *Information technology and authentic learning: Realising the potential of computers in the primary classroom.* London: Routledge.

Mercer, N., and Littleton, K. (2007) *Dialogue and the Development of children's thinking.* London: Routledge.

Pask, G. (1975). *Conversation, Cognition, and Learning.* New York: Elsevier.

Passey, D. (1999). Strategic evaluation of the impacts on learning of educational technologies: Exploring some of the issues for evaluators and future evaluation audiences. *Education and Information Technologies,* 4(3), 223–250.

—— (2007). *Virtual workspace: An independent evaluative review.* Wolverhampton: Wolverhampton City Council and Worcestershire County Council.

—— (2008). *BBC news school report 2007/2008: An independent evaluative review.* London: BBC.

Passey, D. and Rogers, C. with Machell, J. and McHugh, G. (2004). *The motivational effect of ICT on pupils: A department for education and skills research Project* 4RP/2002/050-3. Nottingham: DfES.

Passey, D., Williams, S., and Rogers, C. (2008). *Assessing the potential of e-learning to support re-engagement amongst young people with not in education, employment or training (NEET) status: An independent research and evaluation study.* Overview report: April 2008. Accessed at: http://partners.becta.org.uk/upload-dir/downloads/page_documents/research/elearning_reengagement_neet_overview.pdf

Prensky, M. (2007). How to teach with technology: Keeping both teachers and students comfortable in an era of exponential change. In Becta (Ed.) *Emerging Technologies for Learning* 2 (2007). Coventry: Becta.

Somekh, B., Underwood, J., Convery, A., Dillon, G., Jarvis, J., Lewin, C., Mavers, D., Saxon, D., Sing, S., Steadman, S., Twining, P., and Woodrow, D. (2007). Evaluation of the ICT test bed project: Final report June 2007. Coventry: Becta.

UNESCO (2002). Recommendations addressed to the United Nations Educational Scientific and Cultural Organization (UNESCO) *Youth Media Education* 15–16 February 2002 in Seville. Accessed at:

http://209.85.129.132/search?q=cache:dfPvZ7trAT8J:portal.unesco.org/ci/en/files/5680/10346121330Seville_Recommendations.rtf/Seville%252BRecommendations.rtf+unesco+2002+conference+sevilla&hl=en&ct=clnk&cd=1

Vygotsky, L. (1962). *Thought and language*. Cambridge, MA: MIT Press.

PART III

Digital Literacy Policy, E-Inclusion and Curriculum Development

CHAPTER 7

Digital Literacies: Different Cultures, Different Definitions

Ellen J. Helsper

Introduction

Discussions about what digital literacy is are well underway. Nevertheless, there is still no clarity or agreement about what digital literacy actually means. This chapter will critically reflect on the current definitions of digital literacy and their application in empirical research. There are two main problems with constructing a solid definition of digital literacy:

a. The digital environment keeps changing; the Internet and other information and communication technologies (ICTs) develop rapidly. What was futuristic yesterday is today's prehistory.
b. The cultural composition of the digitally literate keeps changing; those using digital media are not a consistent group of people. For example, Internet users have changed from being white young males to a group more and more representative of the population.

In addition to these changes in the environment there are normative issues to contend with when putting a lot of detail into constructing an exact definition of digital literacy. That is, no one is eager to take a stance in defining which specific activities young people are supposed to undertake to be considered digitally literate. For example, is emailing enough? Is being a proficient gamer sufficient to be considered digitally literate? Should social networking be part of digital literacy training at school? Does it matter what young people do online or is any type of intensive engagement indicative of literacy? In other words, which milestones or minimal requirements do we envision a digitally literate individual complying with? In education all these questions are strongly linked to what researchers and educators think the purpose of education in general is. Are literacy and education solely about information and knowledge gathering or does it also include gaining the skills to survive in society in order to be a confident and well-integrated human being?

With the intention to start a discussion about what it means to be digitally literate, this chapter employs a cultural groups approach. That is an approach that places our engagement with technologies within the context of the variety in people's everyday realities. This approach should be useful within an educational context since the British educational system represents the wider society in its cultural diversity and continuing intergenerational complexities. Digital engagement at school cannot be seen as separate from the world outside school. It is clear that our understanding of digital literacy as an educational goal needs to be placed within this environment.

To construct a picture of the existing differences in cultures around digital literacy this chapter will start with a brief revision of the existing definitions of digital literacy. Then the chapter will examine which cultures could and should be taken into consideration in an educational context for digital literacy. With these definitions of digital literacies and cultures in mind, evidence will be revised for different meanings of literacy in different cultures. The chapter will close by discussing the implications for policy and practice.

Definitions of Digital Literacy

There are a number of researchers, policymakers and educators who have started to define digital literacy and others have no doubt done so in the collection of papers presented in this book. Therefore what follows is only a brief discussion of the different types of definitions of digital literacy. The stance taken here is that there are two main fields of research from which definitions of digital literacy arise, the first is research in relation to digital exclusion and the second the, relatively separate, field of media literacy.

In the first area, related to digital exclusion, the focus has been on defining digital literacy in terms of the technical resources and skills required to access the content available on digital media with a focus on computers and the Internet. This includes: understanding computers, programming language, manuals of digital appliances and the physical ability to read and use these. A discussion of this type of approach to literacy can be found in McMillan's

(1996) paper which compares traditional literacy and computer literacy traditions. Definitions that have come from researchers and practitioners in the area of media literacy tend to focus on creative and critical skills in creating and interpreting digital content. Buckingham and Sefton-Green (1997) discuss the relationships between definitions of media and digital literacy.

Recently these two literatures have become more integrated (e.g., Livingstone, 2004). Policy documents have also started to include the different interpretations of digital exclusion and media literacy approaches to formulating programmes of digital literacy. For example, the Digital European Literacy project (DigEuLit, 2005) defines digital literacy as:

> The awareness, attitude and ability of individuals to appropriately use digital tools and facilities to identify, access, manage, integrate, evaluate, analyze and synthesize digital resources, construct new knowledge, create media expressions, and communicate with others, in the context of specific life situations, in order to enable constructive social action; and to reflect upon this process

The UK's Office of Communications (Ofcom, 2006a) defines (digital) media literacy as 'the ability to access, understand and create communications in a variety of contexts' and the New Zealand Digital Strategy (New Zealand Government, 2008) defines digital literacy as 'the ability to use digital technology, communication tools or networks to locate, evaluate, use and create information'. These definitions all incorporate access, technical, critical and creative skills. Due to the nature of these kinds of documents and the existing literature on which these are based these definitions are by default very broad and do not detail the specific activities and skills that identify the truly digitally literate person. One problem is that to be more specific, as educators have been when it comes to traditional reading and writing literacy (i.e., reading lists), a stable environment is needed. An environment in which people know that their access, technical, critical and creative skills, learned by participating in and being exposed to a range of specific applications and activities, will allow them to continue to realize certain goals in the future. Similar to traditional reading and writing skills, if completely literate, a person would be expected to read a book written 10 years ago as well as a book that will come out in 10 years' time. At this point digital media and the rapid changes in the digital environment seem to lack this guarantee.

Digital engagement, or more precisely high-quality engagement, is not universally experienced in the same way, nor is it stable over time. People who were able to undertake certain activities expertly a few years ago might now find that the digital environment has changed so much that their previous skills are not adaptable to this new environment. Helsper, Dutton, Gerber and Reisdorf (2008) argued that this is the case with the rise of new web 2.0 technologies. People who used to be experts feel less comfortable with the Internet now that it has centred on social networking and interactive applications such as wikis and blogs. Educators and researchers are still struggling to understand which specific skills and activities will be transferable to a future digital world.

This has lead to a general definition of digital literacy which emphasises equality of opportunity, that is, the capability to undertake certain actions and to find and evaluate certain information if the person wishes to do this (DiMaggio, Hargittai, Russell Neuman, & Robinson, 2001; Selwyn, Gorard, & Williams, 2001). However, when discussing digital literacy, researchers and policy makers cannot continue to ignore what users of digital media actually do. There needs to be a 'reading list' or a digital curriculum that reflects the reality of people's everyday lives and the skills they need to survive in this environment. A parallel with traditional education can be used to understand the importance of including specific activities as well as skills in education for digital literacy:

- If young people have access to school but do not go to school, no one seriously thinks there is equality. Access is not enough.
- If young people have the skills needed to learn (and go to school) but they do not actually go to any of the classes, there is no equality. Skills are not enough.
- If young people go to school, have the skills to learn but some (from the first school day onwards) only go to arts classes and others only go to maths classes, this should not be called equality. Narrow engagement is not enough.

Therefore, only if young people have access, have the skills to learn and engage with material in a meaningful way, and only if they have experienced various digital subject matters can we speak of digital equality in education and a universal concept digital literacy.

The framework of corresponding fields used in the Digital Inclusion report (Helsper, 2008a) illustrates this (see Figure 7.1).

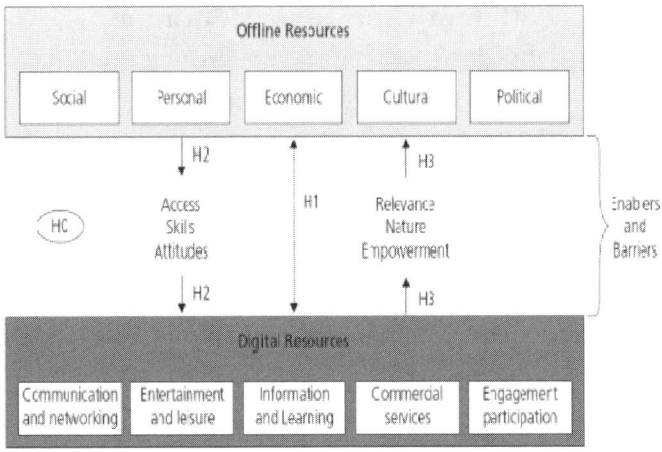

Figure 7.1: Corresponding fields framework. Source: 'Digital Inclusion: An Analysis of Social Disadvantage and the Information Society' (Helsper, 2008a)

In Figure 7.1 offline resources are those areas in everyday life representative of the different capitals which an equal and integrated individual should have access to (Helsper 2008a). The digital resources in Figure 7.1 are those areas which make up different aspects of digital engagement and can be considered the capitals through which they define a complete digital individual.

The underlying principle of this framework is that offline resources influence how people engage with technology (their digital literacy) depending on the type of access, skills and attitudes they have. In the opposite direction, our specific way of engaging with technologies influences only certain and definitely not all aspects of our offline resources (everyday) life, depending on the relevance, nature and type of empowerment that certain types of engagement carry. A mistake made in education is that the introduction of ICTs is expected to influence grades while the biggest influence can perhaps be found in social resources (e.g., friendships and networks) or personal resources (e.g., self-esteem) (Bradbrook et al., 2007). It is therefore important to understand which aspects of offline and online literacy or equality we are referring to.

The implication of this framework and the educational parallel drawn earlier is that digital literacy definitions should cover areas of everyday life in which technology is embedded. Education and thus digital literacy within this framework is about preparing for life and (not just) acquiring formal knowledge and skills.

Different Cultures in Education and Evidence for Varying Engagement

The classroom is a representation of society. In this embedded context, certain social or demographic groups are significant for our understanding of digital literacies especially when education is seen as preparing people for life (and not just for reading and mathematics). From digital inclusion research we should learn that traditional indicators of social exclusion, such as socio-economic status, generation, and disability are all related to the level of engagement and access to digital media (Helsper 2008a; Livingstone & Helsper 2007; Prensky 2001). Other research shows that ethnicity, gender and language influence the way in which we engage with digital media (Calvert, Rideout, Woolard, Barr & Strouse 2005; Dutton & Helsper 2007; Torenli 2006). Classrooms in Europe, and the UK in particular, are increasingly international and national cultures, in addition to the influence of language skills, cannot be ignored. There is sufficient evidence that access and digital skills are different for all these groups. For the UK the evidence for this comes from the ONS (e.g., Office for National Statistics (ONS) 2007), Ofcom (e.g., OFCOM 2008) and OxIS (Dutton & Helsper 2007) studies. To illustrate the basic differences in digital literacy expressed in existing definitions of digital literacy, the Oxford Internet Survey (OxIS) data will be used here to show that these particular cultures can influence digital engagement.

The OxIS conducted by the Oxford Internet Institute (OII) is the British section of the World Internet Project (WIP). WIP consists of a consortium of over 20 countries worldwide that use a set of core questions and comparable sampling techniques to enquire about access, use and attitudes towards the Internet and other digital media. Fieldwork in Britain has been conducted in 2003, 2005, 2007 and the next round will take place in February 2009.[1] Respondents are 14-year-olds and older and face-to-face interviews are used to collect a nationally representative, probability sample of England, Scotland and Wales. The findings of this survey have been compared with the findings in other surveys in this area by Ofcom and ONS and the results were reassuringly similar to OxIS findings (Helsper, 2008b). Since OxIS includes more detailed information on specific uses of the Internet and on different types of skills; OxIS is used here to provide evidence of different digital cultures. In addition, due to its WIP partnership, an international comparison is possible, the results of which are presented later in this chapter.

First, to show that there are differences in basic digital literacy and engagement between different socio-cultural groups, the results are presented for access, skills and breadth of engagement (see Figure7.1 for their significance in the corresponding fields model). In Figures 7.2 through 7.4 digital literacy is operationalised as[2]:

- Access (Media Richness, Quality and Location)
- Skills (Self-efficacy and Multitasking)
- Engagement (Breadth of engagement)

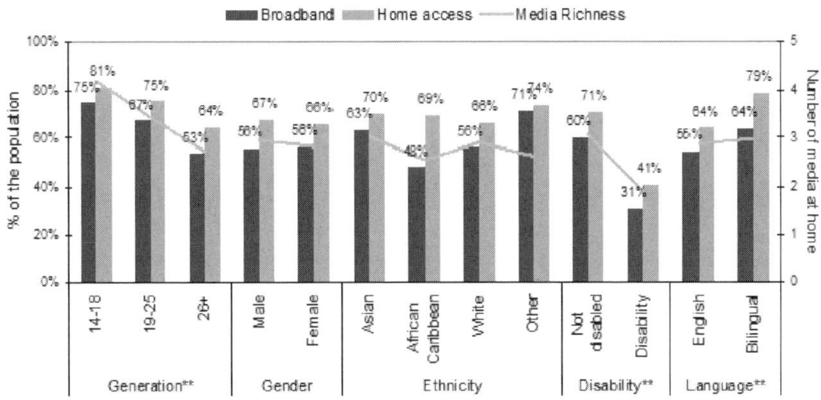

Base. All Internet users and non-users (N=2,350)

** Differences between groups significant at p<.01

Note I. Generational groups were chosen based on the (1st and 2nd generation) digital natives paradigm (See Helsper, 2008b)

Note II. Differences for media richness not significant for language groups.

Figure 7.2: Access to the Internet in Different Groups

Figure 7.2 shows basic evidence that different generations, people with different ability levels and people from different language groups have significantly different levels of access to digital media. The youngest generation (teenagers) are more likely to have broadband, home access to the Internet and to live in environments that are media rich. Not disabled persons are also advantaged in comparison to disabled persons. That is, those without a disability have higher-quality access, in private environments where they are continuously exposed to a large number of different (digital and other) media. The bilingual groups were more advantaged in terms of access than those who were English speaking only, but there was no difference in the media richness of their environments. No significant differences between gender and ethnicity groups were found for the different access indicators.

Figure 7.3 shows that generation, disability and language groups also differ significantly on a basic skills level. The same three groups that had better access levels were more likely to have higher levels of self-efficacy when the analyses focused only on Internet users. However, the differences in multi-tasking were not significant for the disability and language comparisons. There were additional significant differences based on gender. Men perceived themselves to have higher skill levels and were more likely to multi-task than women.

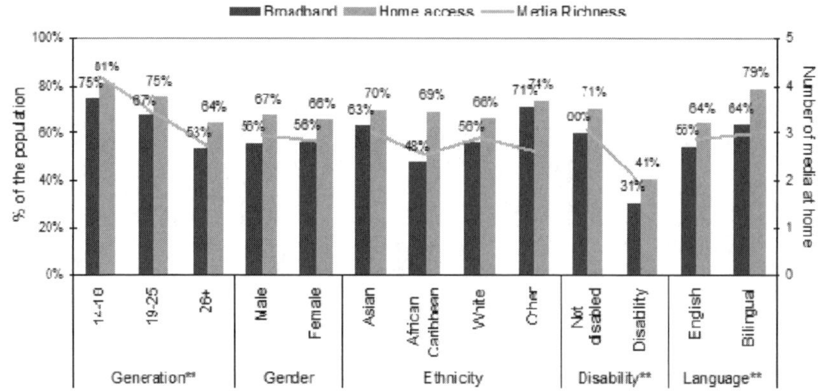

Base. All Internet users (N=1,578)

** Differences between groups significant at p<.01

Note I. Differences in multi-tasking not significant for language groups nor for disability.

Figure 7.3: Skills and digital cultures

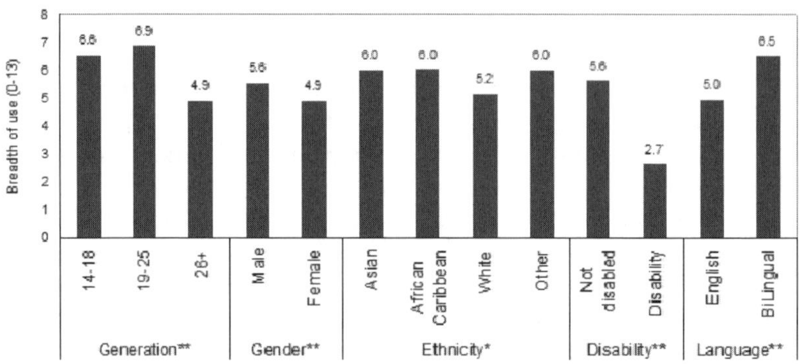

Base. All Internet users (N=1,578)

* Differences between groups significant at p<.05

** Differences between groups significant at p<.01

Figure 7.4: Breadth of use (number of different activities) and digital cultures

Figure 7.4 shows that as soon as it comes to actual engagement with the Internet all different groups examined are related to significant differences in the breadth of their use of the Internet. That is, younger people, men, the non-disabled and those who are bilingual use the Internet for a wider variety of activities. In addition to these group differences, which were also significant for access and skills, ethnic groups showed differences in engagement. The white group was in this case the group who engaged less broadly with the Internet. This might be a counterintuitive finding for those schooled in traditional inequality research, since ethnic minorities are usually socially disadvantaged (Percy-Smith, 2000). However, since the Asian and African Caribbean participants in this study all spoke English, ethnic minority overlaps largely with the bilingual speaker groups and thus represents a particular group of non-White Britons. There is probably a broader validity to this finding, however, since Ofcom studies also showed high participation rates in digital media by these groups (Ofcom 2006b).

The basic evidence presented in Figures 7.2 through 7.4 shows that the everyday context in which different socio-cultural groups interact with a digital medium like the Internet varies. Therefore experiences that students and their teachers of these different backgrounds bring into the classroom can vary considerably and will likely influence how they engage with digital media at school.

Evidence for Different Cultures in Digital Literacy

The previous paragraphs only dealt with the basic aspects of digital engagement, that is access, skills and use or non-use. Since these aspects are mostly quantitative in nature, it is still not clear if those differences are indicative of different cultures. One could argue that differences in access and skills and engagement levels measure social inequalities but not necessarily different digital cultures. The word culture is more qualitative and to a certain extent more normative in nature. When researchers, educators and policy makers discuss digital literacy it is important to make clear whether digital inequalities as well as digital cultures are considered to be part of this discussion. That is, whether digital literacy training should only be a matter of achieving equality of opportunity or also a matter of equality of engagement.

One way to address this issue is to understand what the current substantive, qualitative differences in engagement are between the different groups. This helps our understanding of what digital literacy means in these different socio-cultural groups. An important issue is if, when these different groups have access, they engage with ICTs in the same way or if they experience the digital world in a different way. One way of understanding cultures is by examining which activities comprise basic, intermediate and full (breadth) engagement in these different groups. Using OxIS again to illustrate this within Britain, and World Internet Project (WIP) data for international evidence, this section will first examine differences in types of engagement between generational and ethnicity groups and then show how different national cultures show different patterns of engagement. These same analyses can be done for the gender, language and ability groups but in this chapter the choice was made to focus on generation, ethnic and national groups because they have more often been related to culture.

This section will use the twelve different types of uses of the Internet as described in Helsper, Dutton and Gerber's (2009) report. By examining which uses are taken up by those who have low levels of engagement with the Internet (i.e., a narrow range of activities undertaken online) and comparing those between groups, a rudimentary start can be made in understanding digital cultures. Comparing those with the broadest levels of engagement is less informative because those who do almost everything online in one group are by default very similar to those who do almost everything in another group. Figures 7.5 to 7.7 illustrate this principle for different generations.

Generations

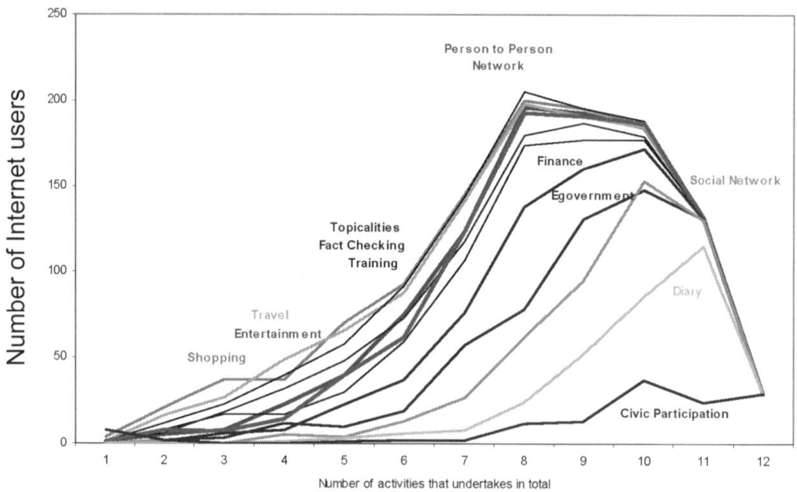

Figure 7.5: Teenagers' patterns of Internet use with increased breadth of use.

Figures 7.5 through to 7.7 show that for the youngest generation (14 to 18 years, second-generation digital natives) the most basic activities are shopping and entertainment. These are undertaken even by those who undertake only 1 or 2 different types of activities on the Internet. Networking and learning are also taken up by those who have a relatively narrow use of the Internet (up to 4 activities).

The recent attention paid to user-generated content such as diary (i.e., blogging, etc.) and social networking activities comes through in these analyses as part of basic set of activities by the youngest generation. Of the teenagers who undertook 4 or less activities 40% participated in social networking and of those who undertook 7 activities 84% participated in social networking. Finance, e-government and civic participation types of engagement were undertaken mainly by those who used the Internet for more than 10 different activities.

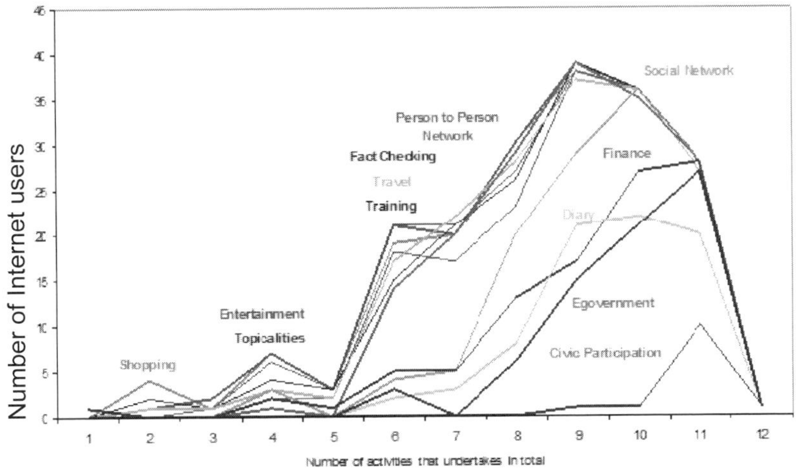

Figure 7.6: Young adults' patterns of Internet use with increased breadth of use

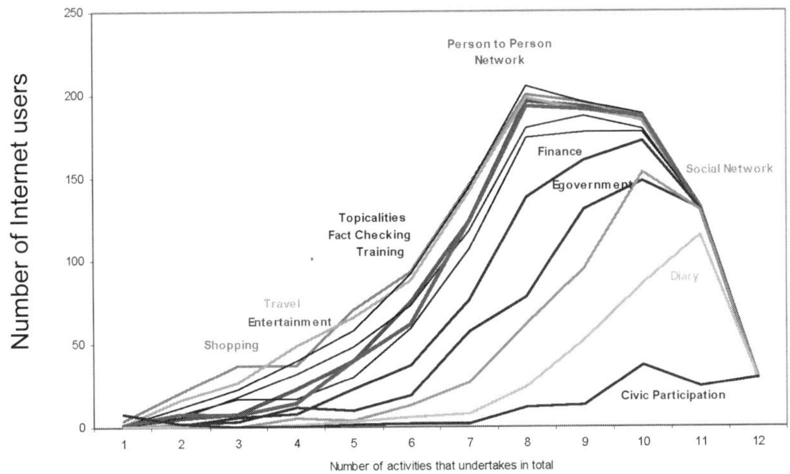

Figure 7.7: Adults' patterns of Internet use with increased breadth of use

In the group of young adults (19 to 25 years, first-generation digital natives) the most basic activities are shopping, training, and looking for topicalities. Entertainment is important for this group as well, but in this group social networking and diary applications are far less common than the attention given to them in the press and research suggests. For the older adult generation the basic activities are shopping and travel, topicalities and entertainment. The main difference between this and the other previously described generations is the relative importance of finance and e-government activities and fact- and information- seeking uses of the Internet, among those who undertake only a few different types of activities online. While diary and social networking activities were part of the first or second 'wave' of activities taken up by younger generations, only the older adults who undertake more than 8 activities are likely to engage in this way with the Internet.

The engagement culture of older adults corresponds to the common definition of digital literacy in education. There it is often defined in terms of high- quality engagement related to learning, participation and critical reflection. Young people are engaged in a creative and social ways even when their digital lives are relatively narrow, while civic and knowledge-gathering activities are not so much part of digital experience of this younger generation. The question could be asked if this is different from other areas in education related to traditional literacy. Have young people (as a group) not always been more open to creation and entertainment than older people, and is it not logical that this is reflected in the digital reality? However, it is important to keep in mind that digital cultures, that is Internet, experiences, differ considerably between generations, especially amongst those with a narrow engagement with the Internet. It is likely that the Internet means something else to teachers than it means to their students.

Ethnicity

A similar analysis was conducted for the different ethnic groups that participated in the OxIS study. This type of analysis is interesting in the context of education because it reflects the British multicultural classrooms, which in turn might be reflected in different digital cultures. A summary of the results follows for the three main ethnic groups in the UK.

The analyses showed that Asian users (N=86) engaged first with fact checking, travel and shopping. There were no Asian Internet users who used the Internet for less than four different types of activities. This shows that the Asian ethnic group as a whole is engaged broadly with the Internet. Of the 12 Asian Internet users who used the Internet for four to seven activities 11 used the Internet for fact checking and 8 for travel and shopping.

African Caribbean users (N=40) with a narrow use of the Internet engaged with topicalities, fact checking, training and entertainment activities. Of the 15

African Caribbean Internet users who used the Internet for five or less activities, 13 used it for fact checking, 12 for topicalities, 9 for training and 6 for entertainment.

The white user (N=1419) was less consistent in the cumulative nature of types of engagement. There was a relatively large group of narrow users who just went online for civic participation (i.e., an older group of white users). Amongst the other users with a narrow range of uses different activities were about equally distributed without a clear focus on a few activities. Nevertheless, shopping, travel and topicalities were the most popular activities amongst those who used the Internet for three or less activities.

The comparison between different ethnic groups shows that there are some interesting differences in digital cultures, especially between African Caribbean and the Asian and White Internet users. African Caribbean users were less likely to have a culture that included commercial activities (i.e., finance, travel and shopping) which were part of the basic engagement package of White and Asian narrow users. This is interesting because Asian and African Caribbean users were equally engaged when access and skills were compared earlier in this chapter.

Nationality

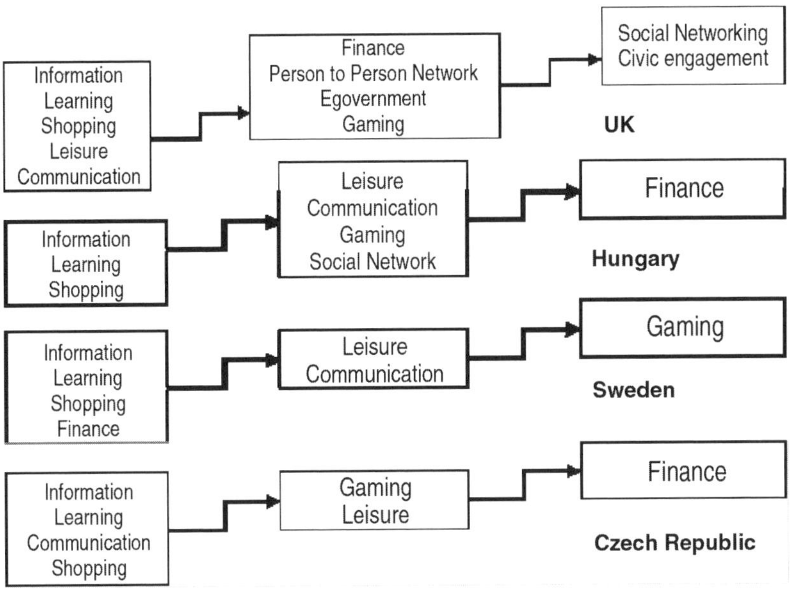

Note. The activities in Figure 7.8 differ slightly from those described in other sections. The activities were reduced based on comparability between countries.

Figure 7.8 Ladders of engagement in different European countries

Recent immigrants from different European countries have come to the UK and started participating in education. Sadly the World Internet Project has no data on Poland, which is one of the largest groups of EU immigrants in Britain. It does have data on other new (Hungary and Czech Republic) and older (Sweden and the UK) European Union member states, and international communities are especially influential in British metropolitan areas and take not only specific generational and ethnic backgrounds to the classroom, but also national digital cultures from their countries of origin.

Figure 7.8 shows schematically the same ladders of engagement as discussed for generations (Figures 7.5 through 7.7) and ethnic groups (described in the previous section). The most basic uses in the UK for all Internet users are reflected in the top of Figure 7.8. Information, learning, shopping, leisure and communication were undertaken by the majority of those who used the Internet for 5 activities or less. In Hungary those who undertook three activities or less were most likely to undertake information, learning and shopping. In Sweden the most common activities were information, learning, shopping and finance. In the Czech Republic information, learning, communication and shopping were the most popular uses amongst those with narrow uses of the Internet.

Basic narrow engagement included information and learning in most of Europe. Social activities (including gaming) and communication were often the second step on a ladder of increasing breadth of engagement. Sweden, however, was the exception to this general trend; there social forms of entertainment were the last step to full engagement.

Swedes and British Internet users engaged with practical applications (e.g., Finances) even when the breadth of their use is relatively narrow, while Eastern EU countries were more likely to engage in this fashion only when completely immersed in the digital world.

Implications in Policy and Practice

The generational, ethnic and national digital cultures described in this chapter are part of people's everyday experiences with technologies. Age and country of origin are influences that find their expression not only within the home context but also in formal educational settings. If definitions of digital literacy continue to be limited to providing access and skills acquisition, ignoring the different meaning and the practical realities that ICTs have for these groups, digital literacy training and policy are likely to be less successful. Equality of opportunity in this context should be related to equality of experience as well as equality of access and skills. In traditional reading and writing literacy programmes certain books from a range of different styles and writers are part of the basic curriculum. A similar strategy might be necessary for digital engagement with a clear idea of which contents and types of activities form part of the digital 'reading list'. To achieve a society in which digital engagement is based on choice, individuals in education should be exposed to the complete spectrum that digital media has to offer. In the corresponding fields model (Helsper 2008a) these are separated into five areas: Communication and Networking, Commercial Services, Entertainment and Leisure, Learning and Information and Engagement and Participation, but other classifications are possible and should be discussed as part of a digital curriculum.

If after exposure to all these different types of digital 'literature' people with different backgrounds decide to engage with only one or a few of the possible range of activities this could be said to reflect a personal or group culture. At this moment definitions and policy related to digital literacy suffer from not clarifying what types of engagement (instead of skills and applications) need to be part of the basic digital literacy package.

The data presented here were lacking in that interpretative or critical skills in themselves were not measured. A recent review of existing research (Helsper 2008a) has shown that there is a gap in current research in Britain as regards our knowledge about measures of critical digital skills. Future research will hopefully be able to address this point. Critical skills measures, in combination with the digital cultures data presented here, would further facilitate the construction of a complete digital literacy programme

This chapter laid out which differences currently exist in digital engagement cultures. Clearly an understanding of current digital cultures should serve as a basis for the development of any future programme that aims to include exposure to types of engagement as well as access, technical and critical skills. What people already know and do at home and elsewhere will doubtless have an effect on what people take up and go home with in formal educational settings. Once researchers and policy makers have a better idea of how current everyday digital experiences differ between teachers and students and between different socio-demographic groups, it will be possible to construct a digital literacy programme that is broad enough to include all possible experiences and interpretations. On the basis of which young people will truly have the equal opportunity to choose the type of engagement that is best for them.

Notes

1 Funding for OxIS comes from various commercial, government and nonprofit organisations.

2 See Dutton and Helsper (2007) for the exact questions asked.

Bibliography

Bradbrook, G., Alvi, I., Fisher, J., Lloyd, H., Moore, R., Thompson, V., et al. (2007). *Meeting their potential: The role of education and technology in overcoming disadvantage and disaffection in young people.* London: Becta.

Buckingham, D., & Sefton-Green, J. (1997). Multimedia education: Media literacy in the age of digital culture. In R. W. Kubey (Ed.), *Media literacy in the information age* (pp. 285–307).New Brunswick, NJ: Transactis.

Calvert, S. L., Rideout, V. J., Woolard, J. L., Barr, R. F., & Strouse, G. A. (2005). Age, ethnicity, and socioeconomic patterns in early computer use: A national survey. *American Behavioral Scientist*, 48(5), 590–607.

DigEuLit. (2005). DigEuLit: A European framework for digital literacy: a Progress Report [Electronic Version]. *Journal of eLiteracy*, 2. Retrieved January 2009 from http://www.jelit.org/65/01/JeLit_Paper_31.pdf.

DiMaggio, P., Hargittai, E., Russell Neuman, W., & Robinson, J. P. (2001). Social Implications of the Internet. *Annual Review of Sociology*. 27(1), 307–336.

Dutton, W., & Helsper, E. J. (2007). *The Internet in Britain: 2007*. Oxford, UK: Oxford Internet Institute, University of Oxford.

Helsper, E. J. (2008a). *Digital inclusion: An analysis of social disadvantage and the information society.* London: Communities and Local Government.

Helsper, E. J. (2008b). *Digital natives and ostrich tactics? The possible implications of labelling young people as digital experts.* London: Futurelab.

Helsper, E. J., Dutton, W., Gerber, M., & Reisdorf, B. (2008). Trust and the Internet: Experience technology or certainty trough models? Paper presented at the *2nd European Communication Conference Barcelona.*

Helsper, E. J., Dutton, W. H., & Gerber, M. (2009). To be a network society: A cross-national perspective on the Internet in Britain. [Electronic Version]. *OII Research Report*, 17. Retrieved January 2009 from

http://papers.ssrn.com/sol3/papers.cfm?abstract_id=1323813.

Livingstone, S. (2004). Media literacy and the challenge of new information and communication technologies. *The Communication Review*, 7(1), 3–14.

Livingstone, S., & Helsper, E. (2007). Gradations in digital inclusion: Children, young people and the digital divide. *New Media & Society*, 9(4), 671–696.

McMillan, S. (1996). Literacy and computer literacy: Definitions and comparisons. *Computers & Education*, 27(3–4), 161–170.

New Zealand Government. (2008). *New Zealand digital strategy.* Retrieved January, 2009, from http://www.digitalstrategy.govt.nz/Resources/Glossary-of-Key-Terms/

Ofcom. (2006a). *Media literacy audit: Report on adult media literacy.* London: Ofcom.

—— (2006b). *Media literacy audit: Report on media literacy amongst adults from minority ethnic groups.*

London: Ofcom.

—— (2008). The consumer experience - Research Report 08. Retrieved January, 2009, from http://ofcom.org.uk/research/tce/ce08/

Office for National Statistics (ONS). (2007). Internet access. 65% of households had access in 2008. Retrieved January, 2009, from http://www.statistics.gov.uk/CCI/nugget.asp?ID=8&Pos=1&ColRank=1&Rank=192

Percy-Smith, J. (2000). Introduction: The contours of social exclusion. In J. Percy-Smith (Ed.), *Policy responses to social exclusion. Towards inclusion?* pp.1–21. Buckingham: Open University Press.

Prensky, M. (2001). Digital natives, digital immigrants. On the Horizon, 9(5).

Selwyn, N., Gorard, S., & Williams, S. (2001). Digital divide or digital opportunity? The role of technology in overcoming social exclusion in US education. *Educational Policy*, 15(2), 258–277.

Torenli, N. (2006). The 'other' faces of digital exclusion: ICT gender divides in the broader community. *European Journal of Communication*, 21(4), 435–455.

CHAPTER 8

Changing the Policy Paradigm for the Promotion of Digital and Media Literacy—The European Challenge

Laura Cervi and José Manuel Pérez Tornero

Introduction

Two recent studies done by our research group[1] show that the policy paradigm for the promotion of digital and media literacy is changing.

Digital literacy is starting to be considered not only as a purely instrumental and technical knowledge but as a tool with a serious cultural dimension and an important potential for institutional innovation.

That's why European experts have started thinking about changing the pedagogical and operative approach that has been given to the promotion policies until now to give more importance to quality, critical thinking towards digital services and contents and to the potential of institutional innovation and transformation itself.

The emergence of the concept "media literacy" itself, that gathers both traditional and digital media, can be seen as a step ahead to the consolidation of a new paradigm.

Media Literacy: Development of the Concept

To fully understand the nature of this new media literacy, we should quickly revisit the historical milestones in the literacy process: classic literacy (reading-writing-understanding) was dominant for centuries and corresponded to the process of reading and writing, in which primary schooling played an essential role; audiovisual literacy, which relates to electronic media such as film and television, focuses on image, and because of that it is the beginning of different educational initiatives early engaged but not sufficiently supported by real policies; digital literacy or information literacy stems from computer and digital media, which brought about the necessity to learn new skills. This is a very recent concept, and is often used synonymously to refer to the technical skills required for modern digital tools.

Finally media literacy, which can be considered as a result of media convergence—that is, the merging of electronic media (mass communication) and digital media (multimedia communication) which occurs in the advanced stages of development of information society. This media literacy includes the command of previous forms of literacy: reading and writing (from understanding to creative skills), audiovisual, digital and the new skills required in this climate of media convergence.

The need to tackle the new media literacy has been recognised by various experts and researchers[2] and has been described with clarity by Sonia Livingstone:

> As media and information technologies converge and pose new problems and challenges for citizens in their everyday understanding of those technologies, two particular traditions are converging. One, broadly, we could call media literacy, the other comes from information literacy, and people here may be more or less familiar with those different traditions. But of course, as technologies converge, skills converge as well, and so we need a convergent notion of literacy. [3]

Media education and media literacy, have been firstly described and defined in an international context by UNESCO, whose work focuses on what is known as media education, which is the immediate predecessor of the broadest definition of media literacy.

It's possible to isolate four stages in UNESCO's formalisation of the concept of media education.

The first step, represented by the Grunwald declaration of 1982, was the creation of the field of media education, which brought attention to the impact of the media on training and education.

The second, with the 1990 Toulouse Conference, was the systematisation and more precise definition of the field.

Thirdly, the 1999 conference in Vienna,[4] took a new look at media education in the context of digital advances and the new communicative era that came about as a result.

Finally, the fourth, the UNESCO seminar in Seville in 2002,[5] which adopted the definition of the field made in the Vienna conference, highlighted the need for action through active promotion policies in four areas: 1) Investigation; 2) Training; 3) Cooperation between schools, the media, NGOs, private businesses and public institutions; 4) Consolidation and promotion of the public sphere of society and its relationship with the media.

In Europe, at the beginning of 21st century, the use of media education was accompanied by media literacy, undoubtedly in order to include and expand digital literacy, which has been a big part of movements to promote the development of information society and to combat the digital divide.

This work has been carried out with the support of the Council of Europe[6] and the European Commission—which for the years 2006 and 2007 has supported a Group of Experts in the field and has launched a Public Consultation on the subject.[7] The work has also been supported by the European Media Charter[8] and a number of public media regulation institutions, such as the United Kingdom's OFCOM.[9]

This institution provided the basic definition, stating that media literacy consists of "the ability to access, understand and create communications in a variety of contexts".[10]

According to the European Charter of Media Literacy,[11] there are seven areas of competences (or uses) related to media literacy:

- Use media technologies effectively to access, store, retrieve and share content to meet their individual and community needs and interests;
- Gain access to, and make informed choices about, a wide range of media forms and content from different cultural and institutional sources;
- Understand how and why media content is produced;
- Analyse critically the techniques, languages and conventions used by the media, and the messages they convey;
- Use media creatively to express and communicate ideas, information and opinions;
- Identify, and avoid or challenge, media content and services that may be unsolicited, offensive or harmful;
- Make effective use of media in the exercise of their democratic rights and civil responsibilities.

Meanwhile, according to the European Commission, media literacy represents a variety of skills and competences related to the media, its images, languages and messages:

> Media Literacy may be defined as the ability to access, analyse and evaluate the power of images, sounds and messages which we are now being confronted with on a daily

> basis and which are an important part of our contemporary culture; as well as to communicate competently using media available, on a personal basis. Media literacy relates to all media, including television and film, radio and recorded music, print media, the Internet and other new digital communication technologies

This definition is complemented with a series of broader considerations, which we will look at below.[12]

On the one hand, the concept of media (with its corresponding messages and languages) refers to all those that form part of daily life and incorporate contemporary culture, independently of their specific nature (image, sound, written word...).[13]

On the other hand, the skills related to media literacy can be summarised in four areas of ability: access, analysis, evaluation and creative production.[14] All of these skills boost aspects of personal development: consciousness, critical thinking[15] and problem-solving abilities.

When considering other elements that help to define the field of media literacy conceptually and thematically, one must remember that it is the result of a process of learning (and teaching) in any given context, but particularly in formal, informal, social, family and media settings. This multi-contextual process leads to the acquisition of specific abilities and competences, in addition to attitudes and values. This process is known as media education.[16]

Media literacy should not be treated as an isolated or independent skill. On the contrary, it is a skill that involves and encompasses other skills and forms of literacy: reading and writing literacy, audiovisual literacy (often referred to as image or visual literacy) and digital or information literacy.[17]

Furthermore, it is a necessary part of active citizenship[18] and is key to the full development of freedom of expression and the right to information. It is therefore an essential part of participative democracy[19] and intercultural dialogue.

> Today, media literacy is as central to active and full citizenship as literacy was at the beginning of 19th century [20]

Study on the Current Trends and Approaches on Media Literacy in Europe

The study on the current trends and approaches on media literacy in Europe—carried out for the Commission by the Universidad Autonoma de Barcelona in the second half of 2007—identified the key factors for the development of an active policy for media literacy. These are as follows:

1. The treatment of media literacy in the educational curriculum of each country.
2. The policy of teacher training in the subject.
3. The policy of assessment of media literacy.
4. The existence of educational material on the subject.
5. The existence of systems for assistance and orientation in the field.
6. The existence of public media literacy campaigns.
7. The existence of stable public departments for the promotion of media literacy.
8. The activity of civic associations in the sector.
9. The activity of regulatory activities in the sector.
10. The participation of the media in activities of media literacy: contents and specific programmes.
11. The participation of the media industry in the sector.
12. Visibility in questions related to media literacy in the public sphere.
13. The existence of incentives and promotion policies for media production by the general public.
14. Field research.
15. Participation in networks of international cooperation.
16. Family participation.
17. Initiatives of media literacy related to commercial communication.

Bearing in mind the objectives of the Commission regarding information society and the analysis of the current state of media literacy in Europe (deficiencies and emerging trends), the research team created the following table of recommendations (Table 8.1). There are five different areas, in each of which strategic objectives and recommendations are outlined. The recommendations have been placed in order of priority: priority 1: short term; priority 2: medium-term.

As a result of this study the 20th of December 2007, the European Commission directed a Communication called "A European approach to media literacy in the digital environment" to the European Parliament.

In this occasion the Commission officially accepted a European definition of Media Literacy stating the obligation for member states to promote this field in their countries. Moreover the Commission called on Member States to encourage the authorities in charge of audiovisual and electronic communication regulation to get more involved and to cooperate in the improvement of the various levels of media literacy defined above; promote systematic research into and regular observation of and reporting on the different aspects and dimensions of media literacy; develop and implement codes of conduct and, as appropriate, co-regulatory frameworks in conjunction with all interested parties at national level, and promote self-regulatory initiatives.[21]

Table 8.1: Recommendations from the "Study on the current trends and approaches on Media Literacy in Europe" (2007)

Area	Strat. Objectives	Priority 1	Priority 2
1. Policy	Develop media literacy *policy*	1.1. Indicators 1.2. Research and monitoring	1.3. Quality standards 1.4. Regulatory authorities 1.5. European media literacy networks
2.Technological innovation	Link media literacy with *technological and economic innovation*	2.1. Spread of technological innovations 2.2. Creation of quality content 2.3. Debate on educational licenses	2.4. Consumers' associations for media and communications services
3. Creativity	Boost *creativity* as an essential part of media literacy	3.1 Media production initiatives for children and young people 3.2 Media literacy resources centers	3.3. Create media in educational settings
4. Active Citizenship	Promote media literacy as an instrument of *Active citizenship in the European public sphere*	4.1. Public awareness campaigns 4.2. Forums on media literacy 4.3. Media literacy Promotion of Europe's audiovisual heritage 4.4. Analysis and debate on commercial communication	4.5 Mediation between media and citizenships 4.6. Codes of conduct 4.7. Regulation, self-regulation and co-regulation
5. Education	Reinforce *Research and Education* in media literacy	5.1. Training teachers and trainers in media literacy 5.2. Media literacy in the media 5.3. Media literacy in the curriculum	5.4. Media literacy in lifelong learning

Media Literacy: New Paradigm of Promotion

As we can see there is a clear trend for linking skills related to new digital media with critical and creative skills related to mass media (film, radio, television and press).

Technological evolution has an important effect on this evolution, though it does not wholly determine it. Cultural and political attitudes are also huge influences. When examined functionally, in fact, computer literacy constitutes an instrumental field of knowledge that allows the implementation of new tasks in the information society. But media literacy is something more than an instrumental, practical education. It involves acquiring awareness; it allows the construction of meaning, and in this way it guides the operative abilities that information society requires.

Socio-political and market demands are quickly encouraging computer literacy, but becoming computer literate does not provide complete media literacy. The former belongs to the paradigm of technological needs, in the sense that computer technologies require users to have certain technical competencies. The latter one lies in the knowledge paradigm, improving civic and human consciousness.

Reducing media education to mere computer literacy would be technocratic reductionism, while including computer literacy within the media education paradigm would lead to the broadest and most meaningful realm of learning. In other words, it would involve including technological knowledge in the broadest realm of acquiring consciousness and meaning.

At any rate, media education must now take advantage of the enormous potential for change in perspective that obligatory computer literacy is imposing as the ideal means to acquire an appropriate critical consciousness. Critical thinking can be more easily developed when the established rules are beginning to be questioned and ways of doing things are subject to brusque changes. And this is precisely what is happening now. In this context, media literacy is starting to take note of the evolution related to the appearance of the so-called Web 2.0.

The paradigm of Web 2.0 is not one of criticism of mass communication, nor of resignation to the technological determinism of the first digital literacy. The underlying political proposal of Web 2.0 and the one which corresponds to the recent technological environment is of media appropriation by individuals and groups and of participation in collective or social media production. In fact all of the Web 2.0's significant tools promote net collaboration and productive activity.

These aspects of the recent technological evolution are directly connected with creativity and production supported by media literacy and media education.

But everything seems to suggest that the most likely evolution is a convergence of models, which would allow for a combination of active participation in media production with critical thinking, that is, the conjunction of the values of traditional media education (centred on mass media) and the current direction of media literacy (centred on production in the new digital environment) of the Web 2.0.

Moreover it's urgent to underline the importance of stakeholders co-operation, that is to say that on the one hand media education must not be confined inside the class, but it has to be a life-long learning process involving all the actors: from school to families, from companies to civil society, etc.

On the other hand it shows that "educate to media" means "educate to participate", to be able to take an active part in the managing of the res publica.

The European Union already foresaw the importance of new technologies in politics being a pioneer in the implementation of the so called e-governance, a tool to make people as close as possible to their government.

But, if e-governance – even with important exceptions – always represent a top-down phenomenon, media literacy can really create a bottom-up change.

In fact, one thing is to be able to use technologies to communicate to our representatives, another is to be media literate and use technologies to create contents and so concretely take part in the decision-making process.

So, coherently with the principles of the Lisbon Strategy, before, and the Lisbon Treaty, after, media literacy becomes a fundamental piece in the construction of a participative democracy for Europe.

The following chart presents media literacy as a creator of active citizenship.

It appears as the result of a process, "media education", which is described through different concepts at the upper-left side of the chart.

Concepts related to "participation and active citizenship" are located on the upper-righ-hand side.

In the lower part, elements that make up media literacy are divided into two main areas, one related to critical thinking, and another related to creation and production skills.

Finally, the three types of literacy that make up media literacy: reading and writing, audiovisual and digital literacy, are positioned to the right of media literacy.

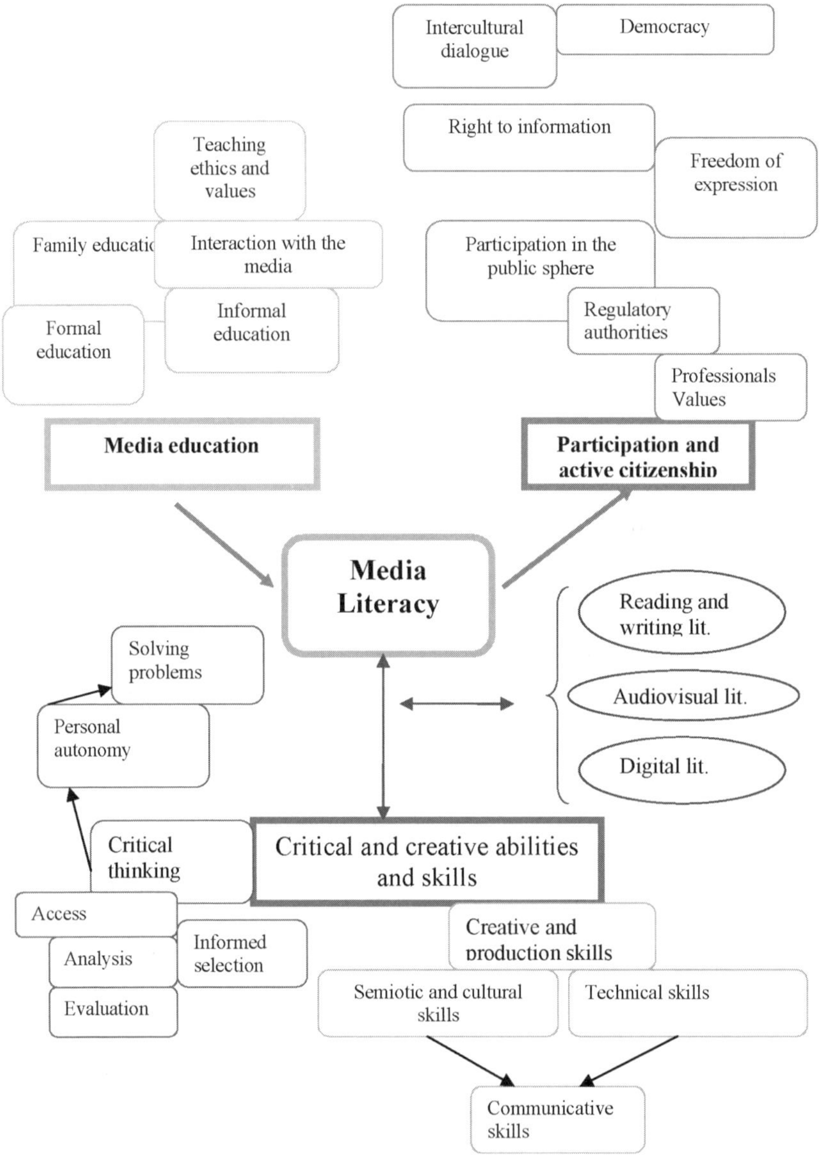
Intercultural dialogue
Democracy
Right to information
Freedom of expression
Teaching ethics and values
Family educatic
Interaction with the media
Participation in the public sphere
Formal education
Informal education
Regulatory authorities
Professionals Values
Media education
Participation and active citizenship
Media Literacy
Reading and writing lit.
Solving problems
Audiovisual lit.
Personal autonomy
Digital lit.
Critical thinking
Critical and creative abilities and skills
Access
Informed selection
Analysis
Creative and production skills
Evaluation
Semiotic and cultural skills
Technical skills
Communicative skills

Figure 8. 1

State of the Art

Despite this intellectual dynamism and some good example of practical application of media literacy in different contexts, generally speaking, this field is therefore affected by problems common to all processes when they start up: dispersion, lack of definition, ambiguity, lack of initiatives and operative networks and also a lack of institutions, etc.

In a context of intense media innovation, of very rapid technological change and the growing power of influence and impact of the communications environment, the importance of deficiencies detected in media literacy increases and takes on a certain significance.

The fundamental barriers to development in the area can be resumed as follows:

- Lack of shared vision: objectives, concepts, methods, resources, research, results evaluation, etc.
- Cultural barriers against innovations
- European visibility of national, regional and local initiatives
- Lack of European networks
- Dispersion and rare coordination among the stakeholders

Media Literacy in the Compulsory Education Curriculum

The introduction of media literacy in curricula can be a good example.

The actual trend in Europe, in fact, is to separate skills related to media education and to digital skills–the former with a more critical emphasis, the latter with a more instrumental emphasis.

There are few curricula – either formal or of lifelong learning – that propose a convergence between media education and digital literacy. If, despite everything, the convergence is taking place, it is more down to technological changes and the integration of all media in a new communicational environment, than to a theoretical discussion or a disciplinary change.

There is no doubt that the inclusion of the media in the curriculum has risen with the educational reforms of the 1990s and 2000s.

Until then, the media was rarely and unsystematically approached via different subjects, but the situation seems to have changed over the last decade.

Many countries have included the acquisition of media and digital skills among the final objectives of their curriculum (Finland, Slovenia, France, Spain); and some have linked these skills to civic education and active citizenship (France, Spain).

Some have created optional subjects (Some in Spain and France) on the media. Others have established evaluation systems for such skills (France).

As a best practice example we may quote Finland. Media education and digital literacy have been central in the Finnish educational approach to dealing with new technologies and communication skills in the 21st century. In early 1996, the Finnish Ministry for Education published a report by a small committee on cultural and media literacy. It emphasized the importance of the new civil and professional skills and competence in the use of the media and net. The report, among other things, pointed out that the field of the media is integrating and becoming interactive while audio-visual communication becomes a central issue. This cultural change requires transforming traditional literacy into media literacy or in broader terms into cultural literacy where it is of central importance to the understanding of how images and meaning are created.

In France, for example, the new law of 23 April 2005 set out the basic skills and objectives in education, among which media studies was established as part of the compulsory education curriculum. It was introduced in subjects dealing with the development of children's abilities of analysis and skills required for living in a free society where technology plays a fundamental role, so as to learn how the technological system works, the laws that govern its operations, and the way technological advances affect their environment. Since October 2006, media education has been a specific objective in the teaching of general skills related with social and civic participation, and is aimed at developing a critical approach to the media. It is important to point out the existence of IT and Internet Certificates, known as B2i, granted to elementary school students who demonstrate competence in ICT.

Regarding the Spanish Educational System, the compulsory school curriculum (Primary and Secondary) contains digital literacy (and media literacy), as a part of the skills that students must attain but currently there are no specific subjects, teaching Media as information sources or tools for learning.

Despite these good examples in many other countries, things are still to be improved.

The Italian educational system—which has recently gone through a period of reform—has been through different phases related with media: during the fifties and the sixties, the educational system focused on film, during the seventies, mainly on TV, and finally in the eighties and nineties mainly on computer science education, multimedia and new technologies. In any case there have been no official and systematic policies created by the Ministry of Education, and development in media education and its application has only been provided by some scholars in the universities and by teachers in the schools.

ICT skills were included as a primary goal in the National Plan for New Technologies in the School (1995), but only from an instrumental, non-critical perspective, with little reference to mass media. In other words, ICT and media education are still not included as a compulsory part of the curriculum, despite the fact that the use of media and the analysis of the mass media has long been normal practice for Italian teachers. The mass media and technology are also considered important support tools for the development of other subjects, such as Italian (language), history, music or art and image.

Although media literacy is present in the Portuguese education system, it has only a discrete presence in the curriculum. There are some references to media studies. ICT is seen as an important subject and a skill to be acquired by all students. In the "*Orientações do Ministério da Educação para a Disciplina de TIC*" it is said that ICT is undoubtedly embedded in the national curriculum and that the subject should not be considered part of IT, but as a subject where skills in informatics are linked with those specific of other areas of learning.

ICT is a core subject for the 8th, 9th and 10th years and is also present in the national curriculum as a basic cross-curricular subject, related to general skills, specific methodologies and acquiring general and specific competences (in handling information, working methods, communication, etc.).

Next Steps

Recently Marianne Miko, an Estonian EuroMP, presented a report[22] recommending including media literacy into the basic formative and the creation of a European curriculum on media.

In October, another MP, Christa Prets, in another communication, *Media Literacy in a Digital World,* underlines that media literacy is fundamental to political culture, suggesting that media education should be an element of formal education to which all children should have access and which should form part and parcel of the curriculum at every stage of schooling, and that media education should, as far as possible, be geared to practical work and linked to economic, political, literary, social, artistic, and IT-related subjects; and she also suggests that the way forward lies in an interdisciplinary approach combined with out-of-school projects. Moreover, the document calls on the Commission, when, as announced, it lays down the media literacy indicators, to take into account both the quality of school tuition and teacher training in this field and underlines that media literacy should feature more prominently in EU support programmes, especially Comenius, eTwinning, and Grundtvig.[23]

Media literacy, in fact, on the one hand underlines the critical thinking component of the relation with media, the idea of giving back to people the power to control the technological context, the capacity of individuals and social networks to create and produce contents—balancing the almost monopolistic impact of big media—and on the other hand it allows the emergence of a new form of citizenship, more active and aware of the importance of media.

Since people's attitudes generate and develop in a specific environment, a proper institutional environment is fundamental to endorse participation, that's why we consider that if the European Union will implement what is stated in this Communication, we're living a concrete step ahead in the development of an active citizenship, allowing media literacy to provide benefit to all the fields of society.

Notes

1 Study on the current trends and approaches on Media Literacy in Europe http://www.mediamentor.org/files/attachments/Study_Media_Literacy_in_Europe_0.pdf José Manuel Pérez Tornero, European Commission, "Promoting digital Literacy", http://ec.europa.eu/education/archive/elearning/doc/studies/dig_lit_en.pdf

2 Cf. David Buckingham, Media Education: Literacy, Learning and Contemporary Culture (Cambridge: Polity Press, 2003) and David Buckingham et al. "The Media Literacy of Children and Young People: A Review of the Academic Research" (London: Ofcom, 2005) http://www.ofcom.org.uk/advice/media_literacy/medlitpub/medlitpubrss/ml_children.pdf); Pier Cesare Rivoltella, J.M.Pérez Tornero

3 Sonia Livingstone, "What is media literacy?" Media@else, (http://www.lse.ac.uk/collections/media@lse/pdf/What_is_media_literacy.doc)

4 Media Education

- deals with all communication media and includes the printed word and graphics, the sound, the still as well as the moving image, delivered on any kind of technology;
- enables people to gain understanding of the communication media used in their society and the way they operate and to acquire skills in using these media to communicate with others;
- ensures that people learn how to:
- Analyze, critically reflect upon and create media texts.
- Identify the sources of media texts, their political, social, commercial and/or cultural
- Interests and their contexts.
- Interpret the messages and values offered by the media.
- Select appropriate media for communicating their own messages or stories and for reaching their intended audience.
- Gain, or demand access to media for both reception and production.

Media Education is part of the basic entitlement of every citizen, in every country in the world, to freedom of expression and the right to information and is instrumental in building and sustaining democracy. While recognizing the disparities in the nature and development of

Media Education in different countries, the participants of the conference "Educating for the Media and the Digital Age" recommend that Media Education should be introduced wherever possible within national curricula as well as in tertiary, non-formal and lifelong education.

- Media Education addresses a wide range of texts in all media (print, still image, audio and moving image) which provide people with rich and diverse cultural experiences.
- In countries moving towards the introduction of new technologies, Media Education can assist citizens to recognize the potential of the media to represent/misrepresent their culture and traditions.
- In situations where access to electronic or digital technologies is limited or non existent, Media Education can be based on available media texts in that context.
- Media Education should be aimed at empowering all citizens in every society and should ensure that people with special needs and those socially and economically disadvantaged have access to it.
- Media Education also has a critical role to play in, and should be responsive to, situations of social and political conflicts, war, natural disaster, ecological catastrophe, etc.

5 Sevilla SeminarCf. http://portal.unesco.org/ci/en/files/5680/10346121330Seville_Recommendations.rtf/Seville+Recommendations.rtf.

6 Cf. http://ec.europa.eu/avpolicy/media_literacy/docs/coe_fr.pdf

7 Cf. http://ec.europa.eu/avpolicy/media_literacy/index_en.htm

8 Cf. http://www.euromedialiteracy.eu/

9 Cf. http://www.ofcom.org.uk/consult/condocs/strategymedialit/strategymedialit/

10 Cf. http://www.ofcom.org.uk/advice/media_literacy/of_med_lit/whatis/

11 Cf. http://www.euromedialiteracy.eu/index.php?Pg=charter

12 The aim of media literacy is to increase awareness of the many forms of media messages encountered in their everyday lives. It should help citizens to recognize how the media filter their perceptions and beliefs, shape popular culture and influence personal choices. It should empower them with the critical thinking and creative problem-solving skills to make them judicious consumers and producers of information. Media education is part of the basic entitlement of every citizen, in every country in the world, to freedom of expression and the right to information and it is instrumental in building and sustaining democracy. Today media literacy is indeed one of the key pre-requisites for active and full citizenship and is one of the contexts in which intercultural dialogue needs to be promoted. Also, media education is a fundamental tool to raise awareness on IPR issues among media users and consumers.

13 The European definition is inspired by the so-called UNESCO Grunwald declaration on the subject, according to which media education covered each and every media.

14 There was an emphasis on creative production, as in UNESCO documents, in the European Union's public consultation on media literacy: "The most commonly expressed concern among the respondents was the importance of adding to the definition the ability to create and communicate messages, as this aspect of media literacy is viewed as fundamental in empowering people to become active and informed consumers of media. Moreover, the communicative aspect of media literacy is considered essential for enabling people to make effective use of media in the exercise of their democratic rights and civic responsibilities".

15 The concept of "evaluation" can be enriched — and in fact was something called for by several experts in the European Union's public consultation on media literacy — with the idea of "critical literacy": Several respondents also stressed the importance of including critical literacy as part of the definition. Again, this aspect of media literacy is regarded as crucial in the creation of an active and discerning citizen. "We would also stress the importance of critical literacy as part of the evaluation component of the definition, for accessing and analysing media messages are not effective if one cannot also critically evaluate those messages, distinguishing the honest from the deceptive, the public interest from commercial persuasion, the objective and trustworthy from the biased or partisan". (Sonia Livingstone, London School of Economics, and Andrea Millwood Hargrave, UK Media literacy Task force). Also: "There exist many definitions of media literacy around the world. More and more often they include the ability 1) to access the media, 2) to understand/critically evaluate different aspects of the media and media contents, and 3) to create media contents/participate in the production process. It is not unusual that the definitions also include aspects of learning to use the media in order to participate in the process for social change, for development, towards increased democracy." (Cecilia Von Feilitzen, The International Clearinghouse on Children Youth and Media, Nordicom, Göteborg University).

16 According to John Pungente, media education "is concerned with helping students develop an informed and critical understanding of the nature of the mass media, the techniques used by them, and the impact of these techniques. More specifically, it is education that aims to increase students' understanding and enjoyment of how the media work, how they produce meaning, how they are organized, and how they construct reality. Media literacy also aims to provide students with the ability to create media products."

We see media education as a process and media literacy as the result of this process.

17 Digital literacy is a natural consequence of the spread of digital technologies and the promotion of information society. For a definition of digital literacy Cf.Pérez Tornero, José Manuel: Promoting Digital Literacy, European Commission.

18 "Media literacy, like print literacy before it, should be recognized as a key means, even a right, by which citizens participate in society and by which the state regulates the manner and purposes of citizens' participation" (Sonia Livingstone, "What is media literacy?" Media@else,

(http://www.lse.ac.uk/collections/media@lse/pdf/What_is_media_literacy.doc)

19 "Media education is a part of the fundamental right of each and every citizen of any country in the world to freedom of expression and the right to information, and is a tool for building and maintaining democracy". UNESCO: ibid. According to Sonia Livingstone, "Indeed, literacy is a concept grounded in a centuries-old struggle between enlightenment and critical scholarship, setting those who see literacy as democratising, empowering of ordinary people against those who see it as elitist, divisive, a source of inequality. Debates over literacy are, in short, debates about the manner and purposes of public participation in society. Cf., "What is media literacy?" Media@else, (http://www.lse.ac.uk/collections/media@lse/pdf/What_is_media_literacy.doc)

20 DG INFSO Commissioner Viviane Reding (Press release IP/06/1326, Brussels, 6 October 2006).

21 *Communication from the Commission to the European Parliament, the Council, the European Economic and Social Committee and the Committee of the Regions.*

A European approach to media literacy in the digital environment http://ec.europa.eu/avpolicy/media_literacy/docs/com/en.pdf

22 http://www.europarl.europa.eu/sides/getDoc.do?pubRef=-//EP//NONSGML+COMPARL+PE-402.864+01+DOC+PDF+V0//ES&language=ES0

23 http://www.europarl.europa.eu/meetdocs/2004_2009/documents/am/743/743320/743320en.pdf

Bibliography

Alvarado, M., Boyd-Barret. O. (Eds.) (1992). *Media Education: An introduction. London*: British Film Institute/The Open University.

Alvarado, M., Gutch, R., & Wollen, T. (1987). *Learning the media*. Houndmills: Macmillan Education.

Aufderheide, P. (1993). *Media literacy. A report of the National Leadership Conference on Media Literacy*. Washington, DC The Aspen Institute. Retrieved May 17, 2005. http://eric.ed.gov/ERICDocs/data/ericdocs2/content_storage_01/0000000b/80/24/78/a6.pdf

Baacke, D. (1979). "Medienpädagogik unter den Konstitutionsbedingungen sozialwissenschaftlicher und medientheoretischer Annahmen", in Wodraschke (Ed.): *Medienpädagogik und Kommunikationslehre*. München Ölschläger: pp.51–65.

Baacke, D. (1994). Jugendforschung und Medienpädagogik – Tendenzen, Diskussionsgesichtspunkte und Positionen, in SWOBODA, H. (Eds.): *Handbuch der Medienpädagogik. Leske+Budrich: Opladen* 1994; pp.37–57.

Bazalgette, C. (1992). Key Aspects of Media Education. In Alvarado, M. y Boyd-Barret. O. (Eds.): *Media education: An introduction*. London: British Film Institute/The Open University, pp.199–219.

—— (Ed.) (1989): *Primary media education: Curriculum statement*. London: British Film Institute, Educational Dept.

Bazalgette, C., Bevort, E., and Savino, J. (Eds.) (1992): *New directions: Media education worldwide*. London: British Film Institute.

Bevort, E. (1994). Esquisse d'un panorama de l'Éducation aux Médias. *Médias-Pouvoirs*, 35, 75–81.

Bevort, E. et Fremont, P. (2001): *Médias, violence et education*. Paris: CNDP.

BLK-Bund-Länder-Kommission für Bildungsplanung und Forschungsförderung (1995):. *Medienerziehung in der Schule*. Bonn: Orientierungsrahmen.

Bloemeke, S. (2003). *Medienpädagogische Kompetenz. Theoretische und empirische Fundierung eines zentralen Elements der Lehrerausbildung*. Munchen: KoPäd-Verl.

Brunner, C. (1999). *The new media literacy handbook*. New York: Anchor Books.

Brown, J. (1991). *Television critical viewing skills education: Major media literacy projects in the United States and selected countries*. Hillsdale: Lawrence Erlbaum Asscociates.

Buckingham, D. (2003). *Media Education: Literacy, learning, and contemporary culture*. Cambridge, U.K.: Polity Press.

—— (2003). New media, new sites of learning. Presentation for "Media Literacy – *Citizenship and Dialogue*": *Brussels* 28.1.03. Retreived May 17, 2007.

http://www.elearningeuropa.info/extras/pdf/brussels_media_literacy.pdf

Buckingham, D. (2004). *Nuevos medios, nuevos lugares de aprendizaje* (www.elearningeuropa.info/doc.php?lng=4&id=44- 26&doclng=4&p2=1) (02-02-04).

Buckingham, D. (ed.) (1990). *Watching media learning*. London: The Falmer Press.

Burton, Graeme (1990). *More than meets the eye: An introduction to media studies*. A Hodder Arnold Publication.

Calvani, A. (2001). *Educazione, comunicazione e nuovi media*. Torino: UTET.

Clemi/Academie De Bordeaux (Ed.) (2003). *Parcours médias au collège: Approches disciplinaires et transdisciplinaires*. Aquitaine: Sceren-CRDP.

Christ, W., & Potter, W. (1998, Winter). Media literacy, media education, and the academy, *Journal of Communication*, 48(1), 5–15.

http://www.blackwell-synergy.com/toc/jcom/48/1

Craggs, C. (1992). *Media education in the primary school*. London: Routledge.

Demo, W. (1986). *The Idea of information literacy in the age of high-tech*. New York: Tomkins Cortland Community College.

Devlin, B. (1997). *Conceptual models for network literacy*. Electronic Library.

http://www.emeraldinsight.com/journals.htm?articleid=1668324

Ebersbach, A., Glaser, M. (2004). Towards emancipatory use of a medium: The wiki, *International Journal of Information Ethics*, 2, 70–77.

http://www.i-r-i-e.net/issue_2.htm

Eshet, Yoram. (2002). Digital literacy: A new terminology framework and its application to the design of meaningful technology-based learning environments. *ED-MEDIA 2002 World Conference on Educational Multimedia, Hypermedia & Telecommunications. Proceedings*. Retrieved May 17, 2007.

http://eric.ed.gov/ERICDocs/data/ericdocs2sql/content_storage_01/0000019b/80/1b/17/fb.pdf

Ferguson, R. (2007). *los Medios bajo sospecha. Ideología y poder en los medios de comunicación*. Barcelona: Gedisa.

Fleming, Dan (1993). *Media teaching*. Oxford: Basil Blackwell.

FloreS-Koulish, S. (2005). *Teacher education for critical consumption of mass media and popular culture*. New York: Routledge/Falmer.

Galliani, L. (2002). Note introduttive. Appunti per una vera storia dell'educazione ai media, con i media, attraverso i media. In Galliani, L. & Maragliano, R. (Eds.) (2002), *Educazione ai media*, in *Studium Educationis*, 3, pp.563–576.

Giannatelli, R. (1996). La media education sbarca in Italia, Postfazione a Masterman. A scuola di media. *Brescia, La Scuola*; pp.111–120.

Gilster, P. (1997). *Digital literacy*, New York: Wiley.

Gonnet, J. (2001). *Education aux médias. Les controverses fécondes*. Paris: Hachette Education/CNDP.

Goodman, S. (2003). *Teaching youth media: A critical guide to literacy, video production, and social change*. New York: Teachers College Press.

Groeben, N. (2002). Dimensionen der Medienkompetenz. Deskriptive und normative Aspekte. In Groeben, N., & Hurrelmann, B. (Hrsg.), *Medienkompetenz. Voraussetzungen, Dimensionen, Funktionen*. München: Juventa, pp.160–197.

Gutiérrez Martín, A. (2003. *Alfabetización digital: algo más que ratones y teclados*. Barcelona: Gedisa.

Hart, Andrew (1991). *Understanding the media. A practical guide*. London: Routledge.

Heidel, A., Elke, D. (2004). *Guideline for media literacy in education*. European Centre for Media Literacy, ECML. Retrieved May 17, 2007. http://ecml.pc.unicatt.it/download/results/Guidelines%20for%20Media%20Literacy_v1.0_en.pdf

Heins, M., Cho, C. (2003). *Media literacy: An alternative to censorship*. (2nd ed.). Free Expression Policy Project. Retrieved May 17, 2007. http://www.fepproject.org/policyreports/medialiteracy.pdf

Hobbs, R., and Frost, R. (1999). Instructional practices in media literacy education and their impact on students' learning. *New Jersey Journal of Communication*, 6(2), 123–148.

http://www.reneehobbs.org/renee's%20web%20site/Publications/instructional_practices_in_media.htm

Jacquinot, G. (1998). Qu'est-ce qu'un éducommunicateur? Les places de la communication dans la formation d'un enseignenant du XXIéme siècle, in Congresso Multimedia e Educação em um mundo globalizado. São Paulo, *S&TM. Sciience & Technology Magazine*, 2 20–23 majo;

http://innovalo.scola.ac-paris.fr/Innovatio/innovatio4/educommunicateur.htm

Jonassen, D., Peck, K., and Wison, B. (1999). *Learning with technology: A constructivist Perspective*. Upper Saddle River, NJ, USA, Prentice Hall.

Kakolewicz, M. (1997). «Edukacja medialna w szkole ogolnokształcacej (Media education in general education), in STRYKOWSKI, W. (Eds.): *Media a edukacja*, publ. eMPi2.

KMK-Kultusministerkonferenz (1995): *Medienpädagogik in der Schule*. Bonn.

Kress, G. (2003): *Literacy in the new media age*. London. New York: Routledge.

Kubey, R. (1997). *Media Literacy in the information age: Current perspectives*. New Brunswick, NJ: Transaction.

http://search.epnet.com/login.aspx?direct=true&db=ufh&jid=Q94&lang=es

Kübler, H.D. (1994). Medienwissenschaft-Produktanalysen als Grundlage medienpädagogischen Urteilens und Handelns, en Hiegemann & Swoboda (Eds.): *Handbuch der Medienpädagogik*. Leske+Budrich: Opladen, 59–100.

Landesinstitut Fuer Schule (Hrsg.) (2004): *Medienkompetenz in Schule und Unterricht – MKSU*, in www.learn-line.- nrw.de/angebote/mksu (06-02-05).

Lanham, R. A. (1995). *Digital literacy*, scientific american.

Larsson, L (2002). *Digital literacy checklist, health services*. Seattle: University of Washington.

Lenox, M.; Walker, M. (1994). Information literacy: Challenge for the future. *NASSP Bulletin*. 78, pp.57–72.

http://bul.sagepub.com/cgi/content/abstract/78/562/57

Logan, R. (1995). *The fifth language*, Toronto, Stodart.

Masterman, L. (1985). *Teaching the media*. London, Comedia.

—— (1988). *Teaching about television*. London: MacMillan Education.

—— (1993). *La enseñanza de los medios de comunicación*. Madrid: Ediciones de la Torre.

Méndez, J.M., and Monescillo, M. (1994). «Orientación y acción tutorial con los medios». *Comunicar*, 71(2).

Méndez, J.M., Monescillo, M., and Aguaded, J.I. (1996). Orientación educativa para un consumo racional. *Comunicar*, 54(7).

Messina, L. (Ed.) (2005). *Andar per segni. Percorsi di educazione ai media*. Padova: Cleup.

Meyrowitz, J. (1998). Multiple media literacies. *Journal of Communication* 48(1), 96–108. http://www.blackwell-synergy.com/doi/ref/10.1111/j.1460-2466.1998.tb02740.x

OFCOM (2005). *Media literacy audit. Report on media literacy amongst children*, London: Office of Communication. Retreived May 17, 2007.

http://www.ofcom.org.uk/advice/media_literacy/medlitpub/medlitpubrss/children/children.pdf

Oliveira Soares, I. (2000). Educommunication: An emerging new field. *Telemedium*, the *Journal of Media Literacy*, 46 (1).

Ottaviano, C. (Ed.) (2001). *Mediare i media*. Milano, Franco Angeli.

Rivoltella, P. C. (1998): Come Peter Pan: Media, educazione, tecnologie oggi. Santhià: GS.

Pérez Tornero, J. M. (2000. *Comunicación y Educación en la Sociedad de la Información*. Barcelona (España): Paidos.

—— (2005). El futuro de la sociedad digital y la educación en medios, *Comunicar* 25, pp.247–258.

—— (2005). *Promoting Digital Literacy*. Brussels: European Commission.

Pielachowski, J., & Kakolewicz, M. (1999). *Program nauczania edukacji czytelniczej i medialnej* (Curriculum of reading and media education). Poznan: eMPi2.

Potter, W. (1998). *Media literacy*. Thousand Oaks, CA.: SAGE Publications

—— .(2004). *Theory of media literacy: a cognitive approach*. Thousand Oaks, CA: Sage Publications, 2004

QvarselL, B. (1998). Studying media and information techniques as educological phenomena. A new research field within education. In Vygotskij, L.S. (Ed.): *Psykologi och dialektik*. (I urval av L-C Hydén). Stockholm: Norstedts.

Ramonet, I. (2000). *La golosina visual*. Madrid: Debate.

Reyzábal, M.V. and Sanz, A.I. (1995). Los ejes transversales: Aprendizajes para la vida. Madrid. Escuela Española.

Reia-baptista, V. (1995). Contribuciones para una pedagogía de la comunicación. *Tarbiya*, 11, 31–44.

Reia-Baptista, V. (2003). *Pedagogia dos media, O caso das linguagens fílmicas na pedagogia da comunicação*. Faro: Universidad del Algarve.

Rivoltella, P.C., & Marazzi, C. (2001). *Le professioni della media education*, Roma: Carocci.

—— (2001). *Media education. Modelli, esperienze, profilo disciplinare*. Roma: Carocci.

—— (2005). *Media education. Fondamenti didattici e prospetttive di ricerca*. Brescia: La Scuola.

—— (2006). *Screen generation. Gli adolescenti e le prospettive dell'educazione*. Milano: Vita, Pensiero.

Salzano, D. (Ed.) (2000). Comunicazione ed educazione, *in Incontro di due culture, Isola dei ragazzi*. Napoli.

Savino, J., Marmiesse, C., and Bensa, F. (2005). *L'éducation aux médias de la maternelle au lycée. Direction de l'Enseignement Scolaire*. Paris: Ministère de l'Education Nationale, Sceren/CNDP, Témoigner.

Schaun, A. (2002). *Praticas educomunicativas*, Rio de Janeiro: MAUAD.

Schorb, B. (1995). *Medienalltag und Handeln. Medienpädagogik in Geschichte, Forschung und Praxis.* Opladen.

Silverblatt, A., and Eliceiri, E. (1997). *Dictionary of Media Literacy.* Westport, CT: Greenwood.

Silverblatt, A., Zoblin, N. (2004). *International communications: A media literacy approach.* Armonk, New York: M.E. Sharpe.

Spanhel, D., and Tulodziecki, G. (2001). *Rahmenkonzept für neue Medien im Lehramtsstudium.* Basis.

Strykowski, W. (1996). Pedagogika medialna i technologia ksztalcenia jako nauki o mediach (*Educational Technology and Media Pedagogy as Sciences of Media*). Poznan: Neodidagmata, XXII.

—— (1997). Pedagogika medialna (Media Pedagogy). *Edukacja Medialna*, 4(97).

—— (Eds.) (2001). Scenariusze zajec z edukacja medialnej (Scenarios of media education lessons). Poznan: eMPi2.

Takenouchi, T. (2004). A Consideration on the Concept of Information Literacy. Is it really 'necessary for all?. *Journal of Information Ethics*, (2) 255–260.

http://www.i-r-i-e.net/inhalt/002/ijie_002_full.pdf

Theunert, H. (1996). Multi-Medienpädagogik, in Medienerziehung, 40. Jahrgang, 96(1), 24–29.

Thoman, E., Jolls, T. (2005). Media literacy education: Lessons from the center for media literacy. In: Schwartz, G., and Brown, P. (Eds.), *Media literacy: Transforming curriculum and teaching* (104) pp. 180 –205. Malden, MA: National Society for the Study of Education.

http://www.nsse-chicago.org/yearbooks.asp?cy=2005

Tulodziecki, G., and Herzig, B. (2004). Medien in Lehr-und Lernprozessen. *Mediendidaktik*

—— (1997). Medien in Erziehung und Bildung. Grundlagen und Beispiele einer handlungs-und entwicklungsorientierten, *in Medienpädagogik*. 3. Aufl, Bad Heilbrunn.

—— (2005). Zur Situation der Medienpädagogik in der Bundesrepublik Deutschland, in Online-Zeitschrif, *in MedienPädagogik* (5): 1–44.

Tulodziecki, G. Six, U. & AL. (2000). *Medienerziehung in der Grundschule. Grundlagen, empirische Befunde und Empfehlungen zur Situation in Schule und Lehrerbildung.* Opladen: Leske + Budrich Verlag.

Tyner, K. (1995). *Aprender con los medios de comunicación: curso de iniciación.* Madrid : Ediciones de la Torre.

Varios (2004). Sobre a violencia nos medios de comunicación: Unha educación necesaria: unidade didáctica, 22. Santiago de Compostela, Seminario Galego de Educación para a Paz.

Von feilitzen, C., and Carlsson, U. (Eds.) (1999). *Children and media. image, education, participation*, Göteborg (Suecia), UNESCO/Göteborg University.

Von feilitzen, Cecilia, and Carlsson, Ulla (Eds.) (2003). *Promote or protect? Perspectives on media literacy and media regulations.* Nordicom, in The International Clearinghouse on Children, Youth and Media, Göteborg University.

Worsnop, Chris (1999). *Screening images: Ideas for media education.* Ontario: Wright Communications.

Declarations

UNESCO (1982): *Challenge of Media Education (The Grunwald Document). International Symposium on Media Education*. Grunwald, Federal Republic of Germany, 1982.

http://www.medialit.org/reading_room/article133.html

Thoman, E. (1990): New Directions in Media Education. *International Conference on Media Education* at the University of Toulouse, France / July, 1990.

http://www.medialit.org/reading_room/article126.html

UNESCO (1999): *Recommendations. The Vienna Conference 'Educating for the Media and the Digital Age'*, 1990.

http://www.mediamanual.at/en/downloads.php
http://mediamanual.at/en/pdf/recommendations.pdf

UNESCO (2002): *Recommendations. Seville Conference "Youth Media Education"*, 2002.

www.coe.int/t/e/human_rights/media/links/events/1DraftVersionFReport_youthmediaeduc_en.pdf

UNESCO (2002) : *Recommendations. Tunis Mentor meeting.*

http ://www.unesco.ru/eng/pages/bythemes/stasya13072005122812.php

WSMCA (2004): *The Rio de Janeiro Charter: Media from All, Media for All. The 4th World Summit on Media for Children and Adolescents* in Rio de Janeiro, Brazil, April 19–23, 2004

http://www.unesco.ru/rus/pages/bythemes/stasya27012005172048.php

MENTOR ASSOCIATION (2004): *Recommendations. Media Education Seminar at the World Forum of Cultures*, Barcelona, Spain.

EU Documents and Studies

Study on the current trends and approaches on Media Literacy in Europe http://www.mediamentor.org/files/attachments/Study_Media_Literacy_in_Europe_0.pdf

José Manuel Pérez Tornero, European Commission, Promoting digital Literacy, http://ec.europa.eu/education/archive/elearning/doc/studies/dig_lit_en.pdf

Marianne Miko, Communication, http://www.europarl.europa.eu/sides/getDoc.do?pubRef=-//EP//NONSGML+COMPARL+PE-402.864+01+DOC+PDF+V0//ES&language=ES

Christa Prets, Communication 'Media Literacy in a Digital World', http://www.europarl.europa.eu/meetdocs/2004_2009/documents/am/743/743320/743320en.pdf

CHAPTER 9

An Alternative Perspective on Curriculum Planning

Georgios Grollios

This chapter is concerned with an analysis of the main perspectives on curriculum planning, which contributed to the formation of the field of curriculum studies in the USA. This analysis becomes the basis for discussing certain positions of an alternative perspective on curriculum planning that is differentiated from the perspectives that have dominated the field. Such a perspective may be important for the development of an alternative approach towards the pursuit of digital literacy that could be responsive to issues and concerns related to the reproduction of social inequalities, power relations, and dominant ideology.

While new technologies have found their way to more and more homes, the more sophisticated tools still remain out of reach due not only to their high cost, but also to the required cultural and knowledge capital that is needed in order to use these new technologies. Firstly is the agenda of access, the range of available technologies as tools, which is inadvertently linked to materialistic conditions. Secondly is the code of access, that is, the cultural capital and discourses necessary to negotiate both the meaning as well as the contents of the agenda of access. The code of access necessarily includes multiple layers of literacy practices. These two factors are mutually informing and dependent upon each other, in that, even if access to new technological tools is granted in technical terms, one still needs the required educational and cultural capital to break through both operationally and discursively. At the same time, somebody who has acquired the discourse necessary to negotiate new media still requires the actual tool in order to materialize access. There are groups situated in the two poles of this reality that have differential degrees of access since access depends on discursive and material resources. Access to new information technologies is further heavily divided along demographic, socioeconomic, and cultural factors.

Also, there is a blind celebration of technological hype as the apotheosis of progress and liberation. ICTs are romanticized and given an illusionary status. Information technology is already thoroughly permeated with such capitalist values as: a tough aggressive individualism, an intensely competitive ethos, commodified images, and an instrumental rationality. The new information/communication technologies are not emancipatory tools by default. Blind over-celebration of new technologies not only fails to link them to real life, it also promotes an instrumentalization of knowledge that has the potential to colonize virtually every realm of social space.

From a critical perspective the traditional meaning of the word *literacy*, as the ability to read and write is rooted in an instrumental/functional ideology that privileges "useful knowledge" through a process of rote memorization of what is deemed worthy. Steeped in positivism, it assumes, pedagogy of transmission where instruction is decontextualized and the audience is passive. In the mainstream educational and public discourse, literacy captures what a given society deems important in terms of knowledge, representations, cultural capital and social experiences. This view situates the responsibility for literacy within the individual person and not within society, since a given society imposes its standards and norms and the individual is called upon to comply. If he/she fails to do so, it is the individual's virtues, skills, capacities and ultimately, his/her character that are called into question and not the way society structures its literacy norms along power hierarchies. Given the inherent instrumentality of technology, a functional approach in the context of the new information and communication technologies means ignoring how particular types of knowledge are reproduced and produced through new media/means of dissemination, who has access to them, and how this information is used beyond skills training. Literacy as simply the acquisition of mechanical skills limits the arena of interpretation and understanding of meaning negotiation.

Literacy should not be viewed as a form of verbalism reduced to a mere codification and decodification of the word decontextualized from the world. Literacy should be the individual's act of reading, decoding, interpreting, producing, and transforming a text that takes on specific meanings in diverse social contexts. This "act" is both action and interaction as it necessarily works on both an individual and a collective level, which are dialectically intertwined. Obviously, this notion of literacy is politicized and invested with ideological meaning since it can produce cultural, political and discursive significations, or reproduce canons, oppressive relations and power asymmetries.[1]

There is no doubt that the conception of literacy that is being used in the context of formal education is represented in the content of the school curriculum. Thus, any conception of literacy, and in particular, any conception of digital literacy that confronts the issues of social inequalities, power relations, and dominant ideology cannot be developed and implemented in the context of curricula that have been planned on the basis of perspectives for curriculum planning that ignore the importance of these issues. Consequently, the importance of considering and developing an alternative perspective towards curriculum planning, that will correspond to such a conception of digital literacy, is obvious.

Curriculum planning refers to a process of organization and synthesis of the structural elements of the curriculum. It is this process that gives meaning to the word *planning*. As a matter of fact, when we speak about curriculum planning we can only refer to a sequence of phases. Furthermore, the process of curriculum planning does not take place automatically but presupposes the existence of the individual or collective subjects that define it. As a result, the concept of curriculum planning is inseparably linked to the process (steps or phases of planning) and the subjects that define this process. Moreover, the concept of curriculum planning is very closely connected to a specific selection of curriculum structural elements. Since any planning process is meaningless without defining the structural elements involved, it is necessary to include here a specific definition of the structural elements that will be used in our analysis. Therefore, we can conclude that the concept *curriculum planning* refers to the process, the subjects that define it, and the selected structural elements of the curriculum.

In this chapter, the term curriculum refers to two structural elements: the goals and the content. I consider these two elements integral to curriculum as a component of pedagogical practice. Goals and content are the two essential elements that any curriculum should contain. Any form of pedagogical practice, because of its sociopolitical nature, is characterized by its incorporation into a sociopolitical strategy that is epitomized by goals and refers to content that mediates between the subjects of the educational process and is approached by them. The content of a curriculum, irrespective of its substance, form, and organization, is essential for the realization of the goals. Other components of pedagogical practices (teaching aids and teaching styles, assessment processes and forms), even though closely related to curriculum, may be studied without being taken into consideration in this process. This means that the curriculum might not necessarily contain them as its integral structural elements. In this sense, goals and content constitute the core of the curriculum concept.

On the basis of the above mentioned considerations, it is essential to clarify that in this chapter the term *curriculum planning* refers to positions regarded with the process, that is, the sequence of the curriculum planning phases and the subjects defining it, as well as its integral structural elements, namely, the goals and the content. Undoubtedly, this is a set of positions that interact with each other and they cannot be considered as ideologico-politically neutral. On the other hand, the term *perspective*—when referring to curriculum planning—entails a specific theoretical and practical approach to the issue of curriculum planning. Having a deontological rather than a descriptive character, this term refers to a number of standpoints concerned with the way in which a curriculum should be planned.

In the USA, curriculum studies became a special field at the beginning of the 20th century, a period in which a variety of curriculum planning perspectives appeared. Later on and in particular during the second half of that century, these perspectives influenced both curriculum theory and practice in other countries. For example, Bloom's taxonomy of educational objectives spread quickly in continental Europe, the Mediterranean and Middle East after 1956.[2] However, it is necessary to add that, when a perspective born within a specific social context spreads to a different social context, this is not accomplished without any changes. For example, the movement for curriculum reform in the United States at the end of the 1950s influenced education in Great Britain, even though it was introduced into a different context and took different forms.[3]

It is not my intention to underestimate the development of the curriculum field in other countries, but apart from what is already mentioned, there are two more reasons that justify my preference to refer to the American curriculum. Firstly, curriculum theory and practice are widely debated in the USA, mainly because of the historical formation of its political and educational systems. In general terms, both of these systems did not hinder educational innovations in a direct way, nor did they limit curriculum decision making to the level of central political authority. This is fairly evident until the end of the 1950s, amid rapid and wide economic, social and ideological changes.[4] The second reason relates to the systematic study of both the history of curriculum, which after the 1970s offers some remarkably well-documented studies on the curriculum debate, as well as to a number of recent studies which offer important holistic approaches to the formation of the curriculum field in the United States.

The Main Perspectives on Curriculum Planning

By the end of the 19th century the traditional perspective towards curriculum planning was dominant in the United States. The main aim of this perspective was to maintain the existing organization of a society, based on the established economic and political liberalism. According to this, curriculum content should be founded on classical tradition, i.e., subjects such as Greek, Latin and Geometry, which were considered appropriate for building rational thought. Faculty psychology, according to which the brain resembled a muscle that developed with exercise, contributed to the definition of curriculum content based on classical tradition. As a consequence, the planning process was primarily the task of those who had expertise in these fields.[5]

At the dawn of the 20th century, however, the economic and social changes were enormous. The Unites States had already been transformed from a rural to an industrial society, big cities had been established through internal and external migration and there was an enormous concentration of production and wealth. This concentration of both production and wealth was evident in the emergence of growing corporate mergers, which is a characteristic representative of the transition to monopolistic capitalism, a process of key importance.

These changes, of course, cannot be considered in isolation from the intricate class struggles that constituted a visible danger to the ruling social classes. As a consequence of the formation of power relationships between capital and labor forces, the first three decades of the century were characterized by a period of reforms, the so-called progressive era (1900–1918) as well as a period of increasing capital profitability, intensified social and political oppression and empowerment of conservative ideas—the so-called *golden age* (1918–1929)—which was surprisingly interrupted by the Great Depression. Progressive education was a movement for educational reform. Its beginning and development were associated with the changes and conflicts mentioned above. It was expressed in many different realms of the educational process and its basic political orientation was the creation of a society that would be exemplified for its harmony, economic stability and growth; an "organic" society, in which the interests of both capital and labor forces would coincide[6].

Until the 1930s, four perspectives on curriculum planning were put forward, revised versions of which are still formulated nowadays. The *social efficiency* perspective was first formulated by Bobbit at the beginning of the golden age in 1918, and it signalled the creation of the field of curriculum studies in the United States. Drawing from Thorndike's behaviourism, Ross's approach of social control, and Taylor's scientific management, Bobbit formed a perspective which became the basis for Tyler's rationale as well as Bloom's and

Mager's proposals and theoretical standpoints, which largely affected the post-war views and practices on curriculum planning.

This perspective was founded on the political goal of increasing the efficiency of the existing capitalist socio-economic organization by means of reducing waste and the subsequent educational goal of peoples' adjustment to this organization. Its departure point for the identification of curriculum content was the formulation of concise, clear and detailed teaching objectives that had to correspond to adult activities whose achievement could be measured. Curriculum planning was an issue to be dealt by the curriculum experts. These experts, starting from the definition of objectives, had to design relevant series of experiences for the learners to acquire, by using scientifically objective processes.[7] It is obvious that the perspective of social effectiveness employed a different starting point for the identification of curriculum content which did not take into consideration the ways learners perceive social reality. Adversely, it was a perspective that in fact advocated the absolute domination of curriculum experts in the planning process, whose decisions were thought to be socio-politically neutral.

There are considerable differences between the social efficiency and the child-centered perspectives in curriculum planning, the latter being formulated mainly by Hall at the end of the 19th century. Child-centered practices had been reinforced in the field of curriculum studies around the end of 1920s. It was about this time that Counts wrote, with regard to Hall's perspective, that it was founded on the individualism of the liberal upper-middle class, whose members were indifferent to the social problems and social injustice but were interested in the everyday tangible comforts of life and their own children's success. Both the political goal of this perspective, which was strived towards the natural development of the child, and its starting point with respect to the identification of curriculum's content, which was based on the child's natural impulses, had a romantic character. In the context of the child-centered perspective, the child was perceived as an entirety of natural inclinations. Furthermore, the differentiation of the curriculum content was based on intellectual provisions, as well as other genetically determined characteristics, such as social gender, and its implementation was left in the hands of child study experts.[8]

Dewey's perspective on curriculum planning, which was implemented at the Laboratory School in Chicago from 1896 to 1904, aimed at the expansion of democracy to every sector of culture in combination with the development/diffusion of scientific thought and the thoughtful coordination of industrial growth. The American liberal educator and pragmatist philosopher did not transcend the boundaries of reforms that converged in building a harmonious society of economic stability and growth, i.e., a society where there would be no socio-political conflicts, alias an "organic" society. According to Dewey, the ultimate educational goal of the curriculum is students' adjustment to the existing social functions and their contribution to the reform of the socio-economic and political regime. Dewey's perspective entailed a kind of unity between what were considered to be a child's natural inclinations, on the one hand, and expert knowledge of the disciplines and social occupations that served basic human needs on the other. He approached the problem of determining the curriculum content and its organization on the basis of the unity between these two elements, i.e., on the basis of a relationship. In Dewey's perspective, however, the experts were influenced only by the way they themselves perceived children's natural inclinations.[9]

The absolute dependence on teachers and experts, who would play a decisive role in the creation of an education powerful enough to bring about social change, characterized the perspective of social reconstruction. This viewpoint had been expressed by Ward's adherence to the importance of cultural capital distribution via education, a condition necessary for the achievement of social progress. Counts, who was the most important representative of this perspective, espoused this position, for as he stated, teachers could lead social reform by representing not the interests of the moment or the interests of a particular social class, but rather the common and constant interests of the people. In this respect, teachers could renovate education into a force of social rebirth and convert schools into centers for study and for the creation of a new culture. Brameld, the post-war representative of social reconstructionism, also supported these ideas by claiming that the common goal of all proposals for social reform was the establishment of a public planning strategy that would work only if people desired cultural rebirth.

The perspective of *social reconstruction* towards curriculum planning challenged the conservative political goals of the *child-centered* and the *social effectiveness* perspectives as well as the inefficacy and the inhumane nature of capitalism which were considered to be obvious after the 1929 depression. Apparently, the Great Depression constituted a precondition for the formulation of the social reconstruction perspective that followed after a decade of criticisms referring to certain characteristics of American education. It stressed the dangers of the complete destruction of culture in the post–cold war era and suggested that technology should be free of restrictions or demands for any kind of privilege, and it should serve the popular masses. However, as far as its political and educational goals were concerned, it did not transcend the boundaries of the progressive education movement that gave birth to this perspective. Nevertheless, it did extend the boundaries of social reform that progressive education demanded in a period of socio-economic crisis. In the context of the social reconstruction perspective, the starting point for the identification of curriculum content was aimed at broadening the curriculum content, so that it did not only refer to all aspects of modern society but also to the solution of social problems in the direction of creating a new culture.[10]

The comparison of the perspectives towards curriculum planning that were formulated in the United States during the post-war era is more facile than the comparison of the ones expressed in the first forty years of the 20th century. The former were articulated after the war and in revised versions, and in this respect they occupy an important part of modern theory and practice in this field. The traditional perspective will find its successors in the work of Adler, A. Bloom and Hirsch. The work of Tyler, B. Bloom and Mager and that of the representatives of "life adjustment education" will be based on the theoretical starting points of Bobbit's social effectiveness perspective. The followers of the child-centered perspective will support similar standpoints to the ones defended at the beginning of the century, in the endeavour of alternative schools. The social-reconstruction perspective was revised by Brameld and Dewey's ideas, which were utilized in the planning of curricula that were based on action research and school experimentations, such as the Coalition of Essential Schools.[11]

The new phase of post-war capitalist development in the United States resulted in the differentiation of the labor force and the transition of a part of it to skilled service personnel. The main characteristics of this development were capital accumulation, the decline of traditional forms of industry, rapid technological growth and its usage in the service of capitalist production. This development and the expansion of the international economic, political, ideological and military influence of the U.S., did not occur without conflict. The basic objective of the dominant social forces was to achieve a form of social and educational consensus that would point towards a closer connection between education and capitalist development as well as the effective control of education. This could be accomplished on the basis of a common framework and objective evaluation standards that demanded a curriculum with a wide scope but little depth,[12] and it was mainly facilitated by the new versions of the social effectiveness perspective for curriculum planning which had emerged in the war period and was at its peak in the first post-war years.

The launch of the Sputnik at the end of the 1950s caused a shock that was experienced by the dominant socio-political forces, and initiated the appearance of another perspective. This perspective attempted to satisfy the criticism of American academics against the depreciation of the importance of certain disciplines. Fundamentally, it attempted to comply with the government's pronouncement to nominate education as a national defence issue, and to establish a national curriculum framework that would place emphasis on technology, mathematics and the sciences.[13] Bruner, based on the findings of the 1959 Woods Hall conference, founded this perspective of curriculum planning.

Bruner's perspective was founded on the political goal of adapting education to the new needs of capitalist development and empowering the United States in the cold war competition. The improvement of teaching efficiency through the approach of the student as a scientist, who had to actively participate in the understanding of the basic structures of each discipline, was associated with considering the whole student population as a reservoir from which some could work their way up to the top of the scientific and technological communities. Thus, these students could become useful to the United States in assuming the leading international roles at an economic, military, political and cultural level.

The emphasis on learning the structure of disciplines was considered a necessary precondition for achieving the above and constituted the starting point for the identification of curriculum content. The position, according to which it is possible to teach the basic principles of all subjects to all students of all ages in an appropriate form, was the basic position for content organization, leading to the design of a spiral curriculum to examine in depth the structures of disciplines. Research could trigger the interest of the "gifted" students without discouraging those "less favoured by nature". As a consequence, the role of the academics that had expertise in the disciplines, became dominant in curriculum planning.[14]

The development of the research spirit and active learning that characterized Bruner's perspective resembled at that specific time and place, Dewey's ideas, thus expanding its influence. Moreover, the emphasis on the structures of disciplines that Bruner's perspective entailed did not contradict the post-war versions of social effectiveness despite the fact that one of the causes of its creation had been the academic criticism towards "life adjustment education".

Within the context of our use of the term *curriculum planning* and to the best of our knowledge, after the 1960s there was no other distinctly different perspective from the ones mentioned above on curriculum planning in the United States. In the 1960s the perspective of learning according to the structure of disciplines was significantly reinforced, having the full support of federal government funding. Federal governments turned mainly to university projects for the instruction of subjects such as physics, mathematics, chemistry, and biology. The movement for the reform of the national curriculum focused on the alignment of secondary education subjects to the academic fields of higher education and the establishment of academic rigor in schools.

To achieve the aforementioned reform, the design and implementation of the curriculum had to be removed from the educators. It was the beginning of a process that was bound to continue in the next decades and included, as its basic component, the shift of the emphasis from local attempts to adjust the curriculum to a kind of centrally controlled reform. In other words, the reinforcement of the role of the central political authority upon controlling the curriculum of schools throughout the country resulted in the appearance and expansion of the use of the so-called teacher-proof curricula.

However, the 1960s was a decade of controversy and social struggles in the United States. The movements for the social and political rights of black people and women, the movement of youth contestation and opposition to the Vietnam War had shaken the country. During the same decade, the formation of the curriculum was being questioned, relating to the wider social, political and ideological dispute and search for alternative solutions.

The dominant paradigms of behaviourism and scientism received the first heterogeneous attacks, which culminated in criticism of the static and limited character of the field. Criticism on educational operations first came to light alongside the radical growth of interest in: various forms of progressive education and research and the pedagogic practices connected to it, in Marxism, in humanistic psychology, in reforming the up to that time prevalent/accepted views in the history of education and in the relations of all these to the theory and practice of the curriculum field. At the beginning of the 1970s it was common ground that the field was in crisis. The disposition to challenge the above, along with downgrading the importance of the work on planning, implementing and evaluating the curriculum so as to guide those working in schools, were among the reasons that led to the so-called reconceptualization of the field.

The term *reconceptualization* is, in my opinion, an exaggeration because the main foundations of the field did not change. So I use the term "movement for the reconceptualization of the curriculum field" which, on the one hand, does not underestimate the relevant confrontations briefly mentioned here and, on the other, does not signify that the curriculum field is a completely new field after 1970. Nonetheless, it was a movement, which, of course, did not mean that traditional work disappeared.

During and following the 1980s, schools were increasingly controlled by businessmen, politicians, bureaucrats and "social engineers", who, mostly attempted to adjust them to the neo-liberal and neo-conservative doctrines that dominated, by taking advantage of the consequences of the economic crisis and the political weakness of the social movements. In the absence of any political will to deal with the issue, experts in the curriculum field tried to remove it from schools and focused on comprehending its complexity. Even though the already loosely connecting bonds of the reconceptualization movement decayed, its influence on the formation of the field was considerable and it could be traced in the ways scholars comprehend the curriculum (as a political, racial, phenomenological, post-structuralist, deconstructed, post-modern, autobiographical-biographical, aesthetic, theological and international text, as well as a text of social gender).[15]

Positions of an Alternative Perspective

An alternative perspective towards curriculum planning must be founded on political and educational goals that are considerably differentiated from the goals of the perspectives that dominated the field of curriculum studies. Such a political goal is the deepening and the expansion of democracy in the context of a wider social transformation with a socialist orientation. In this context and in an age of minimized fundamental political rights and civil liberties in the name of security,[16] the need to support democracy cannot be perceived as the sole concern of political institutions.

The deepening of democracy is linked with changes of the social relations of power. The educational goal which corresponds to such a political aim is the contribution of education to producing citizens who can analyze the social reality they live in, with the ultimate aim to understand and transform this reality. Given that social reality is formed by multiple factors, and among these factors the social, political and ideological conflicts are of most importance, the skills needed to make citizens capable to analyze the world are related to how education deals with the matter of conflict. An education that supports the critical analysis of social reality must not be afraid of referring to any kind of conflict, because citizens belong to social classes and social groups that play the main role in the struggles that change social reality.

Social reality's critical analysis that is connected with social transformation cannot be approached as an abstraction. It must be founded on the forms of social reality that the students themselves experience on an everyday basis, and on the culture they bring to school. When teachers, who support the dominant pedagogy, offer a prepackaged analysis of social reality to students as a given, this is usually accepted in a passive way by the majority of students. But if teachers study the students' knowledge, ideas and practices that have been developed in a concrete cultural context, critical analysis and social change may be meaningful for them.

Founding critical understanding of social reality on the basis of students' culture does not imply that teachers and specialists of various disciplines will not contribute to the identification and selection of curriculum content. A curriculum that contains as its central political goal the deepening and expansion of democracy in the context of a wider social transformation with a socialist orientation needs to use a wide range of knowledge from the disciplines. This curriculum must organize knowledge in such forms that will allow students to learn the basic knowledge of every discipline via approaching the conflicting views inside every discipline and the struggles concerning the social use of that knowledge. Democracy is expanded in school when students learn the conflicting views, and they can make conscious choices. These are preconditions in order to challenge the dominant ideology that is usually presented and established as a dogma in school. Evidently, the aforementioned processes and standpoints must be linked with collective work and dialogue.

The basic knowledge of every discipline must be connected to the social and historical context that has promoted its development. In this perspective, the link between knowledge and labor is of most importance, because labor is crucial for the organization of society and is a main source of knowledge. This does not mean that we should give emphasis to the scientific and technical knowledge while underestimating humanistic knowledge and values. A dialectic synthesis of these two forms of knowledge is both a necessity and a requirement. The critical analysis of social reality that is connected to political action and supports the value of solidarity, is essential for learning scientific and technical knowledge and for the development of citizens' capability to organize and manage the processes of production that are related to the deepening and expansion of democracy.

The position for using a wide range of knowledge from the disciplines does not mean that an alternative curriculum contains the traditional view for the organization of knowledge in school, e.g., the division of content to subject matters that usually correspond to a discipline. This division is antithetical to the need for founding curriculum's content on students' culture, and it contributes to the reproduction of unequal relations of power and of dominant ideology, because the curriculum becomes alien for the majority of the students who come from the working class. Thus, the content of an alternative curriculum should be organized on the basis of themes that would be studied by teachers and students, who would use knowledge from every discipline posing relevant questions. The answers to these questions should be used for posing new questions needed for studying new issues.

The aforementioned process implies a certain structuring of curriculum that gives the opportunity to connect theory with a variety of practices inside and outside school. These practices may contribute to developing students' abilities to understand critically the social life they experience daily, and thus, develop their ability to change it. In this instance, the transformation of the daily experienced social life refers to certain problems that students confront in the context of their community, and to the wider sociopolitical context that determine the conditions of their lives. Thus, students may relate knowledge to their own action with the aim to change the social reality they experience.

Based on the above, we can conclude that the content of an alternative curriculum should not and cannot be strictly predetermined. Its selection should be founded on, mainly, three principles: a) using the conflicts, b) using the forms of social reality that the students themselves experience on an everyday basis and the culture they bring to school, and c) linking theory to practice.

Substantial participation is the key principle that should characterize the process of planning an alternative curriculum. Teachers, representatives of the community, discipline specialists and students have the right to participate in curriculum planning. The perspectives for curriculum planning that dominated the field of curriculum studies do not recognize this right, and the necessary dialogue about the curriculum is being reduced to a conversation among curriculum experts. Apparently, a substantial dialogue must be founded on the collective research of social and cultural reality, and on the ways students perceive this reality, as well as on systematic experimental implementation of different versions of the alternative curriculum. Of course, teachers and specialists, who have a wider horizon of aims, knowledge and experience than students, would play a crucial role and they would take up more responsibilities in the process of curriculum planning. For example, the selection and organization of the sources coming from different disciplines which would be used for studying various issues should be performed mainly by teachers and specialists. In this kind of process of curriculum planning students participate, yet their participation is not based on a conception of fetishizing children's interests that undervalues the teacher's role and the importance of the main elements of disciplines, as well as the social struggles about the uses of knowledge.

Such an alternative perspective may be important for the development of an equally alternative approach towards digital literacy that could effectively confront problems concerned with the reproduction of social inequalities, power relations, and dominant ideology. This happens because such an alternative perspective is founded on both the critique of the naïve position that education is the key for all the social transformations and of the mechanistic position that education becomes important to consider only after the radical transformation of society's substructure. Education is not the key, but no social transformation can be done without education's transformation. And curriculum planning is crucial for the transformation of education.

Notes

1 See Gounari (2009).

2 See Lewy & Bathory (1994, pp.146–163).

3 Holt (1979, pp. 6–7).

4 For more details on the diversity of experimentation in US public schools at the beginning of the 20th century, see Reese (2000, pp. 276–281).

5 See Schubert et al. (2002, pp. 7).

6 See Urban-Wagoner (2000, pp. 201–202), Gonzalez (1986, pp. 28–29, 53–67).

7 See Kliebard (1995, pp. 78–85, 90, 99, 194), Kliebard (1999, pp. 49), Marsh and Willis (2003, p. 43–44).

8 See Kliebard (1995, pp. 35–44), Pinar et al. (2002, pp. 83–87), Counts (1978, pp. 3–7, 25–28, 33–44), Rasis (2003, pp. 4–6).

9 For more details on Dewey's perspective see Macpherson (1994, pp. 110–112), Carr-Hartnett (1997, pp. 60), Karier (1973, pp. 97–99, 104–106), Karier (2002, pp. 85–86), Archambault (1965, pp. vi), Mayhew-Edwards (1965, pp. viii, ix, xiii, 4, 20, 23, 36, 40–41), Schutz (2001, pp. 273–279), Jackson (1990, pp. xxix–xxx).

10 As regards curriculum planning in the social reconstruction perspective see Kliebard (1995, pp. 21–25, 158–162, 171–175), Kliebard (2002, pp. 64–65), Counts (1978, pp. 3–7, 25–28, 33–44), Brameld (1956, pp. vi–vii, 4–5, 31, 160, 166–167, 170, 197–199, 211).

11 See Shor (1992, p.119–122), Beane (1990, pp. 37–38), Pinar et al. (2002, pp. 661–699), Schubert et al. (2002, pp. 261, 382–391).

12 See Noutsos (1983, pp. 43--55).

13 See Rasis (2004, pp. 360–363).

14 See Flouris (2000, pp. 28), Bruner (1960, pp. 26–29), Kliebard (1995, pp. 228–230), Pinar (2004, pp. 7).

15 For more details on the reconceptualization of the curriculum field see Apple (1993, pp. 15–23), Apple (2001, pp. 47–89), Pinar et al. (2002, pp. 159–239), Schumbert et al. (2002, pp. 193–195), Pinar (2004, pp. 72), Marsh-Willis (2003, pp. 249–252).

16 See Giroux (2004).

Bibliography

Apple, M. (1993). Official Knowledge: Democratic Education in a Conservative Age. New York: Routledge

Apple, M. (2001). Eksinhronismos kai sintiritismos stin ekpaidefsi, (Modernization and Conservatism in Education) translation in Greek Deligianni, Athens: M., Metaihmio.

Archambault, R. (1965). Editor's Foreword in Mayhew, K., and - Edwards, A. *The Dewey School: The Laboratory School of the University of Chicago 1896–1903*. New York: Atherton Press

Beane, J. (1990). *Affect in the Curriculum. Toward Democracy, Dignity, and Diversity*. New York:Teachers College Press.

Brameld, T. (1956). *Toward a Reconstructed Philosophy of Education*. New York: The Dryden Press.

Bruner, J. (1960). I Diadikasia tis Paideias, (*The Process of Schooling*), translation in Greek Kliridi, H. Athens: Karavias.

Carr, W., and Hartnett, A. (1997). *Education and the Struggle for Democracy. The politics of Educational Ideas*: Buckingham: Open University Press.

Counts, G. (1978). *Dare the School Build a New Social Order?* Carbondale: Southern Illinois University Press.

Flouris, G. (2000). Analytika Programmata gia mia Nea Epohi stin Ekpaidefsi (*Curricula for a New Era in Education*). Athens: Grigoris.

Giroux, H. (2004). *The Terror of Neoliberalism. Authoritarianis and the Eclipse of Democracy*. Boulder. CO: Paradigm Publishers

Gonzalez, G. (1986). *Progressive Education: A Marxist Interpretation*, Minneapolis: Marxist Educational Press.

Gounari, P. (2009). Rethinking Critical Literacy in the New Information Age. *Critical Inquiry in Language Studies*, 3(6), 148–175.

Holt, M.(1979). *Regenerating the Curriculum*. London: Routledge and Kegan Paul.

Jackson, P. (1990). Introduction. In Dewey, J.. *The School and Society and the Child and the Curriculum*. Chicago: The University of Chicago Press

Karier, C. (1973). Liberal Ideology and the Quest for Orderly Change, in Karier, C., and Violas, P. Spring, J. (eds). *Roots of Crisis: American Education in the Twentieth Century*. Chicago: Rand McNally & Company.

Karier, C. (2002). The Quest for Orderly Change. Some Reflections. In Lowe, R. (ed), *History of Education. Major Themes*. Vol. I. *Debates in the History of Education*. London: Routledge

Kliebard, H. (1995). *The Struggle for the American Curriculum 1893–1958*. New York: Routledge.

Kliebard, H. (1999). *Schooled to Work. Vocationalism and the American Curriculum, 1876–1946*. New York: Teachers College Press.

Kliebard, H. (2002). *Changing Course. American Curriculum Reform in the 20th Century*. New York: Teachers College Press.

Lewy, A., and Bathory, Z. (1994). The Taxomomy of Educational Objectives in Continental Europe, the Mediterranean and the Middle East. In Anderson, L., and Sosniak, L. (eds) *Bloom's Taxomomy: A Forty-year Retrospective*. Chicago: National.

Macpherson, C. (1994). I Istoriki Poreia tis Fileleftheris Dimokratias (*The history of Liberal Democracy*) Translated by Kasimi, E., Athens: Gnosi.

Marsh, C. Willis, G. (2003). *Curriculum Alternative Approaches Ongoing Issues*. Upper Saddle River, NJ: Merril Prentice Hall

Mayhew, K. - Edwards, A. (1965). *The Dewey School. The Laboratory School of the University of Chicago 1896–1903*, Press, New York: Atherton Press.

Noutsos, M. (1983). Didaktikoi Stohoi kai Analytiko Programma. Kritiki mias synhronis paidagogikis ideologias, (*Educational goals and the Curriculum. Ctiticism of a modern pedagogical ideology*). Dodoni: Giannina,.

Pinar, W. (2004) What Is Curriculum Theory? Mahwah: Lawrence Erlbaum Associates.

Pinar,W. , Reynolds, W., Slattery, P., and Taubman, P. (2002) *Understanding Curriculum. An Introduction to the Study of Historical and Contemporary Curriculum Discourses.* New York: Peter Lang.

Rasis, S. (2003). I Krisi tis Proodeftikis ekpaidefsis kai i emfanisi tis anasygkrotikis philosophias tis paideias' in I Paideia stin avgi tou 21 Aiona (*Education at the dawn of the 21st century*), Patra: Ergastirio Istorikou Arxeiou Neoellinikis kai Diethnous Ekpaidefsis.

Rasis, S. (2004). Ta Panepistimia htes kai simera. Symvoli stin Istoria tis Ekpaidefsis. I Agglosaxoniki Empeiria (*Universities in the Past and the Present. Contribution to the History of Education. The Anglosaxon experience*), Athens: Papazisis.

Reese, W. (2000). Grassroots Movements during the Progressive Era. In Lowe, R. (ed.) *History of Education, Major Themes*. Vol III. *Studies in learning and teaching*, London: Routledge.

Schubert, W., Schubert, A., Thomas, T., and Carrol, W. (2002) *Curriculum Books. The First Hundred Years*. New York: Peter Lang.

Schutz, A. (2001) John Dewey's Conundrum: Can Democratic Schools Empower? Teachers College Record, 2(103)

Shor, I, (1992). Culture Wars. *School and Society in the Conservative Restoration*. Chicago: the University of Chicago Press.

Urban, W., and Wagoner, J. (2000) *American Education. A History*. Boston: McGraw Hill.

CHAPTER 10

"Digital Literacy" or "Digital Literacy for Critical Consciousness"!

Anastassios Liambas and Ioannis Kaskaris

Regarding the Theoretical Foundations: School Knowledge (Curriculum)–Digital Literacy

In a period when society seems to experience and be affected by a crisis that questions the links between the civic–the economic–the cultural, education ought to restate its constitutional principles. The 'old' question concerning the type of school and society, education is leaning towards, becomes once again the framework to consider and examine both school curriculum and pedagogic relation.

We reflect, thus, on the nexus between digital literacy and school knowledge, as the theoretical precondition that would clarify the ground upon which we shall elaborate our thoughts since it is necessary to outline the social, political, economic and philosophical foundations of the ICTs in education in order to (and prior to our intent to) elaborate visions of the way(s) "digital literacy" ought to be engaged with and advanced in school pedagogy, hence

> refashioning how we think of power, politics, and everyday life as part of a larger, wired global reality (Giroux 2001, p. 2).

School knowledge, then, is realized as a social and cultural construction that reflects social relations and major historical economic, political and social structures (Kincheloe 2005). Furthermore, school knowledge for the critical pedagogues is understood as the medium for the students to realize themselves because knowledge is recognized as a process that involves and operates through the subjects. That is, school knowledge is more than an over-determined, mechanically applied condition where the institution of education has been set. Quite the opposite, knowledge is an interpretative dynamic procedure where the educational relationship constitutes its logic since knowledge reflects the specialized interests and the power relations of the "re-contextualizing agents" that select—"de-locate" knowledge from its field of production and "re-locate" it into the pedagogic situation (Bernstein 1996).

Nevertheless, simply endorsing a view of knowledge merely as an "act of interpretation"—as a metaphor to acknowledge subjectivities—entails a contingent disregard to understand that such an analysis (i.e., knowledge as an act) actually originated and supports existing power structures and forms of authority, since knowledge "is always local and contextual" (Trend 1992). In contrast, to the epistemology that locates truth in external reality and considers the acquisition of knowledge as simply an inner process conducted in the minds of autonomous (abstract) individuals,[1] the ability to conceptualize is inextricably relevant to culture, power or discourse of the surrounding social world (Kincheloe 2005, pp. 42, 43) (epitomizing and creating the bloc of socio-economic relationships—"historic bloc").

Hence, knowledge in the school has a twofold meaning—it could be analyzed in a framework to define (and derive) the *Personal* and as a blueprint to examine the *Social*. School knowledge, then, is regarded as: (i) the ground to put emphasis on self-existence; and; (ii) a critical meta-cognitive mode to participate in the societal.

The eruptive expansion of literacy/"multi-literacy" involves practices in many contexts, governed by conventions currently evolving, in reverse with traditional notions on literacy (i.e., for books). Consequently, as such, the ICTs require new and enriched competencies, much more decisive than before: skills and abilities (traditional print literacy skills, in addition to visual and aural literacy, analytical, interpretational and critical abilities for various cultural forms and media) are sketched now on a new terrain (textual and semiotic) (Kellner, 2000). The potential for technology in education is enormous—"to motivate and challenge children and adolescents of less favored social classes"— and also to exercise the curiosity that

> convokes the imagination, the emotions, and the capacity to conjecture and to compare in tracing a profile of the object to be known as well as its raison d'être" (Freire, 1998, p. 82).

Furthermore, it is exactly technology that

> holds the secret of the bonds that untie theory and practice, thought and action, logos and technē (Axelos, 1976, p. 331).

It is the flowering of dialectic within technology that offers us all the richness and all its poverty when it meets a human's reflection on his/her connectiveness with cosmos.

Ultimately, the question of "digital literacy" could be reframed into a political concern that ought to provide some plausible guiding course of theoretical-practical action (as "Praxis"), particularly in a historic period where the economy, society and education mirror the fundamental crisis of capitalism (and the ways the organic ideologists of the right tend to re-appropriate the surplus economic and intellectual value), namely, who (and for whom) "demarcates" the limits of the possibilities of the ICTs to direct the students to the production of meaning, to be used as means of self-expression, communication and creation, to make them more motivated and competent participants in a social life for social change?

The personal, thus, suggests a concept of knowledge as a meaningful process that underlines learning as an enriched procedure,

> as both a process of meaning production and a basis for the educational work for social transformation (Simon, 1992, p. 135).

Society, on the other hand, though it could be perceived as an idealistic mono-logical sum of "paradigms" (in terms of thought and consciousness[2] regulatory categories), is a consequential derivative of the historical-political systems where the diffused hegemonic power relationships incubate the ***existing*** structures (material and symbolic/discursive, cognitive and emotional, knowable and unuttered).

Our reference to the ***hegemonic instance*** is explicit since:

(a). we espouse "historical materialism" and "power subjugation" as the essential elements towards an exegesis to examine the social, beyond a simple reduction to a description of the material associations, but as a method to grasp the ways normative processes of legitimization affirm the dominant relations of production (i.e., capitalism) by means of a labyrinthine web of symbolic representations (decoded in the ideologically biased postmodern theorists as the prime ingredients' field of the so called "identities").

(b). we encounter the relation between "society" and "man" as a political and moral practice that works to construct particular notions of agency and common sense, in which the "image" of the learning process is decoupled from the historical, political, economic, and social conditions through which it has already been constituted as a distinctive process.[3]

(c). we argue for a public sphere and a terrain of social struggle synchronized next to a set of ethico-political values over commercial interests: social equality, social justice, solidarity, freedom, participation, democracy.

Revisiting, therefore, the concept of "*school knowledge*", it concerns both the teacher and the pupil in a dialectical manner, that delineates the "pedagogic relation" which in return "nourishes" in the last instance the consistency of theory and practice in critical pedagogy.

In this sense, the process of learning as a cognizant procedure is embedded completely within the "pedagogic relation" to the extent that it is a relation which transforms and advances the subjects (both the teacher and the pupil) to a perspective of having a "conscious" emancipatory interpretation of reality (enhanced, thus, from emotions) rise above necessity and the predominant dispositions.

Consequently, from the moment that school knowledge ("curriculum") fades into the spectrum of the pedagogic relation, the relevant argument on the nexus among formal and/or informal "school curriculum" and "digital literacy" could be considered as a "critical inquiry" which rests upon the interactional commitment

> expressed through the process of writing, talking, debating and struggling over what counts as legitimate knowledge (Giroux 1988, p. 163).

The central question at the end of the day, as Joe L. Kincheloe reminds us is:

> what are the hegemonic and counter-hegemonic dimensions of "digital literacy" and ICTs policies to educational policy and practice? (Kincheloe, 2007, p. 13)

Digital Literacy as a Prospect for Pedagogy of Possibility

The discussion on "digital literacy" could enhance the dialogue within education—and, consequently, in doing that, illuminate the nexus of education with society—to the extent that the discussion

> involves alternative ways of analyzing and producing knowledge, (...), generating questions previously unimagined, that lead to an awareness of the multiple dimensions of the social, (...) thus, perceiving the social structures and the social systems that undermine access to resources and power (Kincheloe, 2005, pp. 137, 138)

The dialectic role of ICTs in the prevailing structural and institutional contexts, in the broader social, economic, political and communicational conditions which were articulated (Zeleza 2007), can become perceptible as "innovations" that create and extend the possibilities of communication, the exchange of ideas and interaction (directness, speed, performance, presentation), expression and creation (Drenoyianni 2006), but also as "innovations" which intensify the social responsibility on power dissemination, as "critical regulators" regarding the borders of oppression and commodification (Giroux 2006).

Furthermore, if the dialogue on "digital literacy" provides the ground to anticipate hope towards a pedagogy of possibility (and be transformed into a "site of possibility and diversity"), then the theoretical principles unfold a schema for an inclusive curriculum (beyond the standardized curricula that fail to account for context, specificity and the complexity of human interaction) that shall embrace humane and democratic knowledge—a prospect that may reorientate the pedagogic approaches in schools towards constructing knowledge for a more just world (Kincheloe, 2005, pp. 167, 168, 169).

The emphasis on "digital literacy", the techno-culturalization of education, involves the dialectic role of ICTs and generates profound transformations to determine pedagogic relation, in the school context. Such a role corresponds to the controversial social function of the institutional school, based on the struggle for the forms of the curriculum, teaching, evaluation and politics.[4] A struggle which is the result that accords to unequal social groups, where the dominant groups define what counts as official knowledge, in order to maintain their power, since the dominant

> must take the concerns of the less powerful into account" (Apple, 2000, p. 10)

Such an institution, in spite of the skills' instruction, transmits knowledge and modes of learning—inscribing, hence, the dominant ideology, reinforcing and reproducing the existing social order (competitive, self-interested individuals formed in accordance with market values and practices) (Althusser, 1983, Bowles & Gintis, 1976). In some manner, schools in advanced capitalist societies undermine the principles to educate

> citizens with critical capacities, modes of literacy, knowledge and skills enabling them both to read the world critically and to participate in shaping and governing it (Giroux 2004, p. 110)

Nevertheless, by virtue the school constitutes a place for democratic action. It could be argued, then, that the struggles among groups in the various levels release possibilities for approaches of critical pedagogy, a pedagogy of possibility that could prepare the students to contest cultural hierarchies, power discourses and consent to domination and exploitation.

Any discourse on "digital literacy" has been confronted with an

> overall approach to schooling–embedding the analysis of education in the evolving structure of the economy and the polity, and giving attention to the non-cognitive as well as cognitive effects of education,(...) expressing the conflicts and limitations as well as the hopes of a heterogeneous and unequal society" (Bowles & Gintis, 2001, p. 21).

If schools continue to be both testing grounds and battlegrounds for building a society, that extends freedom and material benefits to all.

Despite the complex reconfigurations of the discourse on "digital literacy", the socio-political predicament, as Kathleen Tyner has noted, is that the focus on "digital literacy",

> instead of on liberating and democratizing processes in schools, has stunted the debate about the role of technology in education,

nullifying, therefore, the potential for

> educational strategies that blend critical literacy, (...), critical pedagogy to explain the relationship of literacy, technology, and society (Tyner, 1998, pp. 228, 230)

The critical element of the underlying principle/ "*raison d'être*" on "digital literacy" lies on the plausible pathways to overcome "old inequalities" while

> re-framing human elements, in the name of social justice and more humane treatment for all, human and non-human, as well (Lankshear, 1997, p. 190)

Without "a language of critique, hope, and possibility", the categories of intellectual practice on "digital literacy" as a form of cultural politics that dialectically associates discourses-objects-facts-subjectivities, may fall short of filling the gap between the tendency to be technologically "accurate" and our ability to morally and ethically direct technologies, disabling, hence, a prospect to define socially meaningful explanations, that employ–next to pedagogy–a perspective to anticipate contradictions through socio-political transformation.

"Digital Literacy" or "Digital Literacy for Critical Consciousness"— Some Preliminary Appraisals

The discussion on "digital literacy" has been set

> in intentional institutional arrangements and practices within which various forms of images, sound, text, and talk are constructed, presented, and engaged. (...) Implicated

> in the production of the range of meanings that give people a sense of who they are and what their futures might be about (i.e., implicating them in the formation and regulation of identities and desires) (Simon, 1992, p. 42)

Following the logic of the argument,[5] one would maintain that the importance of "digital literacy" as a concept that provides an expanded range of relevance for the notion of pedagogy lies on the prospect that it allows us to

> better understand how the work that goes on in schools may be "articulated" with other forms of cultural work in order to open the possibilities specified and normalized within our social imagination (Simon, 1992, p. 43)

To sustain, through the element of possibility, "empowerment" (Lankshear, 1997, p. 79) open, it is essential to distinguish the partial, the circumstantial, and the incomplete from the actual (real) reproductive mechanisms that uphold current hegemonic capitalist hierarchies. We need to bridge disparate knowledge forms and reconsider the relationship of theory and practice; we need to recognize the artifice of representations (Trend, 1992, p. 63), what most people consider, the natural social world, operating within a multilogical, perplex subjective representational domain that produces knowledge and understandings of the cosmos (Kincheloe, 2007, pp. 13–14). This is not a straightforward process pronounced to us but a set of transhistorical, cultural/epistemological, sociopolitical points of challenge and struggle on meaning.[6] The point of refutation could be situated on what Roland Barthes has termed as the delusive essence of "mythos", the procedure where the meaning becomes an image (Barthes, 1977, p. 230), namely the distance among the image—the object—and the meaning: the route where the image nullifies the essence, via the value it acquires within its social circulation and function (Barthes, 1977, p. 201–211). The "myth", then, institutes a discourse that advances bourgeois ideology of a "scientific or the intuitive kind", that "records facts or perceives scientific or supervisory ideology" to facilitate acknowledgement of the "facts" or the "uses of value" "but refuses explanations", while "the order of the world can be seen as sufficient or ineffable", but "never seen as significant"[7] (Barthes, 1977). The "myth" denies *exegesis* (explanation), to the point that the societal remains either adequate or unutterable (inexpressible). From the moment,

> the myth has the task of giving a historical intention a natural justification, and making contingency appear eternal (Barthes, 1977, p. 245)

Then, the societal has been approached as a "semiotic deposit". Society is delivered as a "deposit", where the "negotiation" and the "dialogue" between the individuals and the socio-economic structures are engulfed within the "mythical significations"; obscuring, consequently, the ideological messages and the political intent of the values conveyed, while the systematical exclusion of certain viewpoints—reproducing, hence, certain social norms—remains intact (Trend, 1992).

Another aspect of critical importance refers to the core of the technological dialectic, that could direct the discussion around the complexity of human act as a new kind of relation between man and nature (that has already been regulated by the relation among men). A dialectic that surpasses/transcends the notion of ICTs and digital literacy as a mere discourse on the links established between the persons[8] and the objects (even as remnants of universal knowledge or even as consequential events of information), that is, to appreciate "digital literacy" as the "coordinating" element that would thrust existing realities that actually amplify reification, injustice, exploitation and coercion. The potential and prospect of such dialectic is at stake as Manuel Castells notes when he writes that,

> the rapid diffusion of virtual reality representation in computer networks creates the possibility of individualized, self-programmable, image representation and perception, which will increasingly disconnect individuals from mass media, while connecting the individualized communication expressions to the individuals' mental world. The social consequence of such technological developments is the growing tension between globalization and individualization in the audiovisual universe, bringing about the danger of a breakdown in the patterns of social communication between world information flows and personal experiences (Castells, 1999, p. 49).

To rephrase Joan Greenbaum, it is not digital literacy or ICTs innovations or limits that necessarily drive change but the ways that organizations and labor interact with them (Greenbaum, 1998, p. 181). The critical moment emerges as soon as we become conscious of our position that any theorizations or practical implementations of ICTs within any educational system would proceed and develop as part and parcel of a political agenda that brings forward an anti-capitalist emancipatory perspective. That is to suggest a pedagogy that leaves more and more in the hands of the learners and the people—educators, students, activists, parents—aiming at their participatory cooperation (Giroux 1998). A pedagogy that develops the "dialogical negotiation", among teachers and students, and creates interactive "spaces" for competing discourses in the classroom on multifaceted views (O'Cadiz et al. 1998), inserting, hence, knowledge approached

> into the larger horizon against which it is generated—the horizon of cultural context, which cannot be understood apart from its class particularities, and this indeed in societies so complex that the characterization of those particularities is less easy to come by (Freire 1994, p. 85).

The question on "digital literacy" and "school curriculum" (school knowledge) appears to be grounded and arranged within a (political, discursive, ideological, and practical-political) context of conflict and variance, especially since "capitalist education is a contradictory phenomenon".[9]

It is crucial to understand that the discussion on the promise of "digital literacy" in education ought to be evaluated—less on the ways that it has been introduced in education, but—on the terms where a discourse on "digital literacy" actually expands the possibilities of critical pedagogy to bear subjects' diversity within a democratic practice in education. In general terms, "digital literacy" is charged with a democratic semantics if it is projected upon a new cultural landscape that encourages dialogue and "free space" according to progressive principles of pedagogy, providing hence

> opportunities for individuals and groups to engage in the creative production of meaning, contributing in diverse ways of public life (Carlson, 2006, pp. 109, 110).

Otherwise, technology as a whole could be incorporated in schools' fulfillment to reproduce dominant ideology— "a task that the ruling class expects the teachers to accomplish", denying therefore another task of an educator—to denounce it— since

> [theoretically] ...education cannot be exhausted exclusively as the reproducer of the subsystem of the dominant ideology (Horton & Freire 1990, p. 118)

This argument frames a reason where schools could embark on a risk process to employ the subjects as entities that act according to (and towards) a critical conscious *Praxis* (i.e., a dialectical interactional sequence among theory and practice) enabling the reflective pedagogue to specify the civic and public function of education. The pledge to "critical consciousness" implies that to argue on "digital literacy"—at the last instance—means "to connect knowledge and the larger society", [...] "making visible, hence, the ethical and political", [...] "combining theoretical vigor with social relevance" (Giroux 2004, pp. 142–143). In the sphere of critical consciousness one can view both the object of analysis and the process involved in such analysis, thus, being able to consider the structural elements that predetermine and situate the socio-symbolic and at the same time to recognize reflective understanding, i.e., the process whereby "meaning" is "produced, represented, and consumed" (Giroux 2001 pp. 154–155). It is then within the construction of critical consciousness where the basis of normative knowledge with the human agents has been established, it is within critical consciousness where the conditions to promote independence of the subject—diverse reasoning and action that leads humans to oppose the contradictions of an oppressive social reality (Giroux 2001).

It is an open stake, since any position on the approach to marry "digital literacy" to school knowledge exposes labor's appropriation in the advanced capitalist societies, where knowledge could be subjugated—through manipulation, indoctrination, and hegemonic dominance—in order to control/organize, intensify class exploitation (McLaren 2000) (translating, hence, "critical pedagogy into another classroom technique"), or it could provide the means to progress into another historical phase where the transforming "self-activating" capacity of labor could be integrated in an emancipatory, liberating trajectory (Rikowski 2002).

> In a world marked by increasing poverty, unemployment, and diminished social opportunities, educators must vindicate the crucial connection between culture and politics in defending public education as site of democratic learning and struggle (Giroux 2000, p. 37)

> Thus, a discourse on "digital literacy" could relate labor-power-knowledge and cultural struggle as a pedagogic, and therefore, political strategy (Freire 1998).

Simply, to attach ICTs in education as a symptom in a strategy by the pupils to acquire low-status knowledge (Apple 2000), and, thus, reflect on knowledge as embodiments of simple acts transmuted to manipulation of symbols by logic-like rules (Kincheloe 2007), leaves the dialogue on "digital literacy" sterile and sanitized from a democratic political prospect; a prospect, which may possibly identify students and teachers, as critically conscious agents, able to understand the complexity of social, political, cultural and ideological factors.

> To confirm, then, and restate such an alternative prospect means to be in a position to adopt clear theoretical argumentation and distinctive standpoint in day by day living. A cultural and political challenge to be ascertained in real life...

Notes

1. Espousing, hence, a position where "the thoughts, moods and understandings and sensations of the individuals are separate from their histories and social contexts" (Kincheloe, 2005, p. 41).
2. As R. Morrow & C. A. Torres argue, a critique that could be applied on the non-critical forms of knowledge could be sketched on the grounds of J. Habermas critique where the philosophy of consciousness used to refer to a cognitive relation that began with an isolated ego that initiated the process of knowing, as opposes to a subject that has already been constituted within a world of interaction (Morrow & Torres, 2002, p. 27) and hence depicting a subject that ontologically is constituted as an agent within a plurality of relations, as an agent which acts, corresponds, feels (Giroux 2006; Morrow& Torres 2002).
3. As Henry Giroux states, this suggests analyzing the spectacle (here, the learning process as a spectacle/manifestation of learning) as part of "a broader constellation of power by examining not only what forms of knowledge and agency it tries to put into place but also

what is screened out and how the latter resonates with subordinate forms of critical knowledge and engagement" (Giroux 2006, p. 74).

4. As Carlos Alberto Torres has noted, "even if schooling could be considered a mostly social reproduction of values, practices, habits, dexterities, or knowledge, in itself it is losing grounds as part and parcel of the socialization devices compared to the mass media and digitalization" (Torres 2006, p. 55), and that leaves us to underlie the possibility to imagine the discourse on "digital literacy" apart from the networks of social reproduction and hegemony, as a discourse open to critical emancipatory conscientization.
5. That is, the logic where "digital literacy" is approached as a mode to examine the acts of representation, comprehension and recognition in order to realize and engage/grasp representations/the symbolic fields that surround teachers-pupils in schools (or other sites conventionally understood as, "educational,") through forms of (visual, written, aural, and gestural) "textualities" (Simon 1992, pp. 42–44).
6. The perils of embracing the discussion on "digital literacy" within a theory of the agent has been noticed by Henry Giroux, when he wrote that: "If a critical theory of literacy is to encompass human agency and critique as part of the narrative of liberation, it must reject the reductionist pedagogical practice of limiting critique to the analyses of cultural products", that is, in our case the introduction and usage of ICTs in schools. "The more narrowly defined theories of literacy tied to this form of ideology critique obscure the relational nature of how meaning is produced, i.e., the intersection of subjectivities, objects, and social practices within specific relations of power", (...) within "the dialectical relationship between human subjectivities and the objective world" (Giroux 1988, pp. 155, 156).
7. "(...) The basic idea of a perfectible mobile world, produces the inverted image of an unchanging humanity, characterized by an indefinite repetition of its identity. In a word, in the contemporary bourgeois society, the passage from the real to the ideological is defined as that from an anti-physis to a pseudo-physis" (Barthes 1977, pp. 243–244).
8. Realized as the subjectivities which are molded and materialized within the relationship of the "individual" with the "communal/collective/class".
9. "On the one hand, it is enmeshed in the capitalization of 'humans'; on the other, it can function as a basis for exposure and awareness of this state of being. [...] The importance of a viable critical pedagogy, which can exposure of the 'horror', as a pedagogic aim, is crucial" (Rikowski, 2002, p. 136).

Bibliography

Althusser Louis (1983). "Ideologia ke ideologiki michanismi tou kratous" [*Ideology and ideological state apparatuses*]. In Thesis [Positions], Athens:Themelio, pp. 69–123.

Apple Michael W. (2000). *Official Knowledge*. New York: Routledge.

Axelos Kostas (1976). *Alienation, Praxis, & Technē in the Thought of Karl Marx*, Austin: University of Texas Press.

Bernstein Basil (1996). *Pedagogy, Symbolic Control and Identity. Theory, Research, Critique.*

London:Taylor and Francis.

Barthes Roland (1977). Mithologies - Mathimata [*Mythologies – Lessons*]. Athens: Kedros.

Bowles Samuel & Gintis Herbert (1976). *Schooling in Capitalist America: Educational Reform the Contradictions of Economic Life*. New York: Basic Books 1976.

—— (2001). Schooling in Capitalist America Revisited, in e\Papers\JEP-paper\Sociology of Education.tex, 2001, pp. 1–26.

Carlson Dennis (2006). Are We Making Progress?: Ideology and Curriculum in the Age of No Child Left Behind. In Lois Weis, Cameron McCarthy, and Greg Dimitriadis (eds.), *Ideology, Curriculum, and the New Sociology of Education: Revisiting the Work of Michael Apple*. New York: Routledge, pp. 91–114.

Castells Manuel (1999). Flows, Networks, and Identities: A Critical Theory of the Information Society. In M. Castells, R. Flecha, P. Freire, H. Giroux, D. Macedo, P. Willis, *Critical Education in the New Information Age*, Lanham, MD: Rowman & Littlefield Publishers Inc., pp. 37–64.

Drenoyianni Helen (2006). ICT in Education: A Chance for Human and Democratic Schools?. *European Journal of Vocational Training*, 39, 3 5–20.

Freire Paulo (1994). *Pedagogy of Hope: Reliving Pedagogy of the Oppressed*. New York: Continuum, New York.

—— (1998). *Pedagogy of Freedom: Ethics, Democracy, and Civic Courage*. Lanham, MD: Rowman and Littlefield Publishers, Inc.

Horton Myles & Freire Paulo (1990). *We Make the Road by Walking: Conversations on Education and Social Change*. Philadelphia: Temple University Press.

Giroux Henry A. (1988). *Schooling and the Struggle for Public Life*. Boulder, CO: Paradigm Publishers.

(2000). *Impure Acts. The Practical Politics of Cultural Studies*. New York: Routledge.

—— (2004) *The Terror of Neoliberalism*. Boulder, CO: Paradigm Publishers.

—— (2006). *Beyond the Spectacle of Terrorism*, Boulder, CO: Paradigm Publishers.

Greenbaum Joan (1998). *From Chaplin to Dilbert: The Origins of Computer Concept*, In Stanley Aronowitz and Jonathan Cutler: *Post-Work*. London: Routledge, London, pp. 167–184.

Kellner Douglas (2000). Multiple Literacies and Critical Pedagogies: New Paradigms. In Peter Trifonas (ed.). Revolutionary Pedagogies. New York: Routledge-Falmer, pp. 196–221.

Kincheloe Joe L. (2005). *Critical Constructivism*. New York: Peter Lang,

—— (2007). Critical Pedagogy in the Twenty-first Century: Evolution for Survival. In Peter McLaren and Joe L. Kincheloe (eds.), *Critical Pedagogy: Where Are We Now?*, New York: Peter Lang, pp. 9–42.

Lankshear Colin (with James Paul Gee, Michele Knobel and Chris Searle) (1997). *Changing Literacies*. Buckingham: Open University Press.

McLaren Peter (2000). Paulo Freire's Pedagogy of Possibility. In Stanley F Steiner, H. Mark Krank, Peter McLaren, and Robert E. Bahruth (eds.), *Freirean Pedagogy, Praxis, and Possibilities: Projects for the New Millennium*. New York: Falmer Press pp. 1–22.

Morrow Raymond A. and Torres Carlos Alberto (2002). *Reading Freire and Habermas: Critical Pedagogy and Transformative Social Change*. New York: Teachers College.

Maria del Pilar O'Cadiz, Pia Lindquist Wong, Carlos Alberto Torres (1988). *Education and Democracy: Paulo Freire, Social Movements, and Educational Reform in Sao Paulo*, Boulder:

Westview Press.

Rikowski Glenn (2002) . Education, Capital and the Transhuman. In Dave Hill (et al), *Marxism Against Postmodernism in Educational Theory*. Lanham *Lexington: Books*, 111 – 144.

Simon Roger (1992). *Teaching Against the Grain. Texts for Pedagogy of Possibility*. New York: Bergin & Garvin.

Torres Carlos Alberto (2006). *Schooling, Power and the Exile of the Soul.* In Lois Weis, Cameron McCarthy, and Greg Dimitriadis (eds.), *Ideology, Curriculum, and the New Sociology of Education. Revisiting the Work of Michael Apple.* New York: Routledge, pp. 47–65.

Trend David (1992). *Cultural Pedagogy*. Art/Education/Politics. New York: Bergin & Garvey.

Tyner Kathleen (1998) *Literacy in a Digital World, Teaching and Learning in the Age of Information.* Manwah, NJ: Lawrence Erlbaum Associates.

Zeleza Paul T. (2007). Knowledge, Globalization, and Hegemony: Production of Knowledge in the Twenty-First Century. In Sveker Sörlin & Hebe Vessuri (eds.): *Knowledge Society vs. Knowledge Economy: Knowledge, Power and Politics.* New York: Palgrave, pp. 79–106.

CHAPTER 11

Digital Literacy Research in the School Environment—Towards the Assessment of Media and Digital Literacy

Tapio Varis

The new literacies can be approached as functional literacies in the same way as traditional reading, writing and calculating. The new abilities are believed to have a strong correlation with the traditional ones but in fact seem to do so much less than expected (Aunion 2009). The evaluation tools are quite advanced in assessment of access (MeAC 2007) and information literacy competence standards (ACRL 2000), for example. But the assessment of media and digital literacy still requires as lot of research work.

In a broad sense the concept of digital literacy is a way of thinking but it can also be understood as complementary to the concept of media education and even synonymous with media literacy. Digital literacy as media literacy aims to develop both critical understanding of and active participation in the media. Digital and media literacy is about developing people's critical and creative abilities. Using a computer requires diverse and complex previous knowledge. It also introduces the individual and humanity to new contexts, which demands mental, intellectual, profound and complex changes. In essence, digital literacy is a complicated process that consists of acquiring a new tekne, ability of art or craft. Creativity and culture become essential raw materials for the knowledge economy (Varis 2008).

One of the best-known internationally comparable assessment tools has been the PISA study which is coordinated by governments of participating countries, through the Organisation for Economic Co-operation and Development (OECD). It may also cover the new literacies soon. Already by 2000, it had been revealed by the mean scores of the countries that Finland showed the highest reading literacy performance. Finland's performance is significantly higher than that of any other participating country. On top of this, in Finland high overall reading literacy performance seems to be combined with comparatively high equality. This is seen from the fact that in Finland, the standard deviation, illustrative of variation in student performance, is among the smallest in OECD countries (Välijärvi 2002).

OECD's latest PISA survey of the knowledge and skills of 15-year-olds shows that some countries have seen significant improvements in student performance since 2000. Based on tests carried out among 400,000 students in 57 countries in 2006, the latest PISA survey focuses particularly on students' abilities in comprehending and tackling scientific problems. It also provides an update on performance in reading and mathematics compared with surveys in 2000 and 2003.

While most students polled said they were motivated to learn science, only a minority aspired to a career involving science: 72% said it was important for them to do well in science; 67% enjoyed acquiring new knowledge in science; 56% said science was useful for further studies; but only 37% said they would like to work in a career involving science and 21% said they would like to spend their life doing advanced science.

At a time when scientific and technological know-how is helping to drive growth in advanced economies, the results of PISA 2006 reveal wide variations in skills levels. Student attitudes to science will be crucial to countries' economic potential in tomorrow's world, and PISA 2006 gives a detailed picture of how well students around the world are prepared for the challenges of a knowledge society.

The top performer in science in PISA 2006 was Finland, followed by Hong Kong-China, Canada, Chinese Taipei, Estonia, Japan and New Zealand. Australia, the Netherlands, Korea, Germany, the United Kingdom, the Czech Republic, Switzerland, Austria, Belgium and Ireland, Liechtenstein, Slovenia and Macao-China also scored above OECD average. Data for science in PISA 2006 are not directly comparable to data in the previous studies as the nature of the tests has changed.

In Australia, Canada, Finland, Japan and New Zealand, at least one in seven students reached the top two levels of scientific literacy. In Greece, Italy, Mexico, Portugal, Spain and Turkey, by contrast, the proportion was lower than one in 20. On average across the OECD, students in private schools outperformed students in public schools in most countries. The picture changed, however, when the socio-economic background of students and schools was taken into account, with public schools taking the lead.

Streaming at an early age tends to increase the impact of socio-economic background on student performance, PISA 2006 indicates. The earlier students were stratified into separate institutions or programmes, the stronger was the impact which the school's average socio-economic background had on performance. Schools that divided students by ability for all subjects tended to have lower student performance on average.

The survey identified considerable interest among students in some scientific issues. Most, for example, were aware of environmental issues such as forest clearing and greenhouse gases. However, they were generally pessimistic about the future, with fewer than one in six believing that problems such as air pollution and nuclear waste disposal would improve over the next 20 years. Those who performed better in science showed greater awareness of environmental issues but were also more pessimistic.[1]

As pointed out by Dr. Ritva-Sini Merilampi in the Ministry of Education, the strong Finnish faith in learning and cultivation is a heritage of the 19th century proponents of Finnish culture and civilisation. It is widely understood that literacy is not inherited, but each generation must build its own literacy. Both young and old Finns, boys and girls alike, are highly literate in the traditional and also in the new media environment.

In Finland, The Ministry of Education and school authorities have promoted media and digital literacy nation-wide. According to international, comparative research carried out in 2000, the Finnish schools are among the top in the world in terms of their access to Internet connections. Almost all Finnish schools (96 %) have Internet connection and only Iceland, Singapore and Canada are more connected.

The use of Internet at schools, however, is limited because of the lack of competence by the teachers. However, compared with other countries the students in Finnish schools use Internet a lot. In 80% of the schools more than every second student utilises e-mail. The Finnish schools also produce a lot of homepages which also include curriculum information. Also other media are used and taught in many ways and levels. Even today, a child can leave the comprehensive school without a real connection to the computer or other media. The courses are voluntary and it is voluntary for the teacher to focus on themes about media. The main problem is the lack of media education in teacher education.

When interpreting the comparative research findings, the Finnish researchers emphasize that the Finnish comprehensive school is not only a system but it is also a matter of pedagogical philosophy and practice. The findings of PISA show that some countries have managed to achieve both high average quality and high equality of educational outcomes. Finland, for example, has been successful in ensuring small parities between schools. Parental socio-economic status also has a less significant impact on student performance in Finland than in many other countries.

In comparison with other countries, Finland has been less successful in ensuring gender equality, particularly as concerns *reading literacy*. The gap, however, is not due to Finnish boys doing poorly but rather to Finnish girls performing exceptionally well.

In *mathematical literacy* on average across countries, gender differences were considerably smaller than in reading literacy. In Finland, practically no differences were found between boys and girls in this domain while in many other countries boys outperformed girls in mathematics. In *scientific literacy*, Finland displayed no significant gender differences.

The Finnish society is characterized by *cultural homogeneity*. Furthermore, radical political conflicts and sudden changes in educational thinking have been very rare. Because of this cultural homogeneity, it has been rather easy in Finland to reach mutual understanding on national education policy and the means for developing the education system. The schools system has also taken care of the needs of the Swedish-speaking minority very well.

In conclusion of the PISA study the researchers suggest that there is no single key factor behind Finland´s successful performance. The high achievement seems to be attributable to a whole network of interrelated factors, in which students' own area of interest and leisure activities, the learning opportunities provided by schools, parental support and involvement as well as the social and cultural context of learning and the entire education system combine with each other.

Also the extensive network of libraries, the prestige of literacy culture and education, high teacher expectations, pedagogical experimentation and recent reading campaigns aimed at fostering students' engagement in reading have contributed to the high performance.

Finland with a population of 5 million inhabitants has a system of comprehensive school education (the primary and lower secondary level), post-comprehensive general and vocational education (the upper secondary level), and higher and adult education (the tertiary level). The system also takes care of low achievers and supports their development by means of remedial teaching. There are only a very few elite schools. As many as 98.4 % of the schools are maintained by local authorities, while the remainder are run by private organizations or the government. Nearly all publicly funded education, from primary to higher, is steered or supervised by the Ministry of Education. (Merilampi 2002).

The media literacy programme for the period 2008–2011 in Finland broadens the approach. The efforts to create a pan-European awareness are combined by efforts to improve the basic information society skills for all. The basic strategy, like the one followed in Finland, implies three dimensions: basic skills while at school, life-long learning, and new vocational skills. The philosophy is based on the assumption that it is characteristic of the information society that information is available through many different media. A new media culture is about to emerge in which people need, in addition to the traditional reading and writing abilities, a new type of ability, "cultural literacy"—the ability to communicate, handle, understand and interpret information. It is the task of general education to provide every pupil with the versatile basic skills in acquiring, managing and communicating information which are necessary in the information society and essential for successful further study.

The aim of the current programme is to improve the prerequisites for media education in basic education, at the secondary level and in teacher education with a view to making media education an established part of day-to-day school activities. It also emphasizes the development of teacher education and the strengthening of media education research.

Understanding Digital Literacy

It is widely understood that the most important skills of the future would be communication skills. Today everyone is able to access vast amounts of data without a mediator. Critical thinking skills are needed as a productive and positive activity. Critical thinkers see the future as open and malleable, not as closed and fixed. They are aware of the diversity of values, behaviours, social structures, and artistic forms in the world. Critical thinking is a process, not an outcome, and it is emotive as well as rational.

In my understanding we face three kinds of problems. First we have to try to understand what is the learning process of becoming literate and what does communication competence and media skills mean in the information society. Second, we have to analyse the increasing neo-illiteracy. Third, we should discuss about what kind of skills we should give to the citizens now as compared to the earlier skills of writing and reading.

Media literacy has been defined as the ability to access, analyze, evaluate, and communicate messages in a wide variety of forms. Media literacy is a concept whose broad definition and range of applications lead to diverse approaches, creating some intriguing conflicts and tensions. Educators and scholars with disciplinary backgrounds in media studies, the fine and performing arts, history, psychology and sociology, education, and literary analysis each may vigorously defend one's own understanding of what it means to access, analyze, evaluate, or create media texts without a full awareness of the extent of complexity, depth or integrity of various other approaches (Hobbs 1998).

In the discussions in UNESCO Communication and Information Sector, for example, digital literacy is understood to enable people to interpret and make informed judgements as users of information supports and sources and it also enables them to become producers of media in their own right. Digital and media literacy is about developing people's critical and creative abilities.

According to José Manuel Pérez Tornero, digital literacy is not just a simple operative and technical consciousness that is made up of nothing more than technical knowledge. Digital literacy is the complex acquisition process of an individual of humanity combined with their abilities and intellectual competencies (perceptive, cognitive, emotive) and practical competencies (physiological and motor). In Pérez's view these correspond to the technological transformation of the last decades in the twentieth century — the technological change of the Information Society.

To reduce digital literacy exclusively to the skills of using a computer is a crude simplification and a loss in meaning. Using a computer requires diverse and complex previous knowledge. It also introduces the individual and humanity to new contexts, which demands mental, intellectual, profound and complex changes. In essence, digital literacy is a complicated process that consists of acquiring a new tekne. This Greek term means the ability of art or craft by an individual or humanity. According to Pérez we are facing the transformation of the most profound tekne that humanity has ever experienced (Pérez Tornero 2004).

The challenges to peace and open, multicultural communication can be characterized by the transition from an industrial society to an information society with the need of digital competences. The dynamics of globalization, mobility and pluralism result in a multicultural world. A higher degree of individual flexibility in combination with the need for tolerance and responsibility are connected to the demand for sustainable development. The promotion of higher-quality and equal educational opportunities become central issues of educational institutions.

The study of complexity has brought science closer than ever to art. Knowledge has gone through a cycle from non-specialism to specialism, and now back to interdisciplinarity, even transdisciplinarity. Art deals with the sensual world (media as the extension of senses) and the holistic concept of human being. Traditional knowledge has been disciplinary based although increasingly interdisciplinary. In the vocational field knowledge is also contextual and needs to be created in application—learning by doing. This also reflects local and regional realities. The Western philosophy is characterized by analytical, scientific, objective, rational and critical thinking while the Eastern approach is characterized by synthesis, literature and art with a subjective and emotional thinking. They cannot and should not dominate each other but should have close dialogues between them. In a sense, many of the basic issues were already discussed in ancient Greece by Socrates, Plato and Aristotle. Aristotle's "Poetics" is of particular importance to understand the balance between different senses of the human being and the combination of sound, drama, and text, like in modern multimedia. Also, Aristotle´s definition of rhetoric as the faculty of discovering in any given case the available means of persuasion is a relevant approach to analyse the influence of modern media.

In order to learn new technologies and become digitally literate, new forms of learning paths have to be developed utilizing all forms of learning, especially at work and non-formal environments. At the same time special attention should be given to teacher education in information and communication skills and competences. The period of transition that we are now living differs from the periods of change of older dominant media. Traditional print and electronic media were introduced within a period of reasonable length and when we moved to the active use of a new form of communication, we could also have a rough estimation of the economic and social impacts of it, and train new professionals for the media and support people for the institutions. Now different forms of communication and technologies integrate and converge with a speed such that hardly anyone has the time or ability to assess all of the consequences, real possibilities, or problems. In a positive sense, people may be able to speak more directly to each other without former restrictions.

The cultural dimension in the communication and technology applications bring also the dimension of emotions and affection and the spirit of sharing and caring to the process. The social dimension requires inclusive policies. The Internet does not automatically promote social understanding and integration. In an intercultural world, communication necessarily mediates different values and cultural behaviours. Great civilizations and cultures have very different patterns of communication and use different senses in a different way. In consequence, if a truly global information society is to be created, more attention should be given to the diversity of cultures and the co-existence of different civilizations and cultures.

The European Union Digital Literacy Expert Group, of which the author is a member, proposed in 2007 concrete measures to evaluate and promote digital literacy. The Group concluded in 2008 that connectedness in the digital world is increasingly becoming integrated with other forms of social and societal interaction. Questions of digital and media literacy and e-inclusion can no longer be artificially separated from wider questions of social inclusion or engaged citizenship. As "quality of use" becomes a dominant theme, it will be necessary to develop appropriate criteria, evaluation methodologies and benchmarks that can be used effectively to target resources to areas of need and to measure impact and value for money.

The Group recommended the development and use of appropriate evaluation and impact assessment frameworks including more socioeconomic background variables and more indicators related to motivation, critical thinking and quality of use. It also supported research leading to the development of more sophisticated evaluation and benchmarking tools for digital and media literacy programmes, and critical academic research.

The Group's study "Current Trends and Approaches to Media Literacy in Europe" (2008) pointed out that the new digital technologies present unprecedented opportunities for far wider participation in the continuing development of Europe's cultural heritage and civil traditions in a global context. At the same time however, these technologies offer profitable opportunities for misinformation, unwanted surveillance, abuse of the vulnerable and infantilization of public discourse. The rapid development of digital technologies has thus made more urgent an issue that has been pressing for some time: the need for European citizens to fully understand the means by which information, ideas and opinions are now created, circulated and shared in modern societies: in other words, for a media literate population.

Promoting media literacy among European citizens has become a *strategic and integrationist objective* for the whole of Europe. A fundamental requirement for the promotion of this new capacity is to have a suitable model for media literacy, and to know all its dimensions, its strategic value and the specific benefits that it can bring to the development of information society in Europe. The question facing the European Commission, therefore, is what can be offered at Commission level that will add value and encouragement to National efforts, diverse as these are. Using this model, we will describe the existing and possible approaches to media literacy and their implications for a policy of promotion and support.

The skills related to media literacy can be summarised in four areas of ability: *access*, *analysis*, *evaluation* and *creative production*. All of these skills boost aspects of personal development: *consciousness*, *critical thinking* and *problem-solving abilities*.

When considering other elements that help to define the field of media literacy conceptually and thematically, one must remember that it is the result of a process of learning (and teaching) in any given context, but particularly in formal, informal, social, family and media settings. This multi-contextual process leads to the acquisition of specific abilities and competences, in addition to attitudes and values. This process is known as *media education*.

Media literacy should not be treated as an isolated or independent skill. On the contrary, it is a skill that involves and encompasses other skills and forms of literacy: *reading and writing literacy*, *audiovisual literacy* (often referred to as image or visual literacy) and *digital or information literacy*.

Furthermore, media literacy is a necessary part of *active citizenship* and is key to the full development of *freedom of expression* and the *right to information*. It is therefore an essential part of *participative democracy* and *intercultural dialogue*.

It is convenient to develop with greater precision the different components of the media literacy and digital literacy abilities. We have distinguished between operative, cognitive, and social abilities:

Operative or technical abilities—that is, the ones related to the technical devices—include capacities related to the comprehension and use of these instruments, as well as others that are developed in order to adapt these tools to the specific users and their needs.

However, due to their very nature, technical abilities include some aspects related to certain decoding capacities (especially interfaces) and of personal appropriation—for specific ends—of the functionalities—and of the interfaces—that media tools have. From this point of view, they could to some extent be integrated in the cognitive field. However, given their relative simplicity, we prefer to see these as belonging to the operative field.

Cognitive abilities include capacities related to the production of meaning that affect media texts (messages) and their signification. In general, they are the abilities of capturing, assimilating and producing information; they include also the use of this information for generating outlines and models of comprehension that allow us to obtain an appropriate diagnosis of the external environment and to use the information obtained for strategies oriented by individuals' actions: problem-solving, strategies of creation and production of meaning, etc.

Finally, *communicative and social abilities* are the result of applying technical and cognitive abilities in the development of communication and social relations. These abilities allow possibilities that range from a simple contact to the creation of complex cooperation and collaboration strategies that use media tools as their base.

Another relevant summary has been given by Henry Jenkins and his colleagues for the Macarthur Foundation (Jenkins, 2007). They found that according to a recent study from the Pew Internet & American Life project (Lenhardt & Madden, 2005), more than one-half of all teens have created media content, and roughly one-third of teens who use the Internet have shared content they produced. In many cases, these teens are actively involved in what we are calling *participatory cultures*. According to them a participatory culture is a culture with relatively low barriers to artistic expression and civic engagement, strong support for creating and sharing one's creations, and some type of informal mentorship whereby what is known by the most experienced is passed along to novices. A participatory culture is also one in which members believe their contributions matter, and feel some degree of social connection with one another (at the least they care what other people think about what they have created).

Jenkins identifies the following forms of participatory culture: *affiliations* (memberships in online communities), *expressions* (producing new creative forms), *collaborative problem-solving* (working together in teams), *circulations* (shaping the flow of media, *the participation gap* (the unequal access to the opportunities), *the transparency problem* (the challenges young people face in learning to see clearly the ways that media shape perceptions of the world), and *the ethics challenge*.

The study emphasizes that schools and afterschool programs must devote more attention to fostering what we call the new media literacies: a set of cultural competencies and social skills that young people need in the new media landscape. Participatory culture shifts the focus of literacy from one of individual expression to community involvement. The new literacies almost all involve social skills developed through collaboration and networking. These skills build on the foundation of traditional literacy, research skills, technical skills, and critical analysis skills taught in the classroom.

The new skills that Jenkins presents could well be the base for assessing digital literacy. These skills include:

Play—the capacity to experiment with one's surroundings as a form of problem-solving

Performance—the ability to adopt alternative identities for the purpose of improvisation and discovery

Simulation—the ability to interpret and construct dynamic models of real-world processes

Appropriation—the ability to meaningfully sample and remix media content

Multitasking—the ability to scan one's environment and shift focus as needed to salient details.

Distributed Cognition—the ability to interact meaningfully with tools that expand mental capacities

Collective Intelligence—the ability to pool knowledge and compare notes with others toward a common goal

Judgment—the ability to evaluate the reliability and credibility of different information sources

Transmedia Navigation—the ability to follow the flow of stories and information across multiple modalities

Networking—the ability to search for, synthesize, and disseminate information

Negotiation—the ability to travel across diverse communities, discerning and respecting multiple perspectives, and grasping and following alternative norms.

Many concepts are related to media literacy, including: Access, Understanding and Create: 3Cs Culture: Critical and Creative: 5Cs adding Comprehension and Citizenship: Read and Write the media; 3Ps Protection; Promotion and Participation; etc. Therefore it may be productive to convert media and digital literacy criteria into social indicators to provide a multilayered instrument and involve different indicators that can be pulled together to form an overall picture of a people´s media literacy competence across different media, different age groups of people and including the dimension of critical understanding. According to the European understanding, media literacy is the **competence** (skill, ability) to cope, autonomously and critically, with a communicative and media environment established by the information and knowledge society.

Note

1 http://www.oecd.org/document/22/0,3343,en_2649_201185_39713238_1_1_1_1,00.htm

Bibliography

Association of Collage and Research Libraries (ACRL) (2000). *Information Literacy Competency Standards-for Higher Education.*

http://www.ala.org/ala/acrl/acristandards/informationliteracycompetency.htm

Aunion, J.A. (2009). *La era digital llega al Informe Pisa.* Madrid: El Pais.

EU Digital Literacy Expert Group *Digital Literacy* (2008) *High-Level Expert Group Recommendations 2008 Current Trends and Approaches to Media Literacy in Europe.*

http://ec.europa.eu/avpolicy/media_literacy/studies/index_en.htm

Hobbs, R. (1998). The Seven Great Debates in the Media Literacy Movement. *Journal of Communication*, Winter 1998, 1(48), 16–32.

http://www.oecd.org/document/22/0,3343,en_2649_201185_39713238_1_1_1_1,00.htm

Jenkins, H. (2007). *Confronting the Challenges of Participatory Culture: Media Education for the 21st Century*, Henry Jenkins, Director of the Comparative Media Studies Program at the Massachusetts Institute of Technology, MacArthur Foundation 2007, An occasional paper on digital media and learning.

Lenhart, A., and Madden, M. (2005). Teen content creators and consumers. Pew Internet and American LifE Project.
http://www.pewinternet.org/~/media//Files/Reports/2005/PIP_Teens_Content_Creation.pdf.pdf

MeAC (2007). *Measuring Progress of eAccessibility in Europe: Assessment of the Status of eAccessibility in Europe*. Executive Summary, Bonn, October 2007.

Merilampi, Ritva-Sini(2002). Facts behind Young Finns´ Success in Literacy Comparisons. Unpublished paper, Ministry of Education, Helsinki, Finland, May 2002.

Pérez Tornero, J. M. (2004). *Promoting Digital Literacy*. European Commission 4th Workshop "Media Literacy, Digital Literacy, e-Learning", 27 February, Brussels.

Varis, Tapio (2008). European and global approaches to digital literacy. *Digital Kompetanse*, 1(3).

Välijärvi, Jouni et al (2002).The Finnish Success in PISA – and Some Reasons behind It. Institute for Educational Research, University of Jyväskylä.

PART IV

Visions of the Future: Digital Literacy and the School in the 21st Century

CHAPTER 12

What Futures for Digital Literacy in the 21st Century?

Keri Facer

Introduction

The terms 'digital literacy' and '21st-century skills' have become almost synonymous in recent years and are often used interchangeably in certain research and policy sectors.[1] This production of an equivalence between 'the needs of the 21st century' and 'digital skills', has been helpful to researchers wishing to advocate for these new competencies to be taken seriously in schools (and to technology companies wishing to promote their products). In the longer term, however, this discursive practice has the effect of conflating the real, long term and global challenges of 'the 21st century', with the immediate, reasonably specialised trend towards pervasive digital technology use. As such, it serves to obscure the much more diverse range of issues that educators, young people and societies are likely to be faced with over the remaining 90 or so years of this century.

In an attempt to challenge this equivalence, this chapter takes a step back from the assumption that current digital literacy practices and the 21st century are fundamentally aligned and asks, instead: What happens if we attempt to take seriously the phrase 'literacy for the 21st century'? What possible socio-technical futures might we see develop over the longer term of this century and what sorts of digital literacies might we need to develop in these different environments?

In asking these questions, I am necessarily arguing that the future should not be assumed to be simply an extrapolation of the present and that it is unlikely to be merely a seamless continuation of existing trends (however all-conquering 'Web 2.0' and other such practices seem today). Instead, I am suggesting that future societies may be fundamentally different in their institutions, values and goals from those we know today; that while incremental progress is possible, significant reversals of fortune or massive changes in values and practice are also potential elements of our future worlds. Where even a year ago, making such a statement was often treated with scepticism by those in stable western countries who never read history, the economic upheavals of the last 18 months have given some insight into how rapidly institutional, governance and economic structures can change.

The field of study and enquiry that provides most insight into these questions is the field of 'futures studies'. This is a diverse field, scattered across governmental, commercial, academic and charitable sectors, drawing on a wide range of methods, theories and resources. What these diverse social actors have in common, however, is a shared commitment to systematic and explicit thinking about the potential for *alternative* futures (Bell 1969/2003) in order to challenge uncritical assumptions about what the future might be. Underlying this commitment is the simple observation that the future cannot be known, cannot be predicted, and can (within certain limits) be influenced. As such, any representation of the future has to be understood as a social construction that can be challenged and interrogated in order to understand the assumptions and, potentially, the political and economic interests that underpin it.

Indeed, looked at from a different field (that of critical discourse analysis), it is possible to see that representations of 'the future' share many characteristics with what Laclau and Mouffe (1985) and later Chouliaraki and Fairclough (1998) call discursive 'nodal points'. Drawing on Lacan's concept of *points de capiton*, 'nodal points' function as linguistic sites in which the infinite play of meaning is closed down and which come to be used as commonsense resources on which people draw in their understandings of the 'natural order' of social relations. 'The 21st century', for example, has been 'naturalised' in discourse as a time of rapid technological change incorporated within globalising economic practices. Such a 'commonsense' vision of the future has become a warrant for investment in digital technologies in schools, colleges and businesses and changes in employment practices, in the patterns of family life, in the relationships between nation states. 'The demands of the 21st century', therefore, can be harnessed in support of seemingly essential policies presented as necessary responses to an unavoidable future reality. This mobilisation of the future as a commonsense discursive resource is an act of 'chronological imperialism' which renders invisible the social and discursive work required to produce it and undermines the capacity of social actors not only to produce new imaginaries of the future, but also to act in and upon the world to create new lived futures.

As a means of problematising this 'closing down' of meanings of 'the future' and of challenging its representation as either inevitable or singular, futures studies sets out to systematically think about how alternative futures might come into being.[2] Its methods range from economic projections, to creative writing, from horizon scanning and reviews of evidence, to mass interviews and surveys. What brings these approaches together, however, is a commitment to presenting a range of possible futures and a resistance to making simplistic 'best guess' predictions. Indeed, these approaches attempt to prevent the fixing of meaning, to resist the desire for certainty, and are fundamentally concerned with enabling social actors to explore uncertainty, change and possibility as a means of empowering them to act in the present. As such, the pre-eminent tools in the futures field are 1) the 'scenario', a set of plausible but highly contrasting visions of possible futures in which existing policies and strategies can be tested and examined, and which can be used as an impetus to stimulate action in the present to avoid or promote different futures (Schwartz 1991; Van Der Heijden 1996) and 2) the disposition to ask the question 'where do these representations of the future originate and what sustains them'? (Inayatullah 2007).

It is these two approaches that I take in this chapter. In it, I want simply to unsettle the orthodox future as it tends to be presented in research and policy accounts of the '21st century' rationale for 'digital literacies'; and to open up the possibility of alternative futures for us to examine. I want to open up the space to ask the questions raised above: what might 'literacy' look like if our orthodox future does not pertain? What sorts of literacies might we need to flourish and function in a range of alternative futures? In so doing, I am attempting to apply critical literacy techniques to our own research field's narratives of the future. After all, as Lankshear and Knobel argue, in order to be able to critique a discourse, it is necessary to have:

> criteria, ideals, alternative experiences and standpoints, values and the like, on the basis of which we can build on our cultural understanding of a Discourse, to critique it (1998).

We cannot have alternative *experiences* of 'the future', but we can explore the alternative possible worlds that might emerge, in order to understand the partiality of our current representations of the 21st century.

Background

Some of the thinking and ideas in this intentionally speculative chapter have been informed by a futures research programme being conducted for the UK Government's Department for Children Schools and Families. This programme, 'Beyond Current Horizons', was established in 2007 with a remit to develop 'a set of long-term scenarios for the future of education in the context of socio-technical change 2025 and beyond'.[3]

The programme, due to report in May 2009, comprises a range of activities. First, we brought together leading academics in the fields of ageing, economics, social psychology, computing and literacy to build a resource bank of reviews from academics in the UK and internationally. These reviews were clustered in five key areas: generations & lifecourse; communication, creativity and information; citizenship, identities and communities; working & employment; public/private/ third sector relationships. The reviews therefore cover areas as diverse as neuroscience and home-working, private sector involvement in education and the politicisation of young people through the Obama election campaign. They collate existing trends and emergent practices in their field and begin to explore possible future directions over the coming 10–20 years. Second, we established a programme of public engagement activities that aimed to identify the aspirations and concerns of educators and learners for the future of education; through online and face-to-face consultation and through citizens panels, we have attempted to understand how diverse groups might wish to see education develop in the future—the roles it might play, the social relationships it should maintain, the knowledge and understanding it should enable. Third, we are in the process of developing a set of future scenarios based both on the reviews and the public engagement activity, and upon a programme of events bringing together specialists from creative and futures fields. These three activities aim to address the challenge in the futures field of exploring 'probable, preferable and possible' futures (Bell 2003; Sandford & Facer 2007).

The scenarios in this chapter are not in any way official outcomes of this programme (which is designed to address very different questions). Instead, they are playfully and speculatively developed 'in conversation' with this project, in order to address the specific issue of the future of literacy in the 21st century.

What Do We Mean by (Digital) Literacies Anyway?

Over the last twenty years, we have come to see literacy (and in particular, literacy as relating to new technologies) not as a set of disembodied technical skills, but as a set of practices comprising three inter-related dimensions: 'operational', 'cultural' and 'critical' (Green 1988; Lankshear & Knobel 1998).

The 'operational' dimension refers to the capacity to use the 'means' of literacy, that is, the development of the technical skills to read and write, to operate and use the tools of communication and representation.

The 'cultural' dimension refers to the capacity to use such skills meaningfully, in contexts and cultures as appropriate. For example, knowing the purposes of language tools in different settings; knowing why one is using those tools in different contexts. Knowing, for example, not only how to operate a spreadsheet, but the purposes for which a spreadsheet needs to be produced in a particular setting, and the way in which it should be used accordingly.

The 'critical' dimension relates to the capacity to perceive the literacy practices in which we participate as always being part of social practice and, as such, as being partial, selective and subject to struggles for power and control. The 'critical' dimension of literacy relates therefore, to the capacity to critique the tools and practices of literacy and the disposition to remake them in new ways that better serve social justice (Lankshear and Knobel 1998, 2003).

These dimensions were outlined over a decade ago and have formed the basis for much of the trajectory of research and practice in the digital literacy field since that time. While there have been further refinements and developments of this model over this time, they function particularly effectively as 'lenses' through which we might ask questions about potential 'futures' for literacy in different scenarios presented later.

Against Universalising Futures?

As outlined above, a primary purpose of futures studies is simply to begin by identifying the assumptions implicit in our conceptions of 'the future'. As such we need to begin simply by pointing out the extent to which the term '21st century skills' serves as a universalising and hegemonic discourse that generalises out a westernised, highly technological and competitive future to the rest of the globe; and which obscures a set of potentially critical geographical and temporal differences.

From a geographical perspective, when we use the term 'digital literacy for the 21st century', some tend to speak as though our audiences were only children, adults and politicians in developed countries with high-quality access to communications tools and networks. What might the future for digital literacy in the 21st century look like for young people living in the flood plains of Bangladesh or on the margins of the Saharah? What tools might be mobilised to support digital literacy in the 21st century for children in the megacities of Delhi and New York or the mountains of Tibet and the Andes? The 21st century is a century in which geographical location will still matter, increasingly so as we continue to fail to reduce the risks of extreme weather events posed by global temperature increases (UNICEF 2008; NIC 2008). There is still, today, no universal electricity network, no 'seamless infrastructure' that would offer real meaning to the terms 'ubiquitous' and 'pervasive' computing (Bell 2007) from a global perspective. Any vision of the 21st century which is premised upon an assumption of universal access is likely to be one which privileges certain well-served groups over others, and which attempts to universalise one set of experiences to the whole of humanity. Moreoever, it will be one that fails to understand, learn from and value the uses, designs and practices of digital literacies that may emerge in the very different socio-economic, socio-technical and geographical contexts outside westernised societies.

It is not only space that matters when we think about the '21st century'; however, it is also time. The question we ask too rarely when we consider the future of digital literacy is: 'how far into the future?' Are we concerned with the possible future of a female child born today in a European country, a child who is likely to live to see the 22nd century? Or are we concerned with the possible future of an adult born in the 1940s and likely (if affluent) to live a healthy life through the 2020s? Or are we concerned only with the 21st century that we are, after all, already living in? Again, the question 'whose future' needs to be addressed, as, depending upon the temporality we are considering, there are likely to be profoundly different needs and concerns for individuals and societies.

The 21st century is geographically and temporally contoured. When we speak of possible futures for digital literacy, therefore, we need to develop a modesty about the extent to which our future imaginaries can be generalised.

Three Possible Future Scenarios

The following three scenarios are produced by creatively exploring how current socio-economic, technical and cultural trends might inter-relate to generate a set of medium term (2020–2030) alternative futures in a European context. Because of the sensitivity at the present time to questions of economic upheaval, I have focused the scenarios around the potential implications of the current economic situation in interaction with computing and bioscience trends. It would be possible to take a completely different emphasis – perhaps starting from questions of the implications of demographic change or environmental risk – but the current interest in economic matters suggests that this focus is one that is likely to have some resonance with a range of readers.

As such, these scenarios also focus primarily on the 'public worlds' of employment and work, rather than on the worlds of family, relationships and homes. They do so because, at the present time, so many of our 'futures' are premised upon particular economic and employment assumptions and the aim of these scenarios is to interrogate these in more detail. Alternative futures could, of course, be written, and arguably, the following scenarios could be considered different or overlapping future developments that emerge at different times over the coming century.

Scenario 1: The Greener Global Economy in 2025?

This future world is the world that underpins many of our assumptions and plans today. In it, our systems, structures, values and institutions have survived reasonably unscathed. In this world, by 2025, we have managed to sustain our existing governance and democratic systems (the previous downward trend in voter participation has been reversed courtesy of the 'Obama technique' of engaging grassroots voters via distributed networks and encouraging enhanced volunteering and political action). The economic infrastructure, while suffering a sustained recession for 3–4 years after the 2008–09 credit crisis, has recovered and the global governance system of light touch regulation has survived enabling global 'free trade' and the maintenance of the WTO. Economies continue to grow and the middle class of China, India and Brazil continues to flourish and demand more goods and services. Low-skill work continues to be 'off-shored' to developing countries, increasingly to Africa as the twin plagues of AIDS and malaria were vanquished due to vaccine breakthroughs. Routine work (many service roles in banks and supermarkets, for example) is also offloaded to machines. An economic rebirth has been stimulated by increased investment in 'green technologies' following the international collaboration and cooperation principles agreed in the 2009 post-Kyoto treaty. As a result, the worst effects of global temperature increase, extreme weather events and water shortages have been mitigated by technological innovation and by resource investment in the poorest countries to support adaptation. In this environment there is a high demand for products and a high demand for a creative workforce, able to develop goods with added value, to identify and exploit new markets, and to innovate and compete not only nationally, but globally. In essence, this future is the orthodox future of 'business as usual'; in it, we manage to avoid some of the worst potential economic, environmental and democratic crises that faced us (and the hidden costs of such a system to the poorest and most vulnerable continue to be managed in ways which reduce the possibility of major social upheaval and unrest).

Moreover, courtesy of the added benefits of massive processing power (Moore's law, in this future, continues to hold true) accessed whenever and wherever we might want courtesy of a pervasive computing network, we are now able to mobilise the information, people and tools we needed on demand and to develop fluid and flexible working practices in response to personal needs and economic circumstances. As innovation and meeting market need become key factors of success in a rapidly responsive economic environment, creativity is democratised in the workplace – whether a hairdresser or a physicist, the individual in this world is constantly on the lookout for new ideas and in developing more effective feedback systems from and with consumers. The individual owns and manages their own intellectual property, sharing this with businesses or colleagues as appropriate through their own personal knowledge networks.

Scenario 2: The Rise of Localism?

This future world is profoundly shaped by the economic crisis of 2008–2009: a shortage of credit and mass unemployment led to an increase in protectionist economic policies and massive reduction in demand for goods and services. 'Every country for itself' became the dominant principle governing world trade discussions, and the global regulation structures began to weaken. At the same time, states, tired of encouraging their consumers to spend money only to discover it was being spent on imports, started to encourage more localised economic exchanges. This upheaval in economic practices coincided with the discovery that oil reserves were significantly lower than the oil companies had previously led the world to believe. Fuel prices rose massively, with the result that global trade and transportation became an expensive luxury rather than an everyday practice; the breakthroughs in mobile nuclear and hydrogen technology were too slow to arrive due to lack of sustained investment funds after the initial state injections of capital in 2009. Protectionism and increased fuel costs meant that increasingly, nations and regions began to look more to home and to their neighbours as their primary markets, workforces and playgrounds.

The massive economic downturn had a number of other consequences – first, it significantly reduced countries' capacity to adapt to global temperature rises and extreme weather conditions meaning that many areas became uninhabitable due to flooding or drought. In European countries and North America, although casualties were fewer than in low-lying and developing countries, the population maps were redrawn as communities moved to areas at lower risk of extreme heat, flooding or water shortages. Such movements caused significant tensions and saw states beginning to fracture and regionalise as 'native' populations increasingly resented having to maintain the costs of refugee populations. The decline in democratic participation that had become familiar from the first decade of the century was exacerbated to the point that 'nation states' no longer retained significant legitimacy. Instead, people increasingly turned to local regional assemblies and economies to reflect their specific needs and interests.

This world never saw the massive investment in fibre optics and infrastructure programmes required to achieve a pervasive computing system. Instead, people had to make do and mend with the infrastructure established by 2010. Resistance developed to purchasing expensive upgrades to software systems and open source and freeware systems flourished. The new local economies saw a mobilisation of social software tools to establish new networks of barter and exchange, the rise of co-operative and 'friendly' societies dependent upon personal knowledge and reputation management, and informal trading practices such as timebanking and local currencies flourished. As transportation of goods became ever more expensive and increasingly highly regulated, there was an increased interest in the previously esoteric world of '3d printing'. Local design and fabrication once again became a desirable practice and the emergence of real renewed interest in design and programming became widespread as such skills enabled access to goods otherwise prohibitively expensive.

Scenario 3: The Emergence of the Superhumans?

In this world, the global economic downturn of the first decade of the 21st century served to shift massive amounts of capital to the rich. Significant government investment in maintaining the banking systems and major corporations saw little impact on the financial and lifestyle expectations of a global 'elite' of highly paid individuals, despite the tax burden placed on the majority of the population. At the same time, the increasing age of western European populations placed increasing burdens on the welfare state of European nations, as the baby boomer generation moved into their long-anticipated retirement. As such, along with increasing economic divides between rich and poor, there were significant pressures placed on public finances leading to a reduction of state investment in welfare and education and a shift of responsibility for achievement of even mid-level skills and welfare from the state to the private sector and the individual. Popular opinion began to turn against massive state investment in capital projects to boost employment and investment; and the state began to withdraw increasingly from such schemes as families resented already high taxation rates.

The banking sectors of Europe, by the mid teens, recovered sufficiently to begin to reinvest in businesses, with a focus on developing ever more streamlined and profitable organisations. This investment continued the trend towards cost reduction and automation. Where low paid workers were already seeing their jobs replaced by machines (in factories and at supermarket checkouts), in this environment, 'middle-class' occupations are increasingly coming under pressure. Highly skilled programmers previously earning tens of thousands are now replaced by younger workers with the same skillsets gained through learning at home; highly educated lecturers in the newly privatised universities are increasingly competing with other lecturers around the world for students being taught online and via video conference to thousands at a time; elite surgeons and technicians are seeing their jobs replaced by precision robots able to conduct routine surgery. In this environment, only the most uniquely skilled and the most affluent individuals experience economic security and there are high costs to pay for falling through the net as the welfare states of most European and North American countries have been cut to the bare bones.

Just as this growing divide between a mass majority of routinised and increasingly insecure workers and a very small highly skilled or economically independent elite begins to become fully visible at the end of the second decade of the century, so too do the pharmaceutical and bio-tech firms begin to make significant breakthroughs. These companies, specialising in those research areas for which there are lucrative early markets, begin to target developments towards areas in which humans can gain competitive advantage in the workplace. Where cognitive enhancement had previously been the preserve of leisured environments (mood enhancers, etc.) by the mid 2020s, bio-technical adaptations through pharmacological or computing means become critical to effective performance in the highly competitive workplace. The ability to achieve high levels of concentration, to integrate and synthesise massive levels of information and data, to manage complex networks of people and resources, all become routinely essential elements of highly paid workplaces. At the top of the scale, these technologies are used to further increase the gap between 'elite' and 'mass' work activities. At the bottom of the scale, pharmacological developments are mobilised by companies to increase the workload and output of their staff.

These technologies do not, in and of themselves, transform human relations – but when combined with emergent socio-economic divides, they can create two different forms of human experience, divided along economic, educational and technological lines. By the late 2020s, we begin to see the widespread adoption of genetic testing pre-birth and the rise of genomics 'treatments'. The divides that have previously played out along economic lines and access to material and technological resources, may by this point begin to play themselves out in the changes to the human genome that are available to different sections of the population.

What Futures for Literacy in These Worlds?

If we return to our definition of literacy as a three-dimensional model of integrated operational, cultural and critical literacy practices, we can ask how these practices might play out in these three future worlds. These skills are necessarily integrated but they are caricatured here in order to challenge assumptions.

Operational Literacy

The primary operational skills required in these three different futures are widely divergent. We could caricature them as follows:

Future 1: Information Management
Future 2: Programming and Production
Future 3: Diagnosis and Prescription

In Future 1, operational literacy skills require the development of the competencies of complex information management. Information working on information remains the defining feature of this 'knowledge economy'–the capacity to operate information search, management and production tools will remain critical. In Future 2, a different set of skills is paramount. In this environment we are talking about functional (old fashioned?) technical skills, the capacity to programme and produce artefacts, to manage your own network systems, to contribute to and use open source systems, to access and operate in online social networks. In Future 3, we are talking about a fundamentally different relationship with technologies, one which does not see them as tools that are external to the individual and which can be operated upon by the individual. Instead, we see a merging of person and technology leading to demand for a new set of skills: the ability to diagnose ones' own performance and to identify the relevant bio-technical enhancements required to improve it. Competence in this environment becomes the competence to act upon one's own body and identity to enable it to more effectively 'operate' within the environment.

Cultural Literacy

The primary cultural skills required in these different futures are also widely divergent. We could caricature them as follows:

Future 1: Market Research, Branding and Communications
Future 2: Community Participation and Reputation Management
Future 3: Human Machine Relations

In Future 1: in this world, the individual becomes her own brand manager, able to market herself to multiple employers and to customers, building loyalty and recognition. She works with market research and data tools to keep up-to-date on what is needed, and rapidly adapts what she is offering. Whether working in major corporations, freelance or in smaller fluid organisations, she needs to work collaboratively, reflectively and flexibly to meet the demands of the market. Meaning is everything in this context—understanding the way in which skills can be mobilised to meet needs will be critical for survival. It will not be sufficient to know how to do things, but to know how these competencies can serve particular economic or social purposes. In Future 2, the individual needs to learn how to participate and work effectively in local and online communities, to manage her reputation and her interactions with others sensitively and effectively. She needs to be able to navigate and make sense of increasingly fragmented and disconnected telecommunications systems, to be able to patch up what she has and to understand how to create and produce her own products. In Future 3, she needs to understand precisely how to complement her skills with the enhancements and resources available to her. She needs to understand how best to integrate her capacities with those of the machines and networks she is able to link up with. She needs to understand and build bridges between human and machine intelligence, and to interact with a wide range of non-human actors acting as extensions of other people she is working with. A key cultural literacy in this future will be the ability to know when to mobilise human capacities and when to mobilise machine capacities.

Critical Literacy

If we examine the three possible futures presented above, what is clear is that the questions common to critical literacy practices will still pertain in all future settings where meaning and human relations are produced through mediating means. Lankshear and Knobel (1998) argued that a key set of questions could be asked in relation to the new meta-languages of the then emergent 'network society':

> *What kinds of practices does this new [meta-language] mediate, and how does it mediate them?*
>
> *What values are 'encoded' in this [meta-language] and the practices associated with it?*
>
> *What sorts of commitments and beliefs does it and its associated practices enlist on our behalf?*
>
> *What forms of identity and subjectivity does it encourage, enhance, enable? And with what actual and potential consequences?*

What can we say about the way it mediates human relationships and social relations? (1998, 5)

These same questions could similarly be asked in any of these future scenarios—for example, how are identity and human relationships produced through these new mediating tools and cultural practices? What values are 'encoded' in the forms of communication that are open to us in these different societies?

The specific technologies may change from the complex information structures of a 'global knowledge economy', the 3d fabrication tools of a 'rise of localism' or the bio-tech enhancements of the 'rise of the superhumans', but in all of these three futures, the same questions still pertain. While there may be a need to develop specific operational and cultural literacies in order to be able to answer these questions, there is not a different set of 'critical literacy' dispositions or processes that need to be developed or learned in preparation for full participation in these different potential futures.

What Is the Purpose of Schools in Supporting Digital Literacy in the Multiple Potential Futures of the 21st Century?

I want now to return to the question: what is the role of digital literacy education in the 21st century? If we take seriously the possibility that there may be multiple possible futures, if we take seriously the idea that the future could be very different from the environment we know now, if we acknowledge that there is a possibility for socio-technical disruptions over the coming twenty years on the same scale that we have witnessed over the last twenty years; we need to ask ourselves whether the digital literacy education that we are currently offering in schools and which many are promoting as '21st-century skills' is one which will really equip young people with the skills, capacities and dispositions to fully engage with and shape the tools of the 21st century?

Operational Literacies

The three 'futures' presented above present a set of very different potential 'curricula' for an education in digital literacy. If young people were to be prepared to operate effectively in all these futures, if we were to try to equip them with the specific skills required to use emergent technologies, it would require a massively diverse curriculum taking up a significant amount of time in order to 'cover all the bases'. The need to ensure that children learned everything from 3d printing processes to bio-computing to database management would exclude from an already crowded curriculum many other subjects and skills that others in different disciplines would fight hard to keep as equally relevant to future survival and flourishing.

The conclusion might therefore be that we simply cannot guarantee to equip young people with the operational skills they will need to use the technologies they will encounter in the mid and long term of the 21st century. What's more, if we look at the experience of the last decade alone, it is clear that schools have, in any case, a poor track record in taking the lead in imparting such technical skills (Facer et al, 2003). Almost always several years behind cutting-edge developments in the digital landscape, stymied by anxieties over child protection and by lack of investment in teacher education, schools often turn to expert groups of young people to access practical skills in use of new technologies. Rather than maintaining the convenient fiction that schools are the sole sites of generational transfer of all knowledge, is it time to suggest that schools move away from a focus on teaching operational digital literacies at all?

A common counter-argument to this is that it is only in schools that we are able to overcome social and economic inequalities. And yet, we know that the inequalities outside the school in terms of access and use of computers, for example, are often amplified in the school setting. Schools don't overcome these inequalities; instead, they can intensify them (Facer & Furlong 2001; Apple and King, 1983). If we are really interested in challenging such social and economic divides, better perhaps that we equip the child rather than the school with the emergent technologies, and create a culture in which it is expected and encouraged that children learn such basic operational skills from each other?

Cultural Literacies

The three futures presented above describe a set of very different potential cultural and social practices in which emergent technologies might be mobilised and a wide range of different socio-economic purposes for their use. It might be argued, therefore, that a function of the school setting is to model these future environments and to allow children to learn 'as if' they were in these future 'real world' environments. Indeed, this is a familiar argument from the '21st-century skills' agenda, in which we often hear calls for children to learn through 'real-world' methods, acting like businessmen or entrepreneurs developing team work and online collaboration skills assumed to be important for the presumed future knowledge economy.

Again, however, we need to recognise two key failings to this approach. First, these future environments are potentially so diverse that we could not reliably generate a model set of cultural practices for which the child would prepare. Any 'future working environment' would necessarily be a partial environment, reflecting a set of implicit assumptions and selections. And, second, we need to acknowledge the historical failings of schools to act as sites for participation in authentic cultural practices: 1) schools are intrinsically sites in which knowledge is transformed from real world knowledge (contingent, unstable, debatable) into 'schooled knowledge' (uncontestable, stable, universalised) (Osborne & Dillon 2008); 2) schools and society over the last 100 or so years, have developed in ways which intentionally and fundamentally separate young people from participation in the worlds of work or the challenges of 'real life' (Aries 1972).

How then, might formal education helpfully prepare young people for the cultural practices in which they might participate in different socio-technical futures? Perhaps by precisely acknowledging these tensions between 'real-world' situated knowledge and disembodied schooled knowledge. Perhaps by precisely acknowledging the limitations of any 'model' cultural practices children are presented with. The goal in school settings, then, might not be to try to second-guess the future and then model it in classrooms, but to create opportunities to participate in a wide range of cultural practices using as diverse as possible a set of tools and resources. The goal then, is not to learn 'the right way' to participate in a dominant set of practices, but to become familiar with the processes of moving between different cultural contexts, of picking up and engaging with new tools and resources, of reflecting upon the differences between different settings and different tools. Cultural literacies are developed in this model not only by understanding how to participate in different situated communities, but in being able to step back from participation to understand difference and the partiality of any form of cultural practice.

Critical Literacies

Unlike the massively divergent operational and cultural literacies that might be required in these three very different futures, the critical literacies that might be required are fundamentally consistent. They require the capacity to ask questions about the values embedded in the tools and resources we use, to explore the sorts of identities and subjectivities they are encouraging, to examine the types of human relationships and social relationships they develop and to imagine and explore alternatives to such arrangements. This bank of questions and this disposition to step back and enquire about the origins of the meditational tools and resources we use to represent ourselves and the world, remain in demand regardless of the future we find ourselves in.

As such, at a time of constrained curriculum, when there is massive uncertainty about potential future developments, there is a strong case for arguing that we intensify our efforts to engender critical literacies through school settings.

A further compelling argument for this emerges when we examine the sorts of digital literacies young people are already developing in informal settings. While young people develop expert operational skills, and are able to mobilise these to support their existing interests, what rarely develops in informal digital cultures is the capacity to critique the political and social contexts in which the tools and resources they are using are produced (Crook & Harrison, 2008). Not only is an emphasis on 'critical literacy', therefore, an emphasis that is likely to be of continued use in all of these three potential futures, but it is also a literacy that is unlikely to be developed elsewhere if it is not promoted in schools.

A 21st-Century Survival Strategy for the Goals of Digital Literacy

Many of us have been advocating the teaching of digital literacy for years because only by so doing, we have felt, can we ensure that we empower young people to participate in and transform their world. In the light of the previous discussion, however, I would argue that we can only achieve these goals of social participation and equity by rethinking our approach to digital literacy education.

First, we need to move away from seeing the school as the means of achieving equitable access to digital technologies and operational skills, and begin to focus on equipping the child with the resources to develop such skills in the non-school setting. This means investing in young people's access to new technologies outside the school setting.

Second, we need to move away from the idea that schools can 'model' a given future environment and that the goal of school should be to move closer and closer to a 'real-world' future work environment. Instead, we need to create the opportunity for young people to participate in a range of different cultural practices and to develop strategies for reflecting upon these differences and moving between them effectively.

Third, we need to place increased emphasis on the teaching of critical literacy skills and to develop the sorts of curricular and pedagogic approaches that would facilitate this. In order to do so, however, we may need to consider whether 'literacy' continues to function as an appropriate term for the sorts of critique and analysis we may require in these future environments, and to explore whether more interdisciplinary collaborations may be required. How, for example, can we learn to 'read' the potentially 'illegible' technologies of cognitive enhancement or synthetic biology? What do we need to know about how such technologies are developed in order to be able to account for the ways in which they produce different social relations?

The future of digital literacy in schools, then, needs to widen out from its focus on the school to an engagement with informal learning; needs to diversify from its advocacy of the development of '21st-century skills' modelled on knowledge economy environments to an exploration of diverse socio-cultural practices; and needs to build on its origins in English, Literacy and Computing to create collaborations with colleagues in Science and (arguably) Philosophy to explore the new forms of identity, social relationships and power that are enabled by diverse potential emergent technologies.

Notes

1. The e-Start Conference November 2008 was titled 'Pursuing Digital Literacy in the 21st Century: Reconstructing the school to provide digital literacy for all'. It was as a response to this discursive articulation of digital literacy with the coming century that this paper was conceived.
2. Of course, it also needs to be acknowledged that commercial futures studies work is also concerned with attempting to understand potential alternative futures for economic gain, for trading purposes and in order to produce futures that are more beneficial to their funders.
3. See www.beyondcurrenthorizons.org for further information on the programme

Bibliography

Aries, P (1962) *Centuries of Childhood: A Social History of Family Life*. New York: Random House.

Apple, M., and King, N. (1983). "*What Do Schools Teach?*" *The Hidden Curriculum and Moral Education*. Ed. Giroux, Henry and David Purpel. Berkeley, CA: McCutchan Publishing Corporation, pp.82–99.

Back, E. and Cameron, C (2008) *Our Climate, Our Children, Our Responsibility: The Implications of Climate Change for the World's Children*. London: UNICEF UK http://www.crin.org/docs/climate-change.pdf

Bell, G., & Dourish, P. (2007) Yesterday's Tomorrows: Notes on Ubiquitous Computing's Dominant Vision. *Personal and Ubiquitous Computing* 11(2): 133–143.

Bell, Wendell (2003) *Foundations of Futures Studies I: History, Purposes, Knowledge*. New Brunswick, NJ: Transaction Publishers.

Chouliaraki, L., and Fairclough, N. (1998) *Discourse in Late Modernity*. Edinburgh: Edinburgh University Press

Crook, C., and Harrison, C. (2008) *Web 2.0 Technologies for Learning at Key Stages 3 and 4: Summary Report*, Coventry: BECTA

http://partners.becta.org.uk/index.php?section=rh&&catcode=_re_rp_02&rid=15884

Facer, K., Furlong, J., Furlong, R., and Sutherland, R. (2003) *ScreenPlay: Children and Computers in the Home*. London: Routledge

Facer, K. and Furlong, R., (2001) Beyond the Myth of the Cyberkid: Young People at the Margins of the Information Revolution. *Journal of Youth Studies* 4(4).

Gramsci, A. (1971/1987) *Selections from the Prison Notebooks.* New York: Lawrence Wishart.

Green, B. (1988). Subject Specific Literacy and School Learning: A Focus on Writing. *Australian Journal of Education* 32(2) 156–179.

Inayatullah, S. (2007) *Questioning the Future: Methods and Tools for Social and Organisational Transformation.* Tamsui and Taipei: Tamkang University

Laclau, E., and Mouffe, C. (1985/2001) *Hegemony and Socialist Strategy: Towards a Radical Democratic Politics*, London & New York: Verso.

Lankshear, C., and Knobel, M. (2003). *New Literacies: Changing Knowledge and Classroom Learning.* Buckingham & Philadelphia: Open University Press, UK

Lankshear, C and Knobel, M (1998) Critical Literacy and New Technologies. Paper presented at *AERA*, San Diego.

NIC (2008) Global Trends 2025:
http://www.dni.gov/nic/PDF_2025/2025_Global_Trends_Final_Report.pdf

Osborne, J., and Dillon, J. (2008) *Science Education in Europe: Critical Reflections*, London: Nuffield
http://www.nuffieldfoundation.org/fileLibrary/pdf/Sci_Ed_in_Europe_Report_Final.pdf

Sandford, R., and Facer, K. (2007) *Futures Review: Looking at Previous Global Futures.* Bristol: Futurelab.
http://www.beyondcurrenthorizons.org.uk/wp-content/uploads/bch_futures_review.pdf

Schwartz, P. (1991/1996) *The Art of the Long View: Planning for the Future in an Uncertain* World. New York: Currency Doubleday

UNICEF (2008) *The State Of The World's Children 2008.* Report by United Nations Children's Fund, New York, USA.

Van der Heijden, K. (1996/1999) *Scenarios: The Art of Strategic Conversation*, Chichester and New York: Wiley

Selwyn, N., Gorard, S. and Furlong, J. (2005) *Adult Learning in the Digital Age.* London: Routledge.

Other sources that were used to stimulate the scenario ideas

Cliff, D., O'Malley, C., Taylor, K (2008) Future Issues in Socio-technical Change for Education. Bristol: Futurelab http://www.beyondcurrenthorizons.org.uk/findings/research-challenges/cross-challenge-papers/

Klein, N. (2008*) The Shock Doctrine*, London: Penguin

Martin, J. (2007) *The Meaning of the 21st Century.* London: Penguin.

Microsoft 'Being Human: Human Computer Interaction in the Year 2020' http://research.microsoft.com/en-us/um/cambridge/projects/hci2020/download.html

The Utopia Experiment http://www.dylan.org.uk/utopia/

Acknowledgments

My thanks to Richard Sandford and to fellow collaborators on the Beyond Current Horizons Programme.

CHAPTER 13

Re-imagining the School as a 'Loose Space' for Digital Technology Use

Neil Selwyn

Introduction

Most discussions of digital literacy and education move quickly towards the wider question of how to best 'reconstruct' the school as a context that supports and strengthens young people's digital technology practices. With these wider concerns in mind, the present chapter shifts the focus of debate away from the specificities of digital literacy and, instead, considers 'the problem' of the school in relation to digital technology use. The chapter commences by reviewing the growing trend amongst education technologists to renounce the school as it currently exists and support the radical reconfiguration of the structures and processes of schooling to meet the technological demands of the twenty-first century. After outlining the weaknesses and impracticalities of such arguments, the chapter goes on to explore alternative possibilities for subtler 'readjustments' to schools' technological practices that do not disrupt existing institutional structures and boundaries. In particular the chapter explores ways in which school-based use of digital technology may be repositioned as a focus for democratic dialogue, cooperation and trust between young people and adults. The chapter concludes by considering how the currently 'tight' regimes, relationships and arrangements that surround school technology use may be adjusted in ways that reconstitute the school as a 'loose space' conducive to less formalised modes of digital practice.

The School as 'Digital Disappointment'

The rather paltry use of technology within schools has been a long-standing source of disappointment to many educationalists and technologists. Whilst appearing to be a high-profile, well-funded and well-resourced element of contemporary education provision, in reality digital technology remains a marginalised aspect of the day-to-day milieu of contemporary schooling. To paraphrase Larry Cuban, new technology continues to be caught in a 'high access, low use' paradox—constituting a highly symbolic but, in practice, highly peripheral element of the drive towards more efficient, standardised and modern forms of education (Cuban et al. 2001). Growing numbers of commentators from within the educational community are now questioning openly the value of education technology reforms. As Michael Apple (2004, p. 513) contended, the time has perhaps come to acknowledge that governments have been "wasting money on computers in schools", and accept that the considerable amounts of time, effort and funding lavished to date on education technology would be more effective if directed elsewhere from now on.

This burgeoning sense of disaffection is rooted in an inconsistent and inequitable pattern of technology use in schools over the past four decades. For many commentators the disappointment of school technology has been exacerbated by the apparent boom in technology use in other areas of society, not least the workplace and the home. Indeed, research studies in North America, Australasia and northern Europe have long reported a relatively extensive and expansive use of digital technologies by children and young people *outside* of the classroom and schoolhouse. In countries such as the UK, for example, domestic usage levels of the internet, mobile telephony and computer gaming now exceed 90 percent of older children and adolescents. In terms of internet use, recent statistics confirm that the majority of young people in the UK maintain profiles on social networking sites, download music and video, and communicate with friends using a range of computer-mediated channels such as instant messaging and chat rooms (see Luckin et al. 2009a). Whilst we should remain mindful of the rather mundane and unspectacular nature of much of this use in practice, it would be fair to conclude that young people's engagements with digital technologies in domestic settings are generally more advanced than their use of technology in school (Livingstone 2009).

Indeed, the school is portrayed regularly within the research literature as a relatively impoverished site of young people's technology use. A body of empirical research over the past three decades has documented a faltering and often awkward integration of technology into the formal organisational structures of schools. Numerous surveys, reports and statistical analyses confirm that whilst the physical presence of digital technology in school systems may continue to rise, it's bearing on institutional practices and processes remains limited and often focused on the management and administration of education. Many teachers' use of new technology at school, for instance, continues to entail little more than the passive delivery of information through 'interactive' whiteboards and the bounded use of 'managed learning systems' and 'virtual learning environments'. Similarly, school use of digital technologies by young people remains dominated by the 'cut-and-pasting' of online material retrieved from search engines such as Google into word documents and PowerPoint presentations (Selwyn et al. 2009a, Luckin et al. 2009b). Students' *and* teachers' in-school uses of the internet are often hampered by a host of blocking procedures and other exclusionary practices of surveillance and filtering (Hope 2008). In this sense, technology use within the school setting continues to be highly formalised and bounded in nature, leading some commentators to conclude that schools offer little more than an artificial facsimile of 'real-world' technology use:

Unlike other spheres of human work in which these technologies are deployed to solve actual problems or re-engineer practices, in education the task is almost always to find useful things to do with the technology. The consequence is that classroom practices typically remain pretend and fabricated. Because the work is chiefly concerned with fitting into the classroom or curriculum logic, scant attention is paid to uses to which the technology is being put beyond the classroom. Computing and communication technologies use in the classroom is therefore almost automatically positioned as inauthentic or, at best, only having meaning in the isolated and largely self-contained sphere in which educational applications of these technologies are discussed and debated (Bigum and Rowan 2008, p. 249).

The long-standing disconnects between schools and technology are now prompting growing numbers of education technologists to argue for the dissolution of the school as it currently exists. Many academics, practitioners and even policymakers are now beginning to highlight what they see as the fundamental incompatibility between digital technology and what is referred to as 'industrial-age' or 'industrial-era' schooling. Such critiques hark back to Alvin Toffler's depictions throughout the 1960s and 1970s of the epistemologically and technologically outmoded 'industrial era school'. Here Toffler (1970, p. 243) decried schooling as an anachronistic by-product of "that relic of mass production, the centralised work place", bemoaning schools' reliance on rigid timetables and scheduling, emphasis on physical presence and ordering of people and knowledge. Now nearly forty years on from Toffler's initial observations, technologists continue to decry the industrial era school as a profoundly unsuitable setting for the more advanced forms of learning demanded by the knowledge age and post-industrial society (e.g., Miller 2006, Warner 2006). In particular, schools' continued reliance on broadcast pedagogies of various kinds, structured hierarchical relationships and formal systems of regulation is seen to leave them 'poorly placed to deal well' with the challenges posed by new digital technologies (Bigum and Rowan 2008, p. 250). As Luke (2003, p. 398) concludes, twenty-first-century educators are failing increasingly to "come to terms with the contradictions" between the technological complexities and fluidities of contemporary learning and the persistence of a model of schooling

> based on static print/book culture and competitive individualism where learning is geographically tied to a desk ... and old-style transmission and surveillance pedagogy.

With these criticisms in mind, it is now received wisdom amongst education technologists that the undoubted education potentials of new technology will only be realised through a radical rethinking of the processes and practices of contemporary schooling – as evident in present calls for the development of 'school 2.0' (e.g., Wang and Chern 2008). Such 'reschooling' arguments are advanced most commonly via proposals for the development of digitally aligned modes of schooling that are built around the active communal creation of knowledge (rather than passive individual consumption), and imbued with a sense of play, expression, reflection and exploration. Indeed it is now argued widely that technology-based practices of collaboration, publication and inquiry should be foregrounded within schools' approaches to teaching and learning. Thus much discussion in the field of education technology concludes with proposals and manifestos for various models of e-assessment, 'remix curricula' and 'pedagogical mash-ups', as well as ongoing debates over the refocusing of the teacher's role and the need to physically rebuild schools to accommodate the spatial and technical requirements of twenty-first-century technology use (e.g., Fisher and Baird 2009, Prensky 2008).

Whilst many education technologists would align themselves with such calls for the radical *re*-construction of the school, in the minds of some commentators the seriousness of the 'school problem' has now passed a point of no return, leaving them with no choice but to renounce the school as a viable site for technology use. This sense of terminal incompatibility is perhaps best encapsulated in Lewis Perelman's (1992) early observation that any attempt to integrate computing into schools

> makes about as much sense as integrating the internal combustion engine into the horse

Now, however, polemic of this sort has been co-opted into mainstream thinking about technology and education, with many commentators willing to denounce the school as an anachronism now rendered obsolete by contemporary digital technology (e.g., Papert 1998). From this perspective, arguments are now being advanced for the comprehensive deschooling of society along digital lines, thus consciously updating the arguments of Ivan Illich (1971) for the early twenty-first century. As Charles Leadbetter (2008, p.44) reasoned recently,

> in 1971 [deschooling] must have sounded mad. In the era of eBay and MySpace it sounds like self-evident wisdom

All of these reschooling and deschooling positions reflect a prevailing willingness throughout the education technology community to 'give up' on the notion of the industrial-era school as it currently exists. The writings of otherwise reasoned, thoughtful and good-natured commentators betray a sense of exasperation at the apparent 'remarkable resilience' of schools to change in the face of digital innovation (Bigum and Rowan 2008, p. 246). This renouncement of the industrial-era school as a viable site of digital technology use is evident across the ideological spectrum of writing on education technology, from the most techno-centric of authors such as Seymour Papert through to economically and socially concerned commentaries from otherwise incompatible neo-liberal *and* libertarian positions. As the sociologist Manuel Castells was led to conclude recently,

> "education is the most conservative system as to changing anything since the Middle Ages [...] the rules, the format, the organisation of the schools are completely different in terms of interactivity and hypertextuality" (Castells 2008, n.p).

Alternatives to Abandoning the School as It Currently Exists

Whilst it may be tempting to denounce the many technological frustrations of the industrial-era school, such thinking sets a dangerous precedent where the interests of technology outweigh all other social, cultural and political concerns. Aside from the presumed requirements of digital technology and the knowledge economy, it could be argued that there are few compelling reasons to assume that formal schooling is set to lose significance and status in contemporary society. In fact, the continued persistence of a top-down, hierarchal configuration of formal schooling could be seen as testament to the

> historical flexibility of schools as organisations, and of the strong social pressures that militate for preservation of the existing institutional structure. (Kerr 1996, p.7)

Thus, whether they like it or not, there is little historical *reason* for education technologists to anticipate the imminent institutional decline of the industrial-era school. Moreover, from a social justice perspective the argument could be advanced that educational technologists (however well-intentioned) have no *right* to legitimise calls for the cessation of the publically provided industrial-era school. For all its faults, it could be argued that the industrial-era school plays a vital role in the improvement of life chances for all young people. Amidst their enthusiasm for new digital technologies, education technologists should therefore remain mindful that whilst functioning as instruments of cultural transmission and state power, systems of compulsory formal schooling also fulfil a societal purpose as a valuable source of 'powerful knowledge' and social mobility for all not just the technologically-privileged few (Young and Muller 2009).

It therefore makes little sense for education technologists to so readily discount the industrial-era school as the principal site of young people's education. Instead, it would perhaps be more constructive for the education technology community to begin to work with—rather than against—the notion of the industrial-era school. In particular, more attention could be paid to the integral roles played by the (albeit imperfect) spaces, institutions and practices of formal education in shaping the realities of young people's educational technology use. In short, it is our belief that education technologists would do well to accept the obduracy of the formal school context in framing learners' use of digital technologies. Instead of giving-up on entire notion of the industrial-era school as it currently exists, it may be more productive to set about addressing the 'problem' of schools and technology in subtler and less disruptive ways.

Negotiating the (In)formalities of Technology Use within the School Environment

So what form may these 'subtler' and 'less disruptive' approaches to the use of digital technology within schools take? One option that we feel worthy of consideration is to view the processes and practices surrounding technology use in schools in terms of a 'formality-informality span'—i.e., the varying "extent and strictness of the social rituals which bind the behaviour of people" in their dealings with technology and each other (Misztal 2000, p. 8). From this perspective, much digital technology use within the school context could be construed as being overly formalised—i.e., planned, goal-directed, determinate, procedural and risk-adverse. Conversely, much technology use outside of the school setting could be characterised as rather more informalised—i.e. spontaneous, indeterminate, fragmented and risky. If we view the 'disappointment' of the school in these terms, then one can see why the informal domestic modes of technology use do not transfer easily into the highly ritualised and regulated school setting and the accompanying formal aims and activities of education institutions and educators.

A pressing priority, therefore, for anyone seeking to 'improve' schools as sites of digital technology use is the development of appropriate ways of lessening the gaps between these differing formalities of engagement—in other words increasing the sense of *informality* surrounding technology processes and practices in school. As Misztal (2000, p. 229) describes:

> Although the process of formalisation is the dominant trend in modern social life, informality is the essential element in constructing trust relationships and, thus, in any cooperative arrangement aimed at improving the quality of life ... only a society that achieves an optimal balance between the informality and formality of interactional practices is in a position to create the conditions for cooperation and innovation.

By suggesting a rethinking of school technology practices along more informalised lines, we are looking to encourage a set of conditions within school settings that may relax and de-restrict the expectations, guidelines, rules and regulations that surround technology use. It is important to emphasise from the outset that we are not proposing the de-regulation of school technology use into some form of digital 'free-for-all'. Instead we are seeking to engender changes 'around the edges' of the industrial-era school that may allow forms of technology engagement that could be considered to be richer and more meaningful to young people, yet pose minimal threat to the overall social order and wider vested interests of the school as organisation. As such, serious thought now needs to be given to how in-school technology use can be refined in ways that *complement* rather than *challenge* dominant institutional priorities of curriculum, assessment, performativity and so on.

As Misztal infers, perhaps the most appropriate means of supporting a meaningful but subtle informalisation is to encourage a negotiated governance of technology use amongst all members of a school community and predicated around conditions of trust, democracy and co-operation. Within most school settings, these conditions are most likely to arise from the encouragement of sustained dialogue between all adults and young people about digital technologies. Indeed, as the ultimate 'end users' of technology in schools it would seem self-evident that more attention is paid to the views, opinions, ideas and expertise of children and young people. As Mimi Ito and colleagues concluded recently:

Although youth are often considered early adopters and expert users of new technology, their views on the significance of new media practice are not always taken seriously. Adults who stand on the other side of a generation gap can see these new practices as mystifying and, at times, threatening to existing social norms and existing standards. Although we do not believe that youth have all the answers, we feel that it is crucial to listen carefully to them and learn from their experiences of growing up in changing media ecology (Ito et al. 2008, p. 35).

Encouraging inter-generational conversations about technology within schools corresponds with a number of wider education policy agendas, not least the interest currently being shown in the development of 'personalised' education systems and 'child-initiated' learning. In the UK, for example, national education strategies are being written with an increased recognition of the benefits of positioning young people as 'partners in learning' rather than passive recipients of schooling (e.g., DfES 2004). Particular interest is being shown in the notion of facilitating 'learner voice' within schools, i.e., allowing learners to enter into dialogue and bring about change with regards to the schools and learning (see Shields 2003, Rudd et al. 2006). The ways and means in which such dialogue can take place are now wellestablished in many European schools, from whole 'school councils' of elected pupil representatives to daily classroom negotiations between individual teachers and their students (see Kirby et al. 2003). Whilst notions of learner voice are considered relevant to many aspects of school life (from encouraging dialogue on the school meals and toilets, to the nature of policies on uniforms and bullying) the topic of technology use is not usually seen to be a suitable area for democratic negotiation. This oversight is curious, as in-school technology use could be considered to be a highly appropriate topic for dialogue and debate between schools and students, not least given young people's presumed expertise and interest in the area.

Of course, establishing technology use as a site for meaningful negotiation and collaboration between all members of the school community should not be considered to be a straightforward or easy task. In the first instance, the relations surrounding school technology will need to be moved on from the 'climates of unease' that presently surround young people's engagement with technology in many schools (Hope 2008), to a set of more cooperative, consensual and civilised relations of *trust*. Whilst school authorities may see increasing trust in young people as a potentially problematic step to take, there is little evidence to suggest that young people cannot be trusted when it comes to reaching sensible, practical and realistic suggestions for technological change. Indeed, empirical studies suggest that most young people have an acute awareness of the educational structures and requirements within which in-school technology use is located. Recent research suggests that young people do not necessarily wish to use technology in educational settings in the same manner as they do at home (Lohnes & Kinzer 2007). Many children and young people appear mindful of the risks involved in fully 'opening-up' classroom settings, often sharing institutional concerns over the 'usefulness' and 'safety' of unfettered technology use (Selwyn 2006, Selwyn et al. 2009b). In this sense there are few reasons to suggest that allowing children and young people an increased role in the *governance* of school technology would result in a slew of unreasonable or unrealistic demands. Whilst the democratisation of other areas of school life may well be more problematic and disruptive, we would argue that technology appears to be an area where increased trust in the opinions and actions of young people is merited.

Towards a 'Loose Use' of Technology within Schools

Assuming that cultures of trust *can* be developed successfully between schools and young people, then what form should negotiations over the informalities of technology use take? Here, it would seem appropriate to focus our attention on a subtle 'loosening' of school technology use rather than seeking to force radical or disruptive change. In this sense, inspiration can be drawn from recent debates amongst academic geographers, planners and architects on the nature of 'loose space' (see Franck and Stevens 2007). From this perspective, school technology use can be conceived as an activity that is situated within a range of spatial, temporal and behavioural boundaries that are the product of continual negotiation and contestation between young people and school authorities. The need remains, therefore, to ask what negotiable boundaries exist within the school setting where 'looser', less formal engagements with digital technologies may take place.

When considering such issues in relation to the general built environment, geographers and planners turn for inspiration to the loose qualities of (quasi) public spaces such as parks, plazas and public squares, as well as more liminal and derelict spaces such as underpasses and side-alleys that are overlooked or disregarded in formal planning process. Such spaces can be described as allowing people to pursue a variety of spontaneous or serendipitous activities often not originally intended for these locations (Franck and Stevens 2007). Of course, the organisational environment of the school is a relatively 'tight' space in contrast to these (quasi) public spaces, but we should remain mindful that looseness can, and will, arise in even the tightest and most formalised of spaces – not least through the activities and actions of individuals that take place with and without official permission and sanction. Indeed, many of the actions most likely to generate looseness may not appear to be especially productive or reproductive, as is the case with the archetypal 'loose' acts of simply playing or 'hanging out'. Yet even the loosest of activities should play a vital role in providing a necessary counterbalance to tighter and more formal arrangements elsewhere. In this sense, permitting a 'loose use' of technology in some areas of the school setting should be seen to be a necessary element of the successful formal use of technology in other areas. Thus sustained and ongoing negotiations between young people and adults over what is (and what is not) permissible within the school space should be seen as a vital element of the healthy ongoing development of technology use within the school.

Questions therefore remain over exactly what opportunities for such loose digital technology use exist within the school setting. Can 'breathing spaces' for informalised modes of digital technology use be negotiated *without* disrupting the wider organisational structures and relationships that constitute the 'school' and 'schooling'? Whilst addressing this challenge fully is beyond the scope of one individual book chapter, we conclude our discussion by offering some initial thoughts on potential areas for dialogue and change within the social contexts of the school setting:

- Firstl, are the formalised rules, regulations, structures and sanctions that currently shape most, if not all, forms of technology engagement within schools–ranging from when and where specific technologies can be used to the form of online content that can be accessed. The rules, regulations and other structures of control that surround these aspects of technology use would seem to be evident areas for negotiation between all members of the school community, exploring the leeway that exists for rules to be relaxed or even subverted at certain times with impunity. The overall aim here would be to make technology use in schools more of a self-governing process that is acceptable both to students and teachers. In this sense, there may well be value in approximating an 'open source' approach within the school community to the development of technology regulations. Indeed, whereas open source approaches are applied usually to the development of software and content, there is no reason why principles of openness, ongoing scrutiny and refinement by a community of 'users' can not be applied to the development of the rules and regulations shaping in-school uses of technology (see Weber 2004). Efforts should therefore be made to increase opportunities for staff and student intervention and participation in shaping the terms on which technology is used in educational contexts (Hamilton and Feenberg 2005).

- Attention should also be given to the negotiated loosening of the nature and scope of technology-based behaviours that are tolerated within schools. From this perspective there may well be opportunities to expand the tacit permission for technology-based activities not necessarily associated with the business of schooling, but nevertheless may provide a balance to more formalised pedagogic and administrative uses of technology. These 'other' activities could include technology-based play and entertainment, informal communication and interaction with others, expressive activities and even the practices of simply 'hanging out' and 'messing around' with digital technologies. Whilst not immediately productive, such activities nevertheless constitute an integral element of participating with new media and have been shown to support young people's acquisition of the "basic and technological skills they need to fully participate in contemporary society (Ito et al. 2008, p. 2)". Thus increased emphasis should be placed on school communities reconsidering their stance towards the seemingly inconsequential, risky and/or transgressive technology-based activities that are often regulated 'away' at present (Hope 2007).
- Many of these changes in behaviours will be associated with a readjustment of the places, spaces and times where digital technologies may be engaged with within the school structure. Whilst some useful debates are already taking place around the longer-term 're-imagining' of the physical spaces and environments of 'schools of the future' (see Mäkitalo-Siegal et al. 2009), here we are more interested in the possibilities for the immediate adjustment 'around the edges' of the current organisation of time and space within schools. In seeking to (re)use the environments that already exist in schools, it would seem appropriate to concentrate on the times and spaces that are connected less directly to the formal bureaucratic concerns of the school. In this spirit, school communities could explore where informal digital technology practices may be encouraged in already 'slack times' of the school day such as lunchtimes, free times before and after school, and in-between lessons. Similar explorations could consider the 'loose spaces' within the physical environment of schools that have no prescribed formal pedagogic function, such as playgrounds, dining halls, atriums and corridors. It may also be that technology use can be encouraged in

less obvious 'found spaces' within the school—i.e., spill-over, liminal or 'niche' spaces such as stairwells, bicycle sheds and other hidden spaces of the school (Rivlin 2007). In short, negotiations could be held over the propagation of various 'technological public commons' within the wider bounded nature of the school, "where definitions and expectations are less exclusive and more fluid, where there is greater accessibility and freedom of choice for people to purpose a variety of activities" (Franck and Stevens 2007, p. 3).

Conclusions

Adjusting school settings in any of these ways would depend on significant shifts in the organisational cultures of schools.[1] It is therefore important to expect any refinements and changes to school technology use to be incremental and gradual (Sørensen et al. 2007). As has already been acknowledged, whilst no public space is absolutely free, the school should be seen as a particularly tight institutional setting,

> where rules, meanings and physical structure are explicit and relatively fixed. (Franck and Stevens 2007, p. 26)

Thus all of the instances of possible 'looseness' described above should be seen in a dialectic rather than an absolute sense, where loosenings and tightenings of technology use within a school setting will develop continually in relation to the other. Yet whilst it would be foolhardy to assume that achieving these increased flexibilities will be easy, it is our contention that shifts in schools' understandings of what is considered acceptable, appropriate and permissible with technology *are* possible.

In mapping out an initial framework for the negotiated adjustment of school technology use, this chapter is certainly not proposing a complete relaxation of the formal aspects of school organisation and provision. Indeed, it should be remembered that the formal provision of schooling provides a valuable certainty, homogeneity and order to technology use, often providing all young people with opportunities to undertake new tasks that they may otherwise not have. Thus whilst calling for increased freedoms from rule-bound conduct, we should remain mindful that

> there will never be a total escape from rules and routines. (Misztal 2000, p. 72)

Indeed, it would be unwise to deny the value of formal schooling at the expense of more informal practices. As Young and Muller (2009, p. 7) contend,

> as learners cannot actually 'construct' their own learning (because, in Foucault's pithy phrase, they cannot know what they do not know) the role of [schools] cannot be reduced to that of guide and facilitator rather than as a source of strategies and expertise

In this sense we would reiterate the belief that, amidst any changes, schools should retain their valuable authoritative role in educating, informing and directing the activities of children and young people.

With all these caveats in mind, this chapter has attempted merely to advance a modest case for exploring ways of loosening up in-school technology use and introducing a degree of informality to digital practice *without* undermining the overall institutionalised social order of the school. Whilst many education technologists may well consider this to be a disappointingly compromised agenda for change, we would contend that the arguments laid out in this chapter are certainly more realistic and achievable than the radical discourses of technological reschooling and retooling currently being proposed by others in the field. To reiterate, we are not calling for a complete, unthinking informalisation where school use of technology is allowed to descend into a learner-driven free-for-all. Instead, careful thought now needs to be given as to exactly how the relationships between formality and informality within schools may be adjusted and altered in ways that can shift the frames of in-school technology use without undermining basic institutional structures and interests. Having put forward an initial framework for change, further discussion and debate is now required to advance ways in which such beneficial *loosenings* may be achieved without incurring a *lessening* of students' and teachers' digital technology use.

APPENDIX

As part of an ongoing project looking at the digital reconfiguration of primary schools (Selwyn et al. 2009b), we are exploring practical examples of such 'loose' changes with young people and technology. Here are some illustrative examples arising from our discussions with young people and schools.

How can we encourage pupils and teachers to negotiate the rules and regulation of technology within schools?

- Place the review of existing school technology policies on the agenda of *school councils*.
- Form '*technology cabinets*' or 'technology working parties' made up of pupil volunteers to propose new school policies and a school technology manifesto. Appoint a pupil leader (a *technology Tsar* perhaps) to chair the group.
- Hold *technology referenda* (across the whole school, or individual year groups or separate classes as appropriate) to vote on contentious topics or decisions
- Appoint individual pupil volunteers as *investigative journalists* to report on the state-of-school-technology and the demands of the pupil body for change,
- Invite *technology providers and gatekeepers* into the school to explain themselves to the pupils, and to discuss their actions – these could include representatives from the local and regional government, or the school's commercial IT suppliers and providers.

What aspects of technology use should be open to negotiation between pupils and teachers?

- Wish-lists of *blocked web-sites* and internet search terms
- Wish-lists of *un-blocked web-sites* and search terms
- *How use of technology should be monitored* within school – and how monitoring information should be used
- Rules relating to what personal technology devices are allowed into school; rules relating to where personal technology use is allowed and when personal technology use is allowed
- Procurement policies–what devices and software are purchased by the school for pupil use

What technology behaviours and activities can be tolerated, facilitated and/or encouraged?

- *Digital graffiti walls*—using plasma screens, digital projectors and whiteboards to project uncensored pupil-created content onto public spaces. For examples, pupils can text-message short slogans and phrases to appear temporarily on the walls of the playground, corridor or reception space.
- *Computer game Olympics*—competitive 'gamer' tournaments held between pupils on games platforms and genres chosen by pupils. Devices such as WII Fit can be used for *Digital Sports Days*. *'Old school' games tournaments* between teachers and pupils can be encouraged, using games played by the teachers in their youth and therefore new to the pupils.

What times and spaces in the school schedule can accommodate the 'loose use' of technology?

- *Technology amnesty days*: allocated days in the school year where pupils can bring in any technology or media device that they wish, to play with or use in their free time. These should not just be the last days of term!
- *Spontaneous and unannounced wi-fi playtimes*, where wireless internet access is provided for a limited period (e.g., a fortnight)
- *'Suggest a technology' question*, asked by the teacher before starting any activity in the classroom. Scheduling in an in-class pause for thought before doing something. 'Is there anything you would like to use to do this?'

'Technology-free lessons' and *'technology-rich lessons'*, spontaneous decisions taken when appropriate to either spend the lesson using no new technology what-so-ever OR ELSE as much technology as possible. These sessions can be akin to the 'let's work outside' decisions that sometime occur in the spring and summer time. Once the high-tech or no-tech sessions have finished, time can be allowed for pupils and teachers to reflect upon what was good, and what was not so good about the session.

Note

1. We recognise that we have written much of this chapter from the perspective of the rigid formal culture of schooling that can be said to exist in countries such as the UK and North America. In developing our arguments we are mindful that the loose/tight, in/formal nature of school technology use will differ between countries, especially those with different national cultures of education (e.g., the social democratic ethos of schooling in some Scandinavian countries as opposed to the more rigid regimes of formal education in the UK). As such, we recognise that not every education system can be said to experience exactly the same issues presented in the chapter.

Bibliography

Apple, M. (2004). Are we wasting money on computers in schools? *Educational Policy*, 18(3), 513–522.

Bigum, C., and Rowan, L. (2008). Landscaping on shifting ground: Teacher education in a digitally transforming world Asia-Pacific *Journal of Teacher Education*, 36(3), 245–255.

Castells, M. (2008). Internet beyond myths: The record of scholarly research. Presentation to London School of Economics, 24 October.

Cuban, L., Kirkpatrick, H., and Peck, C. (2001). High access and low use of technology in high school classrooms: Explaining an apparent paradox. *American Educational Research Journal*, 38(4), 813–834.

Department for Education and Skills [DfES] (2004) *Five - year strategy for children and learners.* London: Stationery Office.

Fisher, M., and Baird, D. (2009). Pedagogical mashup: Gen Y, social media, and digital learning styles. In Hin, L. and Subramaniam, R. (eds) *Handbook of research on new media literacy at the K-12 level* Hershey PA: IGI Global.

Franck, K., and Stevens, Q. (2007). Tying down loose space. In Franck, K. and Stevens, Q. (eds) *Loose space: Possibility and diversity in urban life.* London: Routledge.

Hamilton, E., and Feenberg, A. (2005). The technical codes of online education *E-Learning* 2, 104–121.

Hope, A. (2007). Risk taking, boundary performance and intentional school internet 'misuse'. *Discourse: Studies in the Cultural Politics of Education,* 28(1), 87–99.

—— (2008). Internet pollution discourses, exclusionary practices and the culture of over-blocking within UK schools Technology, *Pedagogy and Education*, 17(2) pp.103–113

Illich, I. (1971). *Deschooling society.* New York: Harper and Row.

Ito, M., Horst, H., Bittanti, M., Boy, D., Herr-Stephenson, R., Lange, P., Pascoe, C. and Robinson, L. (2008). *Living and learning with new media: Summary of findings from the digital youth project.* Chicago: MacArthur Foundation.

Kerr, S. (1996). Toward a sociology of educational technology. In Jonassen, D. (ed.) *Handbook of research on educational communications and technology.* New York: Macmillan

Kirby, P., Lanyon, C., Cronin, K., and Sinclair, R. (2003). *Building a culture of participation: Involving children and young people in policy, service planning, development and evaluation.*

London: Department for Education and Skills.

Leadbetter, C. (2008). *We-think*. London: Profile.

Livingstone, S. (2009). *Children and the internet*. Cambridge: Polity.

Lohnes, S., and Kinzer, C. (2007). Questioning assumptions about students' expectations for technology in college classrooms. *Innovate*, 3(5) [http://innovateonline.info]

Luckin, R., Clark, W., Graber, R., Logan, K., Mee, A., and Oliver, M. (2009a). Beyond web 2.0: Mapping the technology landscapes of young learners. *Journal of Computer Assisted Learning* 1(25), 56-69

Luckin, R., Clark, W., Logan, K., Graber, R., Oliver, M. and Mee, A. (2009b). Do web 2.0 tools really open the door to learning: Practices, perceptions and profiles of 11–16 - year - olds learners. *Learning, Media and Technology* 2(34).

Luke, C. (2003). Pedagogy, connectivity, multimodality, and interdisciplinarity. *Reading Research Quarterly*, 3(38), 397–413.

Mäkitalo-Siegal, K., Kaplan, F., Zottmann, J., and Fischer, F. (eds). (2009). *Classroom of the future: Orchestrating collaborative spaces*. Rotterdam: Sense

Miller, R. (2006). Equity in a twenty-first-century learning intensive society: Is schooling part of the solution? *Foresight* 8(4), 13–22.

Misztal, B. (2000). *Informality: Social theory and contemporary practice*. London: Routledge

Papert, S. (1998). Does easy do it? Children, games, and learning. *Game Developer* June/September, 88–92 [www.papert.org/articles/Doeseasydoit.html]

Perelman, L. (1992). *School's out: Hyperlearning, the new technology, and the end of education*. New York: Avon

Prensky, M. (2008). The role of technology in teaching and the classroom. *Educational Technology*, 48(6), November/December.

Rivlin, L. (2007). Found spaces: Freedom of choice in public life in Franck, K., and Stevens, Q. (eds), *Loose space: Possibility and diversity in urban life*. London: Routledge.

Rudd, T., Colligan, F., and Naik, R. (2006). *Learner voice*. Bristol: Futurelab.

Selwyn, N. (2006). Exploring the 'digital disconnect' between net-savvy students and their schools *Learning, Media and Technology*, 31(1), pp.5–17

Selwyn, N., Potter, J., and Cranmer, S. (2009a). Primary pupils use of information and communication technologies at school and home. *British Journal of Educational Technology*, 39.

Selwyn, N., Potter, J., and Cranmer, S. (2009b). *Primary schools and ICT: Learning from pupil perspectives*. London: Continuum.

Shields, C. (2003). Giving voice to students. *Qualitative Research*, 3(3), 397–414.

Sørensen, B., Danielsen, O., and Nielsen, J. (2007). Children's informal learning in the context of schools of the knowledge society. *Education and Information Technologies*, 12(1), 17–27.

Toffler, A. (1970). *Future shock*. London: Bodley Head.

Wang, S., and Chern, J. (2008). The new era of 'school 2.0'—teaching with pleasure, not pressure in *Proceedings of World Conference on Educational Multimedia, Hypermedia and Telecommunications 2008,* Chesapeake VA, Association for the Advancement of Computing in Education.

Warner, D. (2006). *Schooling in the knowledge era*. Victoria: Australian Council for Education Research.

Weber, S. (2004). *The success of open source*. Cambridge MA: Harvard University Press.

Young, M., and Muller, J. (2009). Three scenarios for the future: Lessons from the sociology of knowledge. Paper for Department for Children, Schools and Families 'Beyond Current Horizons' programme.

Contributors

Helen Drenoyianni is currently Assistant Professor of ICT in Education at Aristotle University of Thessaloniki, School of Education–Department of Primary Education. She is a graduate of the National University of Athens, School of Education and has an MEd and a PhD from the University of Birmingham, School of Education (UK). Her main research interests focus on ICT literacy and its relationship to multi-literacies; the role of ICT in school curricula with an emphasis on integrated, trans-disciplinary and democratic curriculum practices, as well as the investigation of issues of social exclusion and ICT through the lenses of critical pedagogy theory. She has participated in a range of national research, teacher training and professional development projects concerned with ICT literacy, ICT and gender, and initial and in-service teacher education in the pedagogical use of ICT in education. She is a member of the Editorial Board of the journals *Education and Information Technologies* and *Themes in Education.* Furthermore, she is the national representative of Greece in IFIP-TC3 (Education) and a member of the World Digital Solidarity Agency, the NAACE Association (UK National Association of Advisors for Computers in Education) and the Hellenic Scientific Society of Information and Communication Technologies in Education (HICT).

Lampros K. Stergioulas is Reader in the Department of Information Systems and Computing at Brunel University, UK, and a qualified Chartered Engineer. Dr. Stergioulas has published over 150 refereed papers in journals and international conferences and has supervised and examined numerous PhD dissertations in information systems and computer science. He has held many national and EU grants in information systems, technology-enhanced learning, human-centred communications and computing, and medical and health informatics. He is currently one of the academic leads in the UK's RIGHT project, and has been principal investigator in numerous EU projects, including UNIVERSAL (FP5), TIME2LEARN (FP5), PROLEARN (FP6), BASE2 (FP6), OpenScout and iCOPER European research projects. He coordinates the e-START EU Digital Literacy Network and the TEL-Map project in Technology Enhanced Learning futures. He chairs IFIP's Special Interest group in Digital Literacy (TC3–SIG3.9). His research interests include technology-enhanced learning, educational and health information systems, human-centred computing, educational computing, and information systems for society.

Melpomeni Tsitouridou is Associate Professor of ICT in Education in the Aristotle University of Thessaloniki-Greece. Her research interests relate to ICT and children and teacher education in ICT.

Konstantinos Vryzas is Professor of Sociology of Mass Media in the Aristotle University of Thessaloniki–Greece. His research interests relate to children and media and the globalisation of communication and cultural identities.

David Bowden is Professor of Information Science in the Centre for Information Science at City University London, and has a long-standing interest in information and digital literacies.

Lyn Robinson is a senior lecturer in Information Science, at City University London. Her research interests include history and philosophy of information, history of science, information communication and domain studies, use and impact of social media, service evaluation and professional development.

Alivisos Sofos is Assistant Professor for Pedagogy and Media Education, at the University of the Aegean, Primary Education Department. His research interests include Media Education in School, Media Literacy, Media Didactic and Methodology, Multimedia Educational Environments, Safer Internet, and Distance Learning. He is also Consultant Professor at the Hellenic Open University in the Graduate Program "Open and Distance Education".

Ola Erstad is Professor at the Department for Educational Research, University of Oslo, Norway. He has been working both within the fields of media and educational research. He has published on issues of technology and education, especially on 'media literacy' and 'digital competence'. From 1998 until 2005 he was Head of Research at a national centre on ICT research in education, leading large-scale innovation projects in Norwegian schools working on different levels of school development using digital technologies. He is leader of a research group at the Faculty of Education, Oslo, called 'TransActionslearning, knowing and identity in the information society'. Among recent publications is an article on 'Trajectories of remixing – digital literacies, media production and schooling' in *Digital Literacies* by C. Lankshear & M. Knobel (2008, Peter Lang), and two articles in *Digital storytelling, mediatized stories – self-representations in new media* by K. Lundby (2008, Peter Lang).

Joe Cullen is Director of Arcola Research, London; a member of the Board of the MENON Network, Brussels and Principal Associate of the Tavistock Institute, London.

Don Passey is a Senior Research Fellow in the Department of Educational Research at Lancaster University. He has wide experience with developing and using evaluation and research methods to look at technological innovation supporting learning and teaching. He has recently completed studies for the BBC that have focused on aspects of digital literacy, and for Becta that have looked at the potential for technology to support young people 16–18 years of age who are not in employment, education or training. He has worked with government agencies, commercial and non-commercial groups, educational institutions and schools, in undertaking research to inform both policy and practice. He is a member of the International Federation for Information Processing Working Group on Educational Management and ICT, a member of the BCS Schools Expert Panel, and has written widely on aspects of ICT uses in primary and secondary education.

Ellen Helsper is a Lecturer in Media and Communications at the London School of Economics and Political Science. She is on the Advisory Board of the EU Kids Online II project and worked on its predecessor the UK Kids Online survey. Her research and publications focus on vulnerable groups and their use of technologies with a special interest in generational differences in digital literacy and engagement. In particular she looks at digital exclusion and social media use. Previously she was a Survey Research Fellow at the Oxford Internet Institute (OII) responsible for the design, analysis and coordination of the Oxford Internet Surveys (OxIS) and World Internet Project (WIP) Surveys. Further projects she has been involved in are the EU funded 'Youth at risks and ICTs' and 'Social Impacts of ICT' studies, the 'Me, My Spouse and the Internet' and 'Online Gambling' studies.

José Manuel Perez Tornero is Full Professor of Communication at the Communication Department of the Universitat Autonoma de Barcelona. His research interests are communication and education and Media Literacy.

Laura Cervi is Associate Professor at the same Department (above). Her research interests are the relation between new technologies and new forms of participation. She works in Prof. Tornero's research group in Media Literacy.

Georgios Grollios was born in Thessaloniki, Greece and is currently Associate Professor at the Department of Primary Education, Aristotle University of

Thessaloniki. He studied pedagogy and obtained his Phd at the same Department. He is the author and co-author of four books concerned with: a) the European Commission programmes and initiatives for education, b) the scientific activity of Greek teachers, c) an adult literacy research programme, based on Paulo Freire's pedagogy, and d) Paulo Freire's perspective on curriculum planning. Furthermore, he is the author and co-author of more than fifty scientific articles on Pedagogy and Curriculum, published in Greek and international journals and edited volumes.

Anastassios Liambas is a Lecturer at the Department of Primary Education, Aristotelion University of Thessaloniki. He has studied Pedagogy (BEd, PhD). Author and co-author in edited volumes, periodicals and journals. His academic interests are in critical pedagogy, Freire's pedagogy, curriculum, assessment, cultural studies in education.

Ioannis Kaskaris is a primary school teacher at the public/state education, since 1992, and a researcher. He has studied Pedagogy (BEd, DipEd, MEd) and Sociology (MSc). He is an author and co-author of papers in edited volumes and journals. His academic interests are in critical pedagogy, social & political theory in education.

Tapio Varis is a professor of Vocational Education, with particular reference to global learning environments at the University of Tampere, Finland, Research Centre for Vocational Education, and UNESCO Chair in global e-Learning with applications to multiple domains. Principal research associate of UNESCO-UNEVOC. Acting President of Global University System (GUS). Former Rector of the University for Peace in Costa Rica. Expert on media and digital literacy to the European Union. Communication and Media Scholar at the University of Helsinki and the University of Art and Design in Helsinki and the University of Lapland, Finland. Published over 200 scientific contributions. Visiting Professor and Lecturer in many countries in Europe, North and South America, and other regions of the world.

Keri Facer is Professor of Education at Manchester Metropolitan University where she leads the Create research group specialising in digital cultures, social justice and educational change. From 2002–2008 she was Research Director at Futurelab.

Neil Selwyn is sociologist working at the London Knowledge Lab. His research and teaching focuses on the place of digital media in everyday life, and the sociology of technology (non)use in educational settings.

Subject Index

Name Index

new literacies
AND DIGITAL EPISTEMOLOGIES

Colin Lankshear & Michele Knobel
General Editors

New literacies and new knowledges are being invented "in the streets" as people from all walks of life wrestle with new technologies, shifting values, changing institutions, and new structures of personality and temperament emerging in a global informational age. These new literacies and ways of knowing remain absent from classrooms. Many education administrators, teachers, teacher educators, and academics seem largely unaware of them. Others actively oppose them. Yet, they increasingly shape the engagements and worlds of young people in societies like our own. The *New Literacies and Digital Epistemologies* series will explore this terrain with a view to informing educational theory and practice in constructively critical ways.

For further information about the series and submitting manuscripts, please contact:

Michele Knobel & Colin Lankshear
Montclair State University
Dept. of Education and Human Services
3173 University Hall
Montclair, NJ 07043
michele@coatepec.net

To order other books in this series, please contact our Customer Service Department at:

(800) 770-LANG (within the U.S.)
(212) 647-7706 (outside the U.S.)
(212) 647-7707 FAX

Or browse online by series at:

www.peterlang.com